PRACTICE FOR LIFE

PRACTICE FOR LIFE

Making Decisions in College

LEE CUBA

NANCY JENNINGS

SUZANNE LOVETT

JOSEPH SWINGLE

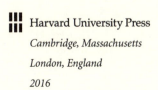
Harvard University Press

Cambridge, Massachusetts

London, England

2016

First printing

Library of Congress Cataloging-in-Publication Data

Names: Cuba, Lee J., author. | Jennings, Nancy E., author. | Lovett, Suzanne, 1958– author. | Swingle, Joseph, author.

Title: Practice for life : making decisions in college / Lee Cuba, Nancy Jennings, Suzanne Lovett, Joseph Swingle.

Description: Cambridge, Massachusetts : Harvard University Press, 2016. | Includes bibliographical references and index.

Identifiers: LCCN 2016003823 | ISBN 9780674970663 (hc)

Subjects: LCSH: College students—United States—Attitudes. | Decision making—Psychological aspects. | Education, Higher—United States—Evaluation. | Academic achievement—Economic aspects—United States.

Classification: LCC LB2324 .C83 2016 | DDC 378.1/98—dc23

LC record available at http://lccn.loc.gov/2016003823

To those who shared their college experiences with us

Contents

Preface

What's it like to be a college student? We answer this question in multiple ways in this book. Although influenced by our collective experience as college teachers for over 100 years, our answers are drawn from interviews with more than 200 students who started college in 2006 and graduated in 2010 (well, most of them did). These students generously agreed to be interviewed every semester from their first year to their last to help us understand how they made their way through college. We are enormously grateful that they took the time to do so.

In making a case for the continuing relevance and value of liberal education, this book argues that becoming liberally educated is a complex and messy process involving making decisions and learning from them. College administrators, faculty, students, and their parents tend to focus more on the formal decisions that happen infrequently—like declaring a major—and not so much on the informal ones that occur almost every day—like striving to balance academic and extracurricular commitments. Yet *all* of the decisions that students make have the potential to shape their college experience. Students sometimes see the decisions they make as obstacles blocking their path through college. At other times, however, they view these decisions as opportunities to learn about themselves and acquire practice for making decisions as adults after college. When they approach decisions as opportunities, college students find themselves caught up in a process of self-creation and re-creation that has significant consequences for students and colleges alike.

In responding to the many decisions they confronted every day, the students you will hear from in this book variously thrived, struggled, and stalled while attending college. In their first year of college, Jessica and Stephanie found themselves trying to figure out how to manage their time and balance competing commitments in an environment much less structured or scaffolded than high school. Dan and Sonya were caught up in another significant challenge facing first-year students: making friends and finding a supportive social network. Oma developed a sense of belonging at college through her academic interests rather than her friends, but she never came to call her college "home." Sam's reluctance to develop meaningful relationships with his faculty advisors resulted in missed academic and professional opportunities, while Nileen's desire to build strong relationships with faculty led her to develop a beneficial network of mentors and advisors in college. Adam's engagement with his courses was limited and episodic: every now and then, and sometimes to his surprise, he would get excited about a course or an assignment. Michael's engagement in physics deepened each year, culminating in collaborative research and a senior honors project, but Dan's engagement grew because he selected courses across fields that strengthened his ability to pose questions, read critically, and debate positions.

Most college students do not attend institutions like the ones we studied. Elite liberal arts colleges differ markedly from many other colleges and universities in the country. For example, they have more selective admissions practices, higher retention and graduation rates, more generous financial aid programs, and greater opportunities for students to study abroad. However, it is not the uniqueness of these students or the colleges they attended, but the commonality and everydayness of the decisions they confronted that animate our discussion of college life. The decision-making processes we identify are not unique to the Jessicas, Dans, and Omas attending liberal arts colleges. Students at four-year public or private universities must decide how to manage themselves and their time, find balance, make friends, develop a sense of belonging or home-away-from-home, select courses, declare a major, and use resources available to them, including faculty advisors. They will also find some of their academic experiences more engaging than others, so acquiring decision-making strategies that maximize opportunities for engagement improves learning outcomes for all students.

In short, our book makes an argument about how students become liberally educated, and that is something many colleges and universities are trying to achieve. We use the term *liberal education* to refer to a broad curriculum grounded in the arts and sciences as distinct from preprofessional, technical, or applied fields of study. This kind of education occurs in many types of colleges and universities, not only residential liberal arts colleges like those we studied. Our book can and should be read as an affirmation of the enduring value of liberal *education* rather than as a defense of liberal arts *colleges* as they are currently constituted. In fact, we are at times quite critical of the practices found at our colleges and offer suggestions for how those practices might be changed to improve the liberal education of all students.

We have written this book with a variety of audiences in mind: high school and college students and their parents; high school and college teachers and administrators; and scholars of higher education. In reading this book, we hope that high school students will come to better understand how college differs from high school and will learn that there is no single path to success in college. We hope that college students will see something of themselves in the narratives we have constructed and, in doing so, realize that they have more control over their education than they may have believed. In ways both small and large, they have many chances to adjust their trajectory through college, if they come to see the decisions they make as opportunities rather than as obstacles.

We hope parents will acquire a greater appreciation for how daily, seemingly mundane choices affect their child's college experience and, as a result, put in perspective the value of "big" decisions, such as choosing a major field of study. We hope that faculty, college administrators, and others who work in higher education will gain greater insight into how the delicate balance between student choice and institutional structure can foster or impede a student's progress toward becoming liberally educated. In particular, we hope that our findings on the variable nature of academic engagement will prove helpful to those seeking to improve college practices and policies.

PRACTICE FOR LIFE

ONE

❧ Restarting College

No man ever steps in the same river twice, for it is not the same river, and he is not the same man.

—*Plato's interpretation of Heraclitus, a sixth-century Greek philosopher[1]*

MONIQUE, JUNIOR: I've said this before, mildly amused, but I'm never the same person. I mean things always change, you know . . . I can't point out one particular thing, but I know that something's changing, or something's different from last year. My summer actually helped me to realize that. It's a fresh year, it's a new year, but it's still different. There are some things that are similar, and there's nothing distinct that I could point out to you right now. But overall, there's something different. Every year, every semester, is something different.

FOR THOSE INTERESTED in higher education—administrators and faculty, parents, and students—the current conversation about the value and viability of a college education can seem bewildering and contentious. On one side, there are almost daily critiques of the expense, structure, and outcomes that traditional colleges produce.[2] Citing data from an array of assessments and surveys given to college students, contemporary critics suggest that college graduates can't write well, think critically, or reason quantitatively.[3] Faculty, they say, do not ask students to engage in serious work, and students wouldn't do it even if asked.[4] Some critics claim that online learning is a more efficient, equitable, and cost-effective way of delivering education.[5] State legislatures attempt to tie funding for public universities to the number of students who find jobs rather than the number of students enrolled.[6]

On the other side, and often in response to these criticisms, scholars and analysts tout both the value and need for liberally educated citizens who will be able to compete in the new knowledge-based economy and be flexible in applying their learning to new situations.[7] They insist that students best acquire these abilities through face-to-face interactions with faculty and peers that challenge their beliefs and expose them to new ways of thinking. Acknowledging the significant costs associated with living and learning on those campuses, proponents of liberal education accuse critics of conflating arguments of cost and obsolescence. While pointing out efforts by colleges and universities to reduce operating costs and to make a liberal education more accessible through financial aid, they ask critics: If the quality of liberal education is doubtful, then why do graduates of liberal arts colleges speak so highly of their experiences and why do so many prospective college students continue to apply to liberal arts colleges?

We enter into this debate by making a case for the enduring value of liberal education, but our affirmation of liberal education is a novel and unconventional one. Based on a five-year study in which we followed over 200 students at seven liberal arts colleges, we argue that becoming liberally educated is a complex and messy process involving making decisions and learning from them. Colleges create spaces (both physical and metaphysical) in which students must make these decisions, often in the face of new and ambiguous situations. Some of these decisions are formal and happen only once or twice during college: what to major in, whether or not to study abroad, whom to choose as an advisor, where and with whom to live next year. Others occur once or twice a semester: which classes to take, organizations to participate in, or lectures to attend. And still others arise every day: whether to invest time and effort in an assignment that seems uninteresting, how to manage time, with whom to hang out, whether to meet with a professor outside of class.

Because most of these decisions have no "right" or "wrong" answers, the choices students make and what they learn from them shape their college experience. For example, a senior who chooses to work on an honors project in her major faces a different set of decisions about her last year of college than a student who quickly finishes up her major requirements in order to take courses in other fields. It may be easy to see how "big" decisions like this one affect students' paths through college, but we found this to be equally true of the seemingly mundane, daily choices that students make, such as how to approach an assignment or whether to talk to a professor during office hours.

Students can see their decision-making as opportunities to change, reflect, and learn something about themselves, or they can see decision-making as an obstacle course for which the best approach is to minimize risk and reduce uncertainty. In figuring things out, seeing decisions as either opportunities or obstacles, college students find themselves caught up in a process of *self-creation* and *re*-creation. This simple observation about the college experience has neither been fully appreciated nor systematically explored. Yet casting students' college experience as a series of choices that offer opportunities for self-creation and re-creation has consequences for students and colleges alike. The decisions that students face, the number of different tasks and experiences that they have, even the structure of college itself (each year, each semester bringing new beginnings and endings) mean that students have frequent opportunities to reimagine and recreate themselves. *Students don't just start college and then finish it. They start and then re-start college many times.*

Students enter college with differing expectations, goals, and priorities. A substantial number enter college looking forward to taking risks, challenging themselves, exploring new subjects and new ideas, and reflecting on them. Admissions officers, in fact, do their best to identify students with these qualities. Our colleges are quite good at nurturing these students and providing opportunities for positive restarts. Other students don't bring these qualities with them; they enter college focused on earning good grades, graduating with the appropriate credentials, and getting on with their post-college lives. They may, in fact, seek to reduce ambiguity and risk in the choices they make by sticking to prescribed paths and avoiding reflection altogether. However, many who start college this way later change and begin to evaluate their college experiences differently. They "restart" college more concerned with what they are learning than with the grades they are making in their courses. In exploring the decisions students make and what they learn from their choices, our research shows how college creates—and sometimes fails to create—liberally educated graduates.[8]

College as Practice for Life

College offers practice at making, and then reflecting on, decisions that build foundational skills, habits, and values associated with liberal education. What are these skills, habits, and values? William Bowen defines these as an "openness to new ideas and new friendships, respect for both evidence and the beauty of language, appreciation of 'difference,' and an ever-deeper awareness of the pure joy of learning." Derek Bok argues that "colleges pursue a variety of purposes" only one of which is intellectual growth. For example, students "need to learn to live and work effectively with other people and enter into fulfilling relationships" and develop "the capabilities, knowledge, and breadth of interests to enable them to enjoy full and varied lives." William Cronon emphasizes the importance of seeing "connections that allow one to make sense of the world and act within it in creative ways," abilities that are fostered by developing skills such as self-criticism, listening, problem solving, and community building. "[I]n our distracted and over-busy age," he writes, "educated people know how to pay attention—to others and to the work around them." Regardless of the language used to describe the goals of liberal education, however, all would agree that it is a *process,* not a state of being, that centers on becoming rather than achieving.[9]

The process of becoming liberally educated is the focus of this book. Rather than frame our analysis of the college experience in terms of the aspirational *outcomes* of a liberal arts education, we claim that how students respond to the many decisions they must make in college is essential to understanding the *process* that can lead to these outcomes. In the chapters that follow, we focus on five areas of decision-making in college that offer practice at becoming liberally educated. The first three areas address decisions related to fundamental reorientations that accompany any move to a new place: managing time and balancing commitments in a new setting, making new friends who can provide personal and social support, and establishing a sense of home in an unfamiliar place. The other two—advice and engagement—both bear on the intellectual and inquisitive orientations we hope students will acquire in college: how to ask for advice, how to become a lifelong learner, and how to find meaning in work.[10]

Time: Decisions about Finding Balance and Focusing on the Present

College is, by definition, a temporal experience, but students don't experience their four (or sometimes five or six) years in college in a uniform way. Absent the highly structured and densely populated schedules of high school, students new to college will often spend a good deal of time figuring out how best to deal with newfound freedoms and unfamiliar course schedules and professors. If they've arrived at viable strategies for managing time, they quickly come to see college as a serial decision-making process punctuated by deadlines. Years in which important decisions have to be made—decisions about declaring a major, fulfilling requirements, studying away, finding a job or applying to graduate school—often feel compressed and stressful, whereas other years may seem—or at least give the illusion of being—more expansive. The series of deadlines attached to the decisions students make in college orients them toward the future. As one student put it, "The first year is for planning for college; the second year is for planning for after college." One consequence that follows from such an intense focus on the future is that college can be seen as a means to an end—rather than an end in itself. However, the frequent decisions confronting students provide numerous opportunities for them to choose to restart college with a new orientation—one that emphasizes living and learning in the present.

Connection: Decisions about Making and Keeping Friends

Friends motivate and sustain students as they confront the uncertainties of college. Recognizing this, colleges jump-start students' initial efforts to make friends by assigning compatible (hopefully) first-year roommates and organizing social events. Most students prioritize making friends, and they tend to do so quickly by connecting to those close to them—roommates, floormates, dormmates. Proximity carries enormous weight in early friendship decisions, yet it would seem to be a poor criterion for meaningful friendships because, as one student described it, proximity merely facilitates relationships of convenience. The beauty of residential college life is that it harbors many restarts that can be, to varying degrees, socially disruptive. Housing lotteries every year can put friends on opposite sides of campus; studying abroad can put them on opposite sides of the globe. Restarts provide fertile ground for students to take stock of current friendships and to consider what they find rewarding—or not rewarding—about them. Restarts can lead students to confront change and uncertainty by choosing to rely on established friendships or they can inspire students to make new ones.

Home: Decisions about Creating Home and a Sense of Belonging

For most students, until they go to college, home has been something they've had little choice in defining. Colleges, however, require them to do their own "home"-making and to do so within a particular geographic, cultural, and social environment. Just as colleges provide a jump start for making friends, they also do much to support students' initial efforts at home-making. Not only do they create conditions to help students quickly establish friendships, they assign students faculty advisors and encourage faculty-student interactions to facilitate the development of an on-campus adult mentor. In addition, they provide support if these things fail. For some, college will be a place where they thrive academically, yet one that never really feels like home. For others, college will quickly feel like home, but a home that they are ready to leave by senior year. The structures and rhythms of college life can interfere with students' efforts to feel at home. Students come and go from college over breaks, often traveling back to their family homes. Students are also required to move residences each year and find new roommates. They choose to study abroad for a semester or year, or their friends make that choice and they are left behind. These moments of coming and going fundamentally shape and reshape students' sense of home. If seen as restarts, these moments of decision serve as opportunities to strengthen their sense of home at college. If not, they serve as obstacles that challenge it.

Advice: Decisions about Asking for and Receiving Advice

Many colleges and universities invest a great deal in designing, debating, and enacting advising programs for first-year students.[11] In particular, first-year students are required to consult with their assigned faculty advisor during course registration. Instead of seeing interactions with their faculty advisors as opportunities to receive personalized advice, however, too many first-year students see them as obstacles to be avoided (and to be fair, some professors share a similar sentiment). They are unable to develop a level of comfort with their advisor for a host of reasons, including failing to recognize the inherent benefits of getting to know faculty. When declaring a major, students often can decide to select a new faculty advisor. This important decision point provides students the opportunity to reflect upon past advising, and restart their advising relationships in order to receive better—more personalized—advice.[12] Developing the kinds of faculty relationships that will facilitate receiving personalized advice takes time, effort, and initiative. Although many students decide to pursue such relationships, others instead decide to "go it alone" and make most of their academic decisions without consulting anyone. They subsequently miss many opportunities to practice the habit of self-criticism that comes from advice-seeking and self-reflection.

Engagement: Decisions about Approaching New Ways of Thinking and Doing

Students experience academic engagement in college when they focus clearly on acquiring or creating new knowledge, are intrinsically motivated to learn, and derive pleasure from doing so. Engagement is linked to students' decisions about specific classes, assignments, professors, pedagogies, subjects, and methodologies. As a consequence, it isn't possible to describe students as being "engaged" or "unengaged" in global terms. They have engaging and unengaging experiences throughout college, and their patterns of engagement vary based on the academic decisions they make. For many students, engagement will be *episodic,* something that they experience only in some semesters. For others, engagement will be *sustained*—experienced to some extent most every semester in college—and some sustained engagement may even be *cumulative,* in the sense that engaging experiences may be linked and build on one another. The typical elements that structure the academic experience at most colleges—requiring students to complete a major and satisfy general education requirements, and using grades as signifiers of achievement and success in college—help some students make choices to become engaged, but for others these elements seem to lead them away from it.

∽ The decisions students make in college are important practice for becoming liberally educated, yet they are also important practice for creating a meaningful adult life. Graduation leads to a series of restarts in each of these five spheres of decision-making. College graduates will need to manage time and balance competing commitments in the context of a new job or graduate school. They will want to make new friends (or re-connect with old ones), and make a new home (or reconstruct their old home, if they return to their family home). They will seek intellectual engagement in new jobs and careers (or seek out intellectual stimulation elsewhere), and try to find new sources of both personal and professional advice.

It is tempting to think that those students who see the decisions they make as opportunities for self-creation are doing so consistently and in all dimensions. We might hope that decision-making improves from the first to the senior year of college in the way that we believe (or hope) that students become better writers each year. However, that's not the way self-creation works—or at least not for most students. Many seem to stumble onto courses or assignments they find surprisingly engaging, and then find other academic experiences—ones they chose because they expected them to be interesting—unengaging. Or students may, at some points, seek out and embrace connections with peers who have quite different lives and who challenge their beliefs, and at other times interact almost exclusively with a small group of close friends who reinforce rather than question their views of the world.

No single college practice or policy (e.g., orientation program, advising system, curricular requirements) can address the complex question of how to educate students to be reflective and engaged graduates. Nonetheless, the array of decisions with the potential to provoke reflection and engagement is large. Every day students face decisions that can serve as opportunities for learning, such as becoming passionate about a paper they are writing for a history course or deciding to limit their involvement in extracurricular activities so they can find more balance in their day or choosing to thoughtfully read rather than quickly skim an assigned reading for class. The many decisions, both large and small, that colleges offer students are invitations to develop skills, practices, and values that will benefit them long after they graduate.

Why Read Yet Another Book on Higher Education?

We believe this is a question worth posing—and responding to—at the outset. Over the past twenty years, many thoughtful, insightful, and field-changing books have been published on virtually every aspect of the college experience.[13] While we have learned much from these and use them throughout to contextualize our own analysis, we believe that our research makes a number of unique contributions to the field of higher education that will interest parents, students, faculty, administrators, and researchers. Our analysis is based on narratives of the student experience that we constructed from repeated interviews with a diverse group of over 200 students who thrived, struggled, or stalled at various points during their college years. Because we interviewed students every semester while they were in college, we were able to gather enormously rich and detailed information about student decision-making. Why did you choose this course, this major, this advisor? Why did you choose to live with these friends, join these organizations, or study abroad? What is most on your mind as you start the school year? And because we asked these questions (and many others) in "real time," we believe that the answers students gave constitute a valid account of their college experience.

Although you will hear from over one hundred students in this book, you will get to know a much smaller number—around twenty—fairly well. The longer narratives we have written about this group demonstrate that students find engaging academic experiences, advisors, friends, balance, or a sense of home in different places and via different routes. They also demonstrate that students' academic engagement, friendships, advisor relationships, experience of time and balance, or sense of home often change over time. We chose some of these students because their narratives were similar to those of many of their peers. We chose others because they were in many respects outliers. Regardless of their typical or atypical nature, each of these students' college experiences offers something instructive about the process of becoming liberally educated.

Very few books about the college experience are based on research that follows students throughout their time in college (or beyond) using a combination of qualitative and quantitative methods. Studies by Catharine Beyer and her colleagues at the University of Washington *(Inside the Undergraduate Experience)* and by Daniel Chambliss and Christopher Takacs at Hamilton College *(How College Works)* are exceptions.[14] Research at both schools provided valuable insights into how students learn and acquire important skills, such as writing and quantitative reasoning, although they offer different views as to whether academic departments or individual students should be the focus of efforts to assess student learning. We extend these earlier studies by addressing additional issues that are important to college students, such as how their experience of time or academic engagement changes during college. As described in more detail later in this chapter, we also conducted our research at seven colleges, rather than at a single institution, bolstering our confidence that we have identified issues that are familiar to many college students.

Other books that rely on qualitative data, such as Richard Light's *Making the Most of College* and Ken Bain's *What the Best College Students Do* offer important advice about student success in college, and our research affirms many of their findings about how students can make decisions that will significantly and positively influence their college education.[15] Bain's book and others like it start with successful students and move backward: What did these students do early on that contributed to later life success? In contrast, we chronicle the array of small and large academic and social decisions that students made and identify strategies that either helped or hindered their ability to navigate college. By looking at what students do before the verdict is in, we direct attention to what worked and didn't work for both successful and not-so-successful students. In addition, our analysis of semester-to-semester, year-to-year, interview data augments and extends ethnographies that have focused only on the first year of college.[16]

Many critics of higher education have attracted attention because they claim that students are shortchanged, aren't learning all that much in college, and spend far more time socializing than studying.[17] For example, in *Aspiring Adults Adrift,* Richard Arum and Josipa Roksa concluded that college students, on average, show limited improvement in critical thinking, complex reasoning, and written communication, especially those who attended "less selective institutions."[18] Students at "more selective institutions," in contrast, demonstrated gains in critical thinking which they attributed, in part, to the more "academic orientation" of these schools, narrowly defined as the length of writing and reading assignments, the number of times students met with a faculty member outside of class in a semester, and the number of hours spent studying in a week.[19] Unlike the standardized learning assessments and decontextualized surveys that provided the foundation for Arum and Roksa's analysis, our repeated, in-depth interviews with students allow us to document the achievement of a more expansive set of college outcomes—such as the development of a "path to purpose" as William Damon puts it—as well as a more expansive set of factors that promote learning and engagement.[20]

Finally, a number of recent books, many of which focus exclusively on liberal arts colleges, inform our discussion of the philosophical origins and debates about the purpose and usefulness of liberal education. Some make claims for the historical importance and present-day value of liberal education,[21] while others argue that the residential liberal arts college model is no longer sustainable.[22] Still others believe that a college degree is, for many, simply not worth what it costs.[23] Although we see our book as aligned with those who affirm the liberal arts, none of these offers a systematic, empirical analysis of how college creates self-motivated, inquisitive lifelong learners. We claim that becoming liberally educated is a messy, complicated, ambiguous process and seek to convince our readers—especially prospective college students and their parents—that this messy, complicated, ambiguous process is, in fact, the point of liberal education.

Our Colleges

Residential liberal arts colleges like ours are often described as "ivory towers," "bubbles," or in other ways that suggest they are insular encampments in which students are cloistered for four years before having to make their way into the "real world." We argue that these characterizations of the college experience not only misrepresent it, but also fail to capture the essence of what these colleges seek to impart to their students. The years students spend in college are indeed "real life," and these years are a critical time in which they are repeatedly asked to make decisions that have the potential to shape practices they will need as older adults. While we are quick to acknowledge that our colleges offer students "a safe space to make hard decisions" (as one student in our study put it), the residential nature of our colleges means that students must make many decisions—the consequences of which can affect both their social and intellectual development. Because students at liberal arts colleges learn, play, eat, and sleep in the same space with the same people, these colleges are especially fruitful sites at which to explore our claim that college is practice for life.

In our research for this book, we followed students at seven different colleges located in New England: Bates College, Bowdoin College, and Colby College, all in Maine; Middlebury College in Vermont; Smith College and Wellesley College, both women's colleges in Massachusetts; and Trinity College in Connecticut. Although three of these colleges have some graduate programs, all are best described as private, liberal arts undergraduate institutions. They all *look* like classic, New England undergraduate institutions—lots of green spaces with trees and grass on which students hang out, throw Frisbees, and walk to classes. All were founded either around the beginning of the 1800s or soon after the Civil War. Vestiges of the past are evident from

Victorian-style red brick buildings and rooms filled with somber portraits of past presidents.

Our seven colleges have much in common. We share the luxuries of numerous applicants, healthy endowments, and well-respected faculty. Small classes taught by tenure-track faculty are the norm at our schools; during the years these students attended our colleges the student–faculty ratios were around 9:1. We have state-of-the-art classrooms, laboratories, and libraries. We are also fairly expensive colleges to attend; tuition and fees in our students' senior year hovered around $40,000, although approximately 40% to 60% of students received financial aid. Enrollments during the years of this study ranged from 1,700 to 2,600 undergraduates (with a median enrollment of 2,300).

Despite these many similarities, there are differences among our institutions that have the potential to shape students' experiences.

- Five institutions are located in small towns or suburbs, one in a midsize city, and one in a large urban area.
- The degree of selectivity among our institutions varies. The acceptance rates for the Class of 2010 at our schools ranged from 22% to 53%.
- Although our first-year retention rates for the Class of 2010 were all over 90%, our six-year graduation rates at the time this class graduated varied from 86% to 94%.
- Our institutions vary with respect to the racial diversity of the student body. Although recruiting more students of color is a goal shared by our colleges, the percentages of students of color ranged from 10% to 39% at our colleges when the Class of 2010 entered in September 2006. When they graduated, the range was 16%–41%.[24] During the time of this study, some of the institutions had hate-speech events or town-gown incidents with racial overtones.
- Two of the institutions are women's colleges, whereas the others have long been coeducational or were men's colleges that became coeducational in the 1970s.
- For three of our colleges, athletics is important both to a majority of students who play on varsity, club, or intramural teams and to the schools themselves that make much of the fact that both men's and women's teams often play in NCAA Division III championship games. Athletics plays a smaller role in the four other schools.

Compared to the vast array of undergraduate institutions in the United States, the differences among our schools may seem minor, yet including students from seven colleges allowed us to examine a broader range of student experience than would have been possible had we limited our research to a single college.

Our Study

Combining qualitative and quantitative methods, involving hundreds of students, and spanning five years, our research captures the academic and social experiences of college students as they unfold across the four years of college and after graduation. Our study of the Class of 2010 was conducted by the New England Consortium on Assessment and Student Learning (NECASL)—a collaboration of our seven liberal arts colleges formed in 2005.[25] The general goals of NECASL were to understand students' transition from high school to college, explore student learning in relation to institutional policies and practices, and understand how students make important academic, social, and personal decisions.

From the outset, NECASL was focused both on research and assessment, so the colleges participating in this study were always interested in how our findings could inform decision-making and change on our campuses. This dual emphasis on research and assessment was important to the foundations that supported our collaboration as well. The cycle of research, assessment, and then change was of particular concern to our largest external source of support—The Teagle Foundation—but it was also appealing to our other funders—The Andrew W. Mellon and Spencer Foundations.

The organizational structure of our consortium was both unique and valuable to our work in several respects. Each college formed a core team of academic administrators, faculty, institutional research staff, and students; other individuals such as student life staff, study abroad directors, and writing program heads also joined us at various times to share their expertise. Having interacted with many faculty and administrators from other institutions who were working on assessment projects, we know of few that effectively engaged these different constituents across all participating colleges. Our inclusion of students at every stage of this project—from developing interview schedules to administering them, from coding the interview data to analyzing those data—benefited our work greatly and has served as a model for others interested in educational assessment.[26] Our student partners also spoke memorably of how their involvement in the project deepened their reflection on and insights into their own college experience.

This book focuses primarily on the qualitative data that we collected as part of this collaborative research project: a longitudinal, interview study of a subset of approximately thirty-six students from the Class of 2010 on each campus. We selected students using a methodology that intentionally oversampled students of color and international students in an effort to better understand the experiences of these less frequently studied populations. At the five coeducational colleges, we selected equal numbers of male and female students. We began interviewing students in the fall of 2006. Starting with just over 250 students, we were able to retain about 200 students who were interviewed in their senior year in 2010. Students were interviewed three times during their first year (2006–2007), once a semester for the next three years (even if they were on leave or studying away) and, finally, one year after graduation (2011). Consequently, we have up to ten interviews with students who persisted in the panel and over 40,000 pages of interview transcripts. We present more detailed information about our study in the Appendix.

We won't quote from all 40,000 pages of interview transcripts here, but we will rely heavily on direct quotations from students throughout this book. Like other scholars whose work features student voices prominently, we have removed most occurrences—although not all—of "you know," "like," "so," "well," and other phrases that make it difficult to read a lengthy quotation. And like others, we believe we have not altered the meaning of those quotations by doing so. In honoring the confidentiality of the students who participated in our study, we do not identify the colleges they attended, the names of specific courses they took, or the professors who taught them. All students' names are pseudonyms. While we routinely let you know if a quoted student is female or male and in what year (and sometimes, semester) the student was being interviewed, we only identify a quoted student's race or ethnicity if it is relevant to the issue at hand. By contrast, for those students we profile more extensively, we often provide greater demographic information (while striving to maintain their anonymity).

Our interviews with students addressed several issues related to their current academic, social, and life management experiences, as well as their aspirations and expectations for the future and their reflections on the past. In terms of academics, we wanted to know how they selected their courses, what they were learning in them, and the extent to which particular courses—and particular experiences in these courses—challenged, excited, or disappointed them. That is, to what extent (and why) were they engaged by their courses?[27] We asked them about their plans for and choice of a major field of study or their interest in studying away. They were prompted to talk about their study habits and changes they made to these, and were asked to assess the knowledge and skills they were acquiring in college. They reflected on the frequency and quality of their interactions with faculty. They told us on whom they relied for academic advice as well as what advice they would have for other students who might follow in their footsteps.

Questions about social experiences focused largely on friendships, residential life, extracurricular activities, and participation in the larger social life on campus. How did they meet their friends, and what did they derive from their college friendships? Did their friendship networks and the benefits they gained from them change over time? To what extent did living on (or off) campus influence their sense of feeling "at home" at college? How did they spend their time outside of class, and did their involvement in athletics, student government, theater, or other extracurricular activities diminish or intensify over time?

We did not ask students pointed questions about drug and alcohol use, partying, "hooking up," or longer-term, intimate relationships. Had we asked such questions of students, we would have been dubious about their answers. Sexual behavior and drug or alcohol use are especially likely to be underreported or not reported at all.[28] Instead, we asked open-ended questions about what students did in their spare time, at night, or on weekends. We gave students many opportunities to talk about these issues; some took advantage of these invitations to explore these topics, but most did not. Consequently, we only occasionally address these aspects of social life.[29]

Questions about how students managed their time and life, coped with living away from home and family, and balanced competing demands helped us understand how they were adjusting to their new roles as college students. One of the principal reasons we interviewed students three times in their first year was to closely track the ways they were managing the many, interrelated transitions from high school to college that affect their academic engagement and social connections in college.

Because we were interested in capturing students' college experience as it was unfolding, most of the interviews focused on what was going on at the time of the interview. At various points throughout their time in college, however, we asked students to think about the past or future in relation to the present: What were your expectations for college, and have these been met? What would make this a successful year for you? Now that your sophomore year is underway, what's most on your mind? If you could speak at first-year orientation, what advice would you give to students about to start college? How have you changed the most since coming to college?

Asking open-ended and non-directive questions of this sort was one of the greatest strengths of our study. Indeed, many of our insights about the college experience came from a systematic analysis of such broad lines of questioning. Had we not asked questions about what students were thinking as a new school year began, we would know little about how they experience time in college. Had we not asked students to talk about each class they were taking in each semester of college, we would never have come to understand that academic engagement is particularistic and often episodic.

In addition to this extensive archive of interview data, we collected survey data from several hundred students in the Class of 2010 at each college from the sophomore year through one year following graduation. (For example, when students in the interview study were sophomores, we surveyed all sophomores at each of the seven colleges.) The focus of these surveys varied each year, although all of them contained questions aimed at assessing academic engagement, connections with peers, and life management skills. When these surveys paralleled topics addressed in the interviews, we reference them in the footnotes to contextualize the experiences of students in the interview study and to demonstrate the extent to which their experiences are typical of their peers.

ɔ We began this chapter with a quote from Monique about change, her own change and changes in her perception of college. As a modern-day Heraclitus, Monique's college experience illustrates the starts and restarts—the messy and challenging process—of becoming liberally educated. The spring of her sophomore year did not end well. Nonetheless, she came back to college in the fall of her junior year with a renewed sense of purpose—as she described, "something's changing, or something's different from last year

... It's a fresh year, it's a new year." Still, Monique found it difficult to hold on to new work habits:

> I actually have made an earnest attempt to organize my life, not in my whole life, but at least my schoolwork. And it worked for a little while. I'm starting to slip back a little bit from maintaining those habits, or keeping up with those habits. Today, for instance, there's a paper due at a particular time, and I was late with the paper. I did not go to class when I was supposed to go to class. But you know, it's [the] little things, and part of me wants to change.

It would be easy to see Monique's restarting as unfolding within an insular bubble of college—something with few consequences and outside of "real life"—yet both what Monique can learn from her restarts and the consequences of them are very much real life. If Monique does indeed "slip back," she may not be in college next year.

The many decisions students make in college provide them with multiple chances to restart college in ways that can benefit them and help them become liberally educated adults. Some of these decisions arise out of college structures, such as academic calendars, course registration systems, advising programs, and housing lotteries. Many others arise out of the day-to-day choices students make about how to spend their time, the value they place on their studies and their friends, or how they respond to unmet expectations. The benefits to restarting college can be great, yet they depend, in large measure, on students confronting the decisions they make as opportunities rather than obstacles, as moments in which to learn about themselves, and as outcomes over which they have much control.

TWO

 Time

What's most on your mind as your sophomore year gets underway?

HENRY: First of all, I felt like, "Wow, my [college] career's about to come to an end!" Maybe that's kind of early to start thinking about it, but I felt like, "Wow, I only have my junior and senior year left!" And so that kind of hit me. And then I started thinking about graduate school and stuff, like what do I need to do for that? What are the requirements? I'm taking my tests next year, you know, all that stuff. So I started planning for that. And picking a major. I felt like I was pretty set [with that] because I kind of knew what I was doing.

COURTNEY: Nothing—other than it's going by quick.

TIME PLAYS A PIVOTAL ROLE in the structure and meaning of college, even before students set foot on a college campus. The students in our study started college in the fall of 2006 having been admitted months earlier as members of the Class of 2010, defining the college experience as one of four contiguous years and defining students by the moment in the future when they will hopefully graduate. Once students arrive, class year continues to significantly impact decisions that mean a great deal to them, such as where they choose to live or what courses to take. Throughout their time in college, students are reminded of the uniqueness of this temporal experience ("These are the best years of your life," "You won't ever be able to do this again") to encourage them to get the most out of college. These admonitions to seize the day are reinforced by the high price tag of a college education. Time is money, in college as elsewhere, so it is not surprising that some students will describe unengaging courses, or courses in which they have little interest, as a "waste of time."[1]

Although students become familiar in high school with some of the ways that time shapes learning—following a different calendar, sitting in classes of varying duration, the privileges of seniority—the relatively greater number of opportunities and more "free time" in college present them with much greater challenges regarding how best to manage time and self.[2] With rare exceptions, college courses don't meet five days a week, and it is not unusual for students to meet in classes for only a few hours a day and to have days on which they have no classes at all. Expectations for what it means to "do homework" for courses are more ambiguous. Some instructors assign text-books (the standard medium for the conveyance of knowledge in many high school courses), but many do not. Some courses require students to produce a tangible product each week—perhaps a problem set or a short writing as-signment—but many do not. What does it mean to "do the reading for next Thursday" or "come to class well-prepared?"

Many students, even those who thought they managed their time well in high school, come to college concerned about how they will deal with their newfound freedoms and unfamiliar course schedules and professors. Managing time can take a lot of work (and time) and, because there is no simple formula for figuring out how to best manage one's time, finding the right "balance" necessarily involves ambiguity. How much time should be devoted to study? To hanging out with friends? To participating in clubs? Failure in this project of self-management can negatively affect both academ-ic engagement and social life.[3]

In addition to managing themselves and their coursework, students ex-perience college as *a serial decision-making process punctuated by deadlines*. They must register for courses, declare a major, plan for study abroad, apply for internships or fellowships, and find a job or apply for graduate study. Some decisions are seen as more important than others—declaring a major, for example—and concomitantly harbor the potential to be more anxiety producing. Once one decision is made, another presents itself, and the se-ries of deadlines attached to this decision-making process orients students toward the future, rather than the present. As students find themselves plan-ning their way through and *out of college*, they often come to experience their time *in college* as short and compressed.[4]

We begin with student narratives about the college search, an activity which for many begins early in high school and exemplifies the future orientation that will shape the way students experience time in college. Once they arrive, the starts and restarts that accompany the beginning of each academic year play heavily into the different ways that students think about their time in college. Although each year is not marked by a singular orientation toward time, some modal patterns emerge as students move from one year to the next. Absent the structure of high school curriculums, multiple extracurricular activities, and the logistical support of families and friends, first-year students find that time is something they need to manage in order to profit from the academic and social opportunities college presents. By sophomore year, there is a shift in how time is experienced. It's no longer the proactive, trial-and-error project of self-management. Rather, time is experienced as reactive, deadline-driven responses to the academic decisions students must confront, chief among them the declaration of a major field of study and whether to study abroad.

Returning to college having made these decisions, many view their junior year as a time for implementing the plan crafted the previous year, freeing them up to focus on time out of college, on their futures. For those who spend all or part of their junior year studying abroad, however, time takes on a wholly different phenomenology. The time spent away from campus underscores the sense that time is compressed in college. It is no surprise, then, that the senior year presents students with a temporal dilemma: trying to stay grounded in the present so as to enjoy classes, friends, and activities, while dealing with the uncertainties of the future that signal the end of their college experience.

High School: Time to Get into College

Virtually all of the students in our study planned to go directly from high school to college.[5] An outstanding athlete may have considered trying professional sports for a year, another student may have contemplated a postgraduate year at boarding school to improve her chances of getting into a highly selective college, and yet another may have toyed with the idea of taking an adventurous gap year before attending college. But these students were exceptions to others in their cohort, many of whom had been thinking about college for a long time. And when these students thought about the colleges to which they might apply, they aimed high. Assumptions about going to college were, for the most part, assumptions about going to a highly selective, prestigious college. The search process was largely about narrowing the field to determine which elite college they would attend.

We first talked to students about six weeks into their first semester of college. These interviews began with a series of questions about their college search: When did they first start looking at colleges? What kinds of things were they looking for in choosing a college? Who influenced their selection and decision-making process? To which schools did they apply? It was not surprising to find that students had a great deal to say about their college search, given that many of them started this process in earnest in their junior year of high school or in the summer before the junior year. But for a number of students, thoughts about going to college began as soon as they entered high school. In some cases, high school guidance offices had put in place programs that forced students to think ahead to college. Jessica (whom you'll hear more about shortly) attended such a high school and offered the following recollection:

> I started looking at colleges my freshman year of high school. Our counselor actually required us to make a list of about thirty schools that we were interested in. In between freshman year and junior year we had to do research, visit, you know, all that kind of stuff to make a final decision as to where we wanted to apply, and the final list consisted of about ten to fifteen schools. So my actual final list was done by the second week of my senior year.

Early formal interventions of this detail and magnitude were, however, uncommon among students. For some, thinking about college early on was a more generalized byproduct of the culture of their school or local community. A student who went to a "super academic high school" in a university town recalled, "People had been talking about college forever, maybe even in middle school." Another, soon after she found out she had been accepted to a private high school, remembered that "a whole bunch of parents were asking me where I was going to college, so I guess that's when I started thinking about college." (Note that this student is describing a set of interactions she had *before* entering high school.)

Parents or others close to them also played a role in getting even first-year high school students to think ahead to their future as college students.[6] "My parents would always say, 'Have you looked at this school,' or 'you should look at that school,'" one student recalled in thinking back to her first year of high school. The expectations of family members could likewise signal the importance of getting into a good college and the steps needed to make that happen. This was sometimes a prominent concern for students living in other countries who were hoping to attend college in the United States. When asked when she first started thinking about college, one international student replied:

> It was always in my family that I would be going to college, and it was always like, "Aim high." So I've always been introduced and exposed to a lot of colleges since I was very little. Since seventh grade, I started looking into colleges, starting to feel like which ones I wanted to go to and was considering, and starting to prepare in terms of my high school workload and preparing for [International Baccalaureate exams].[7] Because I was living overseas at that time, I wanted to keep my options open with IB, so that if I happened to go overseas I would have some credential other than like an average high school.

But the role of parents in getting young high school students thinking about colleges was often much less instrumental. Family vacations, for example, offered a low-stakes way of exposing children to a generic "college experience." Although it is not clear that these early encounters with college had much of an effect on the searches students had as juniors and seniors, these visits may nonetheless reaffirm the importance of thinking about college early on: "My family went on 'official' college visits my junior year. But before that, whenever we went anywhere there was a college, we would go look at it. So I remember seeing Berkeley when I just got out of eighth grade, and UCLA when I was in ninth grade, and just random colleges when I happened to have been in those areas."

The college search of siblings often increased the likelihood that students would develop a nascent interest in the college search process. For parents, trips to visit colleges for one child served as a kind of educational "twofer" whereby the younger, not-yet-seriously-looking-at-colleges student gets to tag along with her older, seriously-looking-at-colleges sibling. Unlike the "vacation as excuse for visiting colleges" experiences of the students quoted above, here the college search for one child served as the impetus for a family vacation. As one student put it: "I started [looking at colleges] early because my brother's a year older than me and, when he started, my parents weren't going to waste the opportunity to take me with them. So I started probably in my freshman to sophomore year, less freshman year, but a lot of looking in sophomore year."

From the younger student's point of view, the search experiences of older siblings provided a standard against which their own college search would be evaluated. Likes and dislikes about colleges were assessed; similarities and dissimilarities to siblings were considered. Having gained familiarity with major features that distinguished one college from another—size, location, areas of study—students with older siblings were more likely to be "restarting" their college searches as high school juniors or seniors. They were, in a sense, retracing the paths that their brothers and sisters had followed to college.

One final impetus for starting the college search early stemmed from the desire to pursue college athletics. Although our colleges don't offer athletic scholarships and are not competitive in signature college sports (e.g., football, basketball, hockey, or baseball), serious athletes at a variety of levels saw the college application process as instrumental to continuing their passion for sports. Knowing that most student athletes are recruited before coming to college (even those at Division III schools), high school students may start looking at colleges sooner than others with the hope of finding a good fit—the right coach, welcoming teammates, top-notch facilities—that will increase the likelihood that athletics will remain an important part of their college experience:

> I started my sophomore year with trying to get recruited to play sports between field hockey and lacrosse. So I was really active in those two things out there in high school. I just started sending recruitment forms my sophomore year, which is really early, but by the time the summer [before] my junior year, I had already, could get a little bit of feedback, you know, [from] coaches and go to camps at schools that I thought I would like. But other than that, yeah, that's how it started and then it kind of developed from there.

For many reasons—programs designed by high school guidance counselors, subtle (or not so subtle) nudges from parents, trips with and advice from older siblings, or the general context of the communities or networks in which they live—students spend a good deal of time in high school focused on getting into college.[8] Although our interviews provided little insight into how this orientation toward the future affected students' academic engagement and social connection in high school, that so much of their time in high school was taken up with thinking about college is significant in its power to frame students' expectations about college. If getting into college takes so much time and effort, then isn't high school really just about getting into college? And if high school is really about getting into college, isn't college really just about getting a good job, a prestigious fellowship, or a spot in a top-notch graduate program?

Many students enter college with a temporal framework shaped by their high school experiences, a framework that encourages them to be continually focused on the future. The admonition that "College will be the *best* four years of your life" is quickly set aside in favor of one more akin to "College will be the *next* four years of your life." That shift has significant implications for how students view decisions they will make and how they experience time in college.

The First Year: Time Management and Balance

Given the amount of time students spend trying to get into college, it is somewhat ironic that they arrive knowing very little about what college will be like. They understand that "College is not high school," because this is a message that colleges repeatedly convey to students as they recruit them. But one problem with this message is that high school students—even those who have siblings in college or college professors as parents—can't really know what college is like until they experience it. As a consequence, they don't always have realistic expectations about college and find that they don't "get the most out of college" until they've been there for a while.

Many students new to college assume a certain linearity about the transition from high school to college. They see college as a kind of "super high school" where classes will be harder and good grades more difficult to earn, where homework will consist of more reading, and where writing assignments will be more frequent or longer. Students may indeed find that these things are a part of their first-year experience, but they will also find that they are being asked to think, speak, write, read, and study differently. That is why some students who had been told that they were good writers in high school are (rightfully) surprised when their professors tell them they have serious writing problems. That is why beneficial study habits acquired in high school may not work well in college (maybe because lots of people are around all of the time and they can't seem to find a time or place to study). And that is why the history course a student may be taking (which she's not liking) bears little resemblance to the ones she had in high school (which she adored).

To help new students cope with the many ambiguities they face, colleges treat the first year as different in a number of ways. They invite students to come to campus early for orientation programs that address a host of issues ranging from academic integrity to diversity and inclusion to time management. Some offer (and others require) small seminars or writing courses only open to new students. First-year students are assigned faculty advisors and are directed to peer academic and residence advisors who give them advice about course selection and general information about how to navigate their way through college. Roommates are assigned and living arrangements structured in ways that are supposed to help them make new friends. These institutional practices serve as visible acknowledgments of the significant transitions confronting first-year students as they attempt to create a new home at college: leaving community, family, and friends behind and moving to an unfamiliar place where virtually everyone is a stranger and where the routines of everyday life can no longer be taken for granted.

Institutional structures and practices, of course, are never sufficient to guarantee every student a successful transition from high school to college. Students respond to the newness of college in various ways and to various ends but, for most students, managing themselves and their time effectively is essential to constructing the foundation on which their college experience will be built. It is difficult to learn and make good grades if your study habits do not allow you to prepare for class discussions or turn in work on time. It is difficult to enjoy hanging out with friends or to attend campus events if you feel the need to study all of the time. And it is difficult to enjoy most anything in college—academic, social, or otherwise—if you are forever running from one thing to another, experiencing time as though it were without punctuation.

We found that the earlier students learned to manage time and achieve a workable balance among academic and social experiences, the greater their academic engagement and social integration.[9] Conversely, students who had not been able to achieve these goals by the end of the first year were likely to be frustrated, stressed, and sometimes panicked by their inability to adjust to college. But what distinguished students who succeeded at time management and balance from those who did not? As might be expected, given the success that our students had in high school, it was not simply that some worked hard at these goals and attained them while others "slacked off," treating the first year of college as an extended vacation. Many students worked hard at managing their time, but some struggled to translate that work into a successful day-to-day, week-to-week plan for college. Why didn't their work pay off?[10]

The first-year experiences of Jessica and Stephanie provide some insights into how we might answer this question.

Jessica: Seeking Balance

In choosing her first-semester courses, Jessica decided to balance required classes with classes she was just interested in taking. She also carried over this sense of balance to her social life. She explained that most of the people in her dorm were able to find a good balance because everyone could be very studious, "but no one is really to the point where like they're studying 24/7." She acknowledged that it was still the first month of school, but she thought that this would be a good living situation. Jessica also got involved with several campus groups (too many by her own account), but she hadn't spent much time with them yet. She hoped that these groups would keep her from becoming "that person who's just like school, school, school . . . and nothing else." While her "grades definitely come first," she thought it was important to value life outside of the classroom.

During her second semester, Jessica commented that she got "ahold of everything" in the first few weeks of the semester, and adjusted to "being new and understanding the way classes worked, and office hours, and how to manage your free time, and do homework, and just to stay on top of things." Her good time management skills helped her to maintain a balance of academic work, extracurricular activities, and relaxation throughout her first semester. To begin with, she had a good set of study skills. As she explained, "I knew how to allot time well to study for different things." She also recognized that, although some subjects required her to work alone so that she could concentrate, there were others that she would benefit from by studying with others. Although she generally did well handling her classes, she wished that she had sought help earlier. She knew about available resources, such as professors' office hours and student tutors, but she didn't use them soon enough. She hoped to improve this in the future: "just not waiting until I desperately needed it but at the first signs of weakness, or struggling, to go seek help."

Because she managed her schedule well, Jessica was able to make time for extracurricular activities: "I think that went well, just making a schedule of my own and finding time to concentrate on the academic aspect as well as talk to my parents, or go into town, or just to really find a balance I think helped a lot." She went to church every week and appreciated the opportunity to leave campus and "do something for me." She valued her "down time" during her first semester. For instance, every Thursday she got together with friends to watch a favorite television show. It was "a nice refreshing time," and "it was just that time for me to relax and remember to be human and laugh for a little bit." She also would go to one or two campus events a week, judiciously choosing which ones to attend so that they didn't interfere with finishing her homework.

Jessica also found time to participate in many student organizations and to have a job. Although she considered cutting back on her extracurricular activities, she didn't because she realized that most of them didn't take up much time: "I thought it was going to be a lot when I sat down and did the list, but some of them met every other week or once a month or like for an hour one day every week, so it wasn't really a huge time commitment, so it wasn't that bad." She waited a week or two at the beginning of the semester before getting a job because she wanted to "make sure that [she] had enough time."

Jessica signed up for a more challenging course load during her second semester, but she scheduled her classes to ensure she had time to both relax and do her homework. She had a better feel for "the way things work" and "what's expected" of her. Jessica changed her study techniques to accommodate her two labs and her work hours: "I found that it's better, and it helps me to stay focused and on task if I have a schedule. Time is so precious now because I don't have a lot of it, like I did last semester, so every moment that I have, I need to be using it wisely." She acknowledged that last semester she "spent an equal amount of time on everything" rather than allotting her time differently to study for different things as had been her goal. So this semester, she planned her time more carefully: "If I know it's only a short quiz that counts for 10 points, I might study a little bit, for maybe thirty minutes two or three days before the quiz, as opposed to if it's like an exam that's worth a lot. I might begin to study the week before."

Looking ahead, she hoped to maintain the balance she achieved throughout her second year. "Everyone says that sophomore year is really crazy," she remarked, so she wanted to "remain calm and try to think ahead and try to do what I can to make it less stressful next year." She explained that part of her good balance came from her parents' encouragement. They "knew about my college's reputation and how people here are, so they would constantly nag and tell me to put down my book and to go for a walk or do something like that." She also saw the way that some students devoted all of their time to academics, and she didn't want to end up like them: "I saw a lot of different people and I didn't want to be like them because, I mean there's nothing wrong with studying but I pay for room and board, so I'd rather sleep in my bed than in the library."

Summing up the importance of finding balance, Jessica offered the advice she would give to incoming students: there is more to school than just academics.

> The college experience is not only about books and getting good grades. Yes, you can get good grades. Yes, you can get the A's, but what else suffers? What are you missing out on? Because how does that serve you if you get all A's or if you do very, very well, but you don't know how to carry on a conversation with someone because you're kind of socially awkward?

She would encourage new students to "do what you have to do to keep your sanity," ranging from walking around the campus to going out to dinner. "It's not only about the books. They are important. But life is important, too."

Stephanie: Managing Time

Although Stephanie got off to a good start at college—she enjoyed most of her classes, made some friends, and joined a few organizations—she was concerned with how she would be able to manage her time because of the lack of structure in her schedule: "I guess the lack of time [in high school], made me really, really stay on track." In college, though, she had big blocks of free time: "For example, today I finished at 9:30, and then I had a class at 4:00 . . . I have all this time and, I'm like, 'Maybe I should watch TV or maybe I should check my email.' I feel like I end up getting sidetracked. But I need to have a set schedule." Stephanie printed out a schedule where she "can fill things in and keep reminding" herself that she had "to stay on task." She wanted to put in enough effort to achieve good grades in her classes, in particular "an A in math and A in biology," so she needed to manage her time to make sure she could do all of the work. She discussed time management when explaining what would make for a successful year: "If I take the time and effort, then I can do well in the classes . . . If I have the time and I take the time to do what I need to do, then I don't think I have to worry."

Stephanie's first semester did not go as well as she had expected, so for her first college restart, she actively tried to improve her study techniques and time management skills in the second semester. She had thought her study habits were "fine" because she was "getting good grades in high school," but now realized she needed to learn to study differently in college: "It's a lot more about outside learning; you have to do a lot more outside of class. And I think I had to adjust to that for some of my courses." She read a book about how best to study, which "makes you see what you've done wrong and how you could easily improve them. And it's not about making big changes or anything. It's mostly about studying and finding out if being alone works better." The advice from this book, along with her lived experience of first semester, made her think about what she needed to change: "Studying with friends does not help me at all. Last semester I didn't have set hours, which was not very good either, because I didn't think about how many hours of free time that I had."

After assessing how she spent her time the previous semester, she "just realized how much time I was wasting . . . I would just sort of sit in my room and waste time online, do very little homework and just waste the time." She had much more free time first semester compared to this semester. Responding to this change, she realized that she works better in the afternoon, so she set aside time to study after lunch. She also continued to construct "a master weekly schedule." "It sounds very anal," she commented, "but it really, really helps." She used it to keep track of time for classes, studying, work, and free time, and "so far it's been working very well."

Despite having some issues with time management, Stephanie was fairly active outside of her studies during her first semester. She went to several campus events and was also a member of many extracurricular organizations and planned to continue with most of them. She also got a job in a dining hall that "worked out pretty well," but she had to miss out on events that were scheduled when she worked. Also, since she wouldn't consistently manage her time well during the day, Stephanie would "have to hurry up and try to finish everything" after work when she was tired. She adjusted her work schedule this semester, but she wasn't sure if she'd keep this particular job next semester because she got "too exhausted" from her Friday morning shift. Because Stephanie had to work to contribute to her financial aid, she couldn't stop working but she hoped to find a less taxing job.

At the end of the semester, Stephanie admitted that her time-management restart—the ways she tried to cope with time management—did not work out. She was often stressed and got sick a few times throughout the semester, which took a toll on her schoolwork. For one thing, most of her academic work was condensed into a few days every week: "I think with the way my schedule was set up, it made me really tired really quickly." While her master schedule was helpful at first, it also contributed to her stress because she felt that she could not catch up when she strayed from it. She explained what would happen if, for instance, she napped instead of doing her work: "If I slept fifteen minutes over the time that I had set, I would feel stressed out like I still have a lot of work to do and I haven't gotten to it yet." She also became more involved with her extracurricular activities, which "didn't work out too well." These took up a lot of time, and she assumed "sub-positions in almost everything." She realized that she "took on too much," but that she would still volunteer "for a lot of other things that I probably did not have time for."

The low point of her first year was "being stressed out and being sick." She explained that a lot of the stress was "from being tired and not sleeping enough. Sometimes it was because of work. Sometimes it was just my fault." And when she was stressed, she wasn't able to keep up with her coursework: "I think with how stressed I got this semester I stopped enjoying my classes because I know I would feel really tired and not really feel like going." Her poor health had a big impact on her work: "If I hadn't been sick, I think I would have felt better. Maybe not as homesick or not as tired. Not as stressed out. And I probably would have done better in my classes." Overall, Stephanie realized that she was trying to do too much: "I was stretching myself too thin."[11]

When Stephanie returned to campus for her sophomore year, she was "looking forward to coming back and sort of starting over or starting new." She was excited to take new classes and to assume new leadership positions and was hopeful she would improve her time-management skills: "Last semester was really hard and I was really, really stressed out, and I thought maybe I could fix all of the mistakes I made last semester."

∾ In the years that followed, both Jessica and Stephanie continued to work on managing competing demands on their time, but Jessica remained more successful at these tasks. Why? In many respects Jessica and Stephanie confronted similar challenges in making the transition from high school to college. Both had to adjust to less structured course schedules, decide which organizations to join and how much time to give to them, make time to attend campus events that interested them, and work a job. And both shared many background characteristics when they arrived at college. Jessica and Stephanie had lived at home with both parents, neither of whom attended college. They both attended public high schools and received financial aid from their colleges.

Perhaps Jessica was more successful in making the transition from high school to college because she was more adept at coping with ambiguities in ways that reflected her particular individual practices. In the process of making changes to her study habits or her extracurricular commitments, she did a close reading of both herself and her environment in order to keep her goal of balance on track. It was not just about finding enough time to do everything she wanted to do; it was about realizing that some course assignments take more time and effort to complete. It was about realizing that some organizational commitments weren't all that time-consuming, so they could be retained. Although she also reflected on what was working and what was not, Stephanie adopted a more generic approach to managing her time. She read a book about how to study more effectively that she described as a straightforward guide that was "not about making big changes or anything." At the same time, she took on leadership roles in the campus organizations which, she discovered, carried with them increased—and more open-ended—time commitments.

Jessica and Stephanie used different mental schema to address these and other ambiguities that students new to college face. Jessica approached these tasks from the standpoint of creating *balance* in her life. From the beginning she was worried that she would spend too much time studying and not enough time doing other things. She saw other students who do this and didn't want to be like them. Stephanie, by contrast, confronted large blocks of "free time" as something to be *managed*. She created a detailed schedule to impose order on her days, but this master plan soon became a source of anxiety in and of itself. She felt "stressed out" and became ill as a result. Jessica's holistic focus on balance might have contributed to her relative success in relation to Stephanie's segmented focus on time management.

Of course, the differences in Jessica's and Stephanie's responses to how they were balancing things or managing time might be attributed to their expectations about what it meant to succeed at those tasks. Coming to college concerned about her ability to manage time, Stephanie may have had more exacting expectations than Jessica for what is means to manage time effectively. Her comments about straying from her daily schedule—napping for fifteen minutes instead of finishing her homework—suggest this might be the case. As a consequence, she experienced a good deal of stress in failing to live up to what were perhaps unreasonable standards. Furthermore, although Stephanie's interviews don't tell us very much about the support she received in managing the move from high school to college, Jessica explicitly called attention to how her parents nagged her and told her "to put down my book and go for a walk." Maybe this social affirmation led Jessica to believe that she was doing better at managing the transition from high school to college than most would expect. As a result, she felt like she had things pretty well under control.[12]

Jessica—who maintained a comfortable sense of balance throughout college—and Stephanie—who never seemed to be satisfied with her efforts at time management—are but two exemplars of how first-year students experience time. Some students were self-described "pendulums," swinging back and forth between the academic and social dimensions of the college experience, and taking three or more semesters to find a workable balance between the two. Others—only a few—would never do so, no matter the number of times they restarted college. Their failure at this task led some into a downward spiral of academic and social disengagement, which culminated for some in taking time off from college (either because they chose to do so or because their colleges told them they had to do so). No matter the path traveled, however, all of these students' experiences underscore the importance of achieving balance and managing time in transitioning from high school to college.[13] The significance of these achievements was much on the minds of students as they ended their first year and anticipated the "busyness" of their sophomore year—the year when they believed they would make the most consequential decisions of their college careers.

The Sophomore Year: Time to Get Serious

From the student's point of view, the sophomore year can seem like a big puzzle with moving pieces that change shape and size over time: What will I major in? Will I study abroad or stay on campus my junior year? How will I fulfill my general education requirements? What kinds of internships can I apply for next summer? Solving this puzzle is complicated and riddled with ambiguities because the pieces are often interrelated: If I major in this subject, will I be able to study abroad or take courses in other fields that interest me? If I study abroad, will I be able to continue my participation in sports or other extracurricular activities when I return? In confronting questions such as these, sophomores are likely to feel that there is much at stake and very little time to arrive at answers. Consequently, many students experience their sophomore year as a watershed in their time in college.

Students begin this pivotal decision-making year, of course, with the great advantage that they are restarting—not starting—college, returning to a place over which they have some mastery. They know where things are. They have some friends and have been involved in some activities. They know what it is like to be in a college classroom and have a sense of the expectations professors have of them. Most have taken a range of courses giving them a sense of the field in which they might major. Most have acquired a better sense of how to manage time and competing commitments.[14]

Students routinely acknowledged that the experience and knowledge gained during their first year carried great benefits as they started their second year of college. When asked what it was like to be back on campus as a sophomore, one student said:

Different. Sometimes I still want to say, "Freshman." When people ask me about school I say, "Yeah, I'm a freshman. Oh no, I'm not!" And you have a reinforced assurance of yourself and your capabilities because you made it through a year. It's like, if you made it through one, chances are you can probably do it again and again and again. So you have a little more confidence. Even though you go through the same things, you're less quick to jump the gun. If you get a test grade that you're not too happy with, you probably won't, like last year, freak out and not know what to do. But this year I'm like, just regroup and try to talk to your professor. You have connections, not just with people but mental connections where you know the proper protocol for when things happen. So you have more experience, and with experience you know how to navigate better.

At the same time that returning to college as a sophomore can inspire a sense of confidence, the multiple decisions students will soon be asked to make can evoke a sense that things are moving much more quickly, maybe too quickly. From both their colleges and their friends, sophomores receive messages stressing the need to act now in order to realize the benefits of their college education in the years to come: "The halcyon days of the first year are gone." "No more playing around." "It's time to get serious." "It's time to focus on the future." But what do these somewhat daunting and often ambiguous calls to action mean to students embarking on their second year of college?

Talking about his experience of returning to college as a sophomore, one student spoke about how the benefits of restarting college were countered by pressures to think about the years ahead:

Well, you're no longer a freshman. Boy, did that go by fast! Now you're a sophomore, but where do you go from here? That's the question on the minds of many sophomores. As a sophomore you're ready to have more fun. You're more excited about doing things. You know [the college], [the college] knows you. But at the same time, in the back of your mind, it's like, "Shoot, college is going to be over before you know it!" You're starting to think about things you never thought before, [like] your GREs, your LSATs.[15] So sophomore year to me is about I know things now, but where am I going to go with these things that I know.

Talking about returning to college as a sophomore, another student acknowledged that:

> It feels different because I've been here for a year. I feel like there's a lot
> more pressure of the real world encroaching on my little bubble because
> we're talking about going abroad and about getting internships for the
> summer. Last year you were just starting out and you didn't have to
> worry about that kind of stuff. But this year I feel like there [is] a lot
> more planning for the future.

Others voiced similar sentiments about how the decision-making and planning they would do in their sophomore year were consequential for both the remainder of their time in college as well as their lives after college. The impending decisions about choosing a major, planning for study abroad, and completing requirements provided a portal through which students began to imagine life many years down the road.[16] When we asked first-semester sophomores: "What's most on your mind as your sophomore year gets underway?" they expressed a variety of sentiments reflecting the need to "get serious" about the future and the sense that time was indeed "flying by" in college:[17]

> I still don't know what I'm going to major in. That's sort of the same
> thing as last year. That's definitely the main thing on my mind right
> now. Different things. Just thinking about the future even more. As a
> freshman you're like, "Ah, it's freshman year just do whatever, just find
> yourself." I didn't really think much about later in my college career
> or later in my life. But I'm definitely doing more of that now this year
> because it's getting even closer and you better start getting prepared and
> decide what you want to do.

> This year they say, "Oh, it's the beginning of the year where things really
> matter." Because if you want to participate in a special program for your
> junior year, if you want to figure out what you want to do for your major,
> or for whatever else you want to do [for] the rest of your college career,
> now is the time to do it. It's your sophomore year. Not that I didn't have
> to worry about [figuring things out sophomore year], but, it's definitely

here now, something present now for me. So it's a lot more pressure for me to do that. And that's different from what I had to feel last year but you know, you deal with that when it comes. And I feel like this year it's really coming in my mind, to figure out what exactly is it that I want to do instead of being vague and [only] having an idea. I came in thinking I wanted to do something, then that changed so then I have to figure out again what I want to do.

When confronted by the sense that time is rapidly accelerating in the sophomore year, some students pointed to what they saw as mixed messages being sent by their colleges. The themes of exploration, risk-taking, and breadth are central to the tradition of liberal education, and they get prominent play in the first-year orientation and advising programs at our colleges. New students, who had been told they have plenty of time to "find their passion" and pursue newfound interests, returned as sophomores to find that their "time is up": majors need to be declared, study abroad options explored, degree requirements fulfilled.[18] It is not surprising then that some students saw this as a form of bait-and-switch whereby they questioned the advice they received as first-year students. Thinking back to her first year, one sophomore said:

I just remember the first year, like a lot of people—professors, deans or whatever—said you have four years to complete your requirements, and you have plenty of time to find your major. And all of a sudden sophomore year, they tell you: "The time's approaching. You need to declare a major if you want to study abroad and there are deadlines."

Given the emphasis liberal arts institutions place on graduating in four consecutive years, these mixed messages can heighten the sense that time in college is short and compressed:

I feel like first year they told us don't worry about what you're going to major in. You know, take any classes that you want and follow your interests. And then you get to sophomore year, and it's like that's over. Like that sort of honeymoon period at [college]. So I don't feel like I got a lot of advice that was pertinent to sophomore year first year ... It's just funny that it's kind of what they tell you first year and then you really do have to decide sooner than they make it seem. And it goes by so fast.

Even if students didn't complain about being misled about how much time they had to make decisions, they often felt that their college put them back on the application treadmill in their sophomore year. Sandwiched in between the external process of applying to colleges in the senior year of high school and the internal process of declaring a major or applying to study abroad, their first year, in retrospect, seems all the more a "time out" from applications and paperwork. For one sophomore, who was making plans to study abroad her junior year at the same time that she was dealing with deadlines for declaring her major, the year was "going by really, really fast already . . . I feel like that's sophomore year. It's just everything happens at once. And you still have to be doing all your schoolwork, too. But there's just all these deadlines and applications."

Another student, who was feeling "completely overwhelmed by study abroad" at the beginning of her sophomore year and was "really worrying about next year," compared the application process to taking another class:

> I have to declare a major because I want to study abroad. And so I have this checklist that I carry around with me. It's just sort of in my notebook. Things like in my calendar, and it's all paperwork stuff that I have to do. So I feel like, even at night when I'm going to bed, I'm sitting there and I'm like, "Did I print out that form? Did I fill it out? Did I remember to take in my birth certificate?" And so that's heavily hanging over my head. It's like taking another class.

Echoing many of the same concerns, another sophomore reflected on how the application process was taking precedence over her academic and extra-curricular involvement:

> It really seems like there's so much more expected as far as being on top of your game with paperwork-y type stuff like figuring out your major, or I'm trying to declare [a special program], so figuring out who I need to contact for that and trying to get your study abroad [application] done, and just all of these extra components besides focusing on your

school work. This year I feel like I have so much less time for [my extracurricular activities] because of all this other stuff going on. So, it's not that it's necessarily a bad thing. It's just a different challenge I think as opposed to trying to figure out schoolwork. Now it's like, "Schoolwork? I hope I get it done." Because there's not really time to stop and work at it.

We began our discussion of the sophomore year employing the metaphor of a puzzle. By the end of the sophomore year, almost every student will have finished that puzzle. Not unlike the feeling one gets snapping in the last three pieces of a 1,000-piece jigsaw puzzle, many students will end the year with a sense of accomplishment and satisfaction. Others, less joyous, will think that the puzzle took too long to complete or that it should have been easier to solve or wonder why they wasted so much time working on it and worrying about it. Yet others will, at some later date, worry that the puzzle they completed is no longer the one they wish they had started. Regardless of how they look back on their sophomore year, virtually all will believe that they have made the most important decisions of their college lives.

The Junior Year: Thinking about Time after College

Not unlike the start of college in their first year, juniors restart college feeling as though they've crossed a threshold. The big decision—the declaration of a major—is over, and plans to study abroad have either been made or abandoned. This restart is more of a coast than a climb. Responding to the question of what's most on her mind at the beginning of her junior year, one student expressed these sentiments clearly:

I feel like last year there was a lot to decide. It was, okay, what am I going to major in, where am I going to study abroad, what classes do I want to take? And sort of once I decided all that, I feel like there's nothing more to decide this year. Now it's just following the plan and everything's laid out. So I feel like there's less to decide this year.

The sense that the important decisions of college are behind them can lead students to turn their attention (and worries) to the future, to after college.

Although we saw this focus on the future emerge in the sophomore year, it quickly comes to predominate in the junior year:

> I guess definitely it would be grades, the internship, my junior internship, because after that I'll have to graduate. And then I think it's also just more about finding myself. I mean, I have more definitions of myself now since I've accumulated two years of friends, social life experience, courses, sort of about what I don't know and what I do know. I already have a major, so there are a lot of things that are becoming more clear in my life, but I still feel like after [college], then definitely I will have to change what I am, or just what I am will change as a [college] graduate, as someone with a B.A. degree. I'm just going to say it's a little scary at this point.

For students beginning their junior year the future intrudes into their lives in three prominent ways. Some students focus on academic goals they have for their senior year or for after college (which often are related to one another): Which topic will I choose for my senior thesis, and whom will I ask to be my thesis advisor? Do I have the courses, grades, and test scores to get into graduate school? Many more will think—and worry—about whether they will have a job after graduation: What kind of work am I interested in, and will my degree help me secure a job in that field? Would a summer internship help me get a job, and how do I find it? Finally, anticipating studying abroad later in the year or interacting with seniors who will soon be graduating, some juniors will emphasize social concerns: How can I make the most of my friendships before I graduate? Although academic and career-related objectives serve to advance students' focus on the future, social concerns tend to anchor them in the moment. But regardless of the directional forces at play, all of these heighten the sense of time compression in college.

Academics

At some of our colleges, all students must write a thesis as a capstone requirement for the major. At others, students who have demonstrated great interest and promise in their major field will be invited to do thesis work.

The cultures at all of our colleges support the belief that these semester- or year-long projects are "a big deal," ones that require a lot of forethought and planning. At the start of the year, one junior spoke about this in a vexed way: "I'm about to graduate, and you have to plan now for what you want to do with [your] thesis. I just talked to my advisor and she said, this summer you should plan what you want to do for your thesis so that you can do it for fall. So I guess a lot of the planning has to happen now. And, you know, I really have to be on top of things."

This student's response to "What's most on your mind as your junior year gets underway?" is notable in two ways. Although she is only midway through the first semester of her junior year, she begins her answer to this question by declaring that she's "about to graduate." And when her major advisor tells her that she should think about her thesis topic *next summer*, she declares, "a lot of the planning has to happen *now*."

The junior year will, for some, present itself as the stage on which (hopefully) strong graduate or professional school applications will start to be assembled. Grade point averages—never high enough—need to be raised. Kinks in study habits must be ironed out. Standardized tests for medical, business, law, or graduate school need to be studied for, practiced, and taken. Resumes have to be created and polished. All of these may combine to make the junior year of college all too reminiscent of the junior year of high school: too early to apply to schools but not too early to be preparing to apply to schools.

What's most on your mind as your junior year gets underway?

I'd say grades have become more significant to me. I'm not sure if this is true, but I feel like your junior-year grades are pretty important for med schools. And the classes that I'm taking now are kind of crucial classes for being able to prove that I'm good. I'm taking neuroscience, and I'm a neuro major. So obviously if I don't do so great in that class, it's not a good sign. And I'm taking [organic chemistry], and that's important for med school. So I guess it's that the classes that I'm taking now, I really want to be able to prove that I can handle the coursework and get good grades in them.

Well I guess because I've been thinking about [junior year] all summer. I came back and a lot of my friends are seniors. I came back sort of thinking about the whole grad school thing and a little worried about it. Because the best way to eventually get there is to do more research, because that's what they like to see. But in order to do a thesis, I need to improve my GPA and work hard academically this year.

Jobs

Just as students planning to go to graduate school find themselves in limbo in their junior year—"too early to apply but not too early to prepare"—those hoping to work after graduation are worrying about how best to prepare for their entry into a mysterious and turbulent job market.[19] But unlike students who have their sights set on business, medical, law, or graduate school, students who will look for jobs as college graduates see their futures as much more nebulous. That they will be graduating from colleges that do not offer pre-professional majors adds to concerns about what kinds of jobs they might be qualified for or want to do. This uncertainty and ambiguity about the future was expressed by several students in their answers to the question of what was most on their minds at the beginning of the junior year. "I think just thinking about what I'm going to do after [my college]," one junior replied. Or simply "Life after [my college]," answered another. The insulating "college bubble" that students so often referred to was starting to thin. No longer a first-year student and soon to be a senior, figuring out life after college became a priority as one junior commented: "Like really trying to figure out what I want to do is really happening now. I thought about it freshman year, but it didn't really matter because it was so far away. But now it's coming up really quickly. I haven't done it yet, but I know it's on my agenda." Another said: "Some of my senior friends or the people that have graduated, either they're looking for a job or they have jobs. I'm kind of terrified from the ads. Next year I'm going to be a senior, and I'm going to have to start on that process also. So I'm actually trying to figure out what I might want to do. So that's like been on my mind."

One way in which students responded to their concerns about employment after graduation was through seeking a summer "internship" rather than a summer "job" after their junior year. For a student majoring in sociology, the beginning of the junior year found him "trying to figure out an internship, just thinking like what comes after college. It's really started hitting me more as a junior than it did at the end of my sophomore year and over the summer. It really kind of set in when I came back to school." For another majoring in economics, focusing on getting a consulting internship helped allay his fears about a bad economy, something that was "freaking him out." Making the distinction between summer *jobs* (e.g., lifeguarding, camp counseling, grocery store stocking) and summer *internships* (e.g., consulting, working for state or federal representatives, running programs for NGOs), one student was hoping to "get a more resume-filling job than I've been doing [in past summers]. Just more preparation for the future."

Social Life

Seniors who were looking for jobs might be making their friends who are juniors anxious, but they were also making them mournful. Unlike school or job hunting that moved juniors to focus on being out of college, friendships with seniors could orient them toward making the most of their time left in college. As one junior put it:

> At the beginning [of the semester] I was just trying to have a good time, because I felt like I had so little time here left. I have some good friends who are seniors and, I just get really sad about this kind of stuff, but it makes me figure out how much I'm going to miss them. It's my last time to have this kind of time with them.

Study abroad can similarly intensify a focus on the social aspects of college life. Students who have friends studying off campus find that restarting college in their junior year presents them with the challenges of finding new friends and new activities—at least until their friends return. Commenting on the difference between beginning her sophomore and junior years, one student spoke of these challenges:

> All my friends are abroad this year. So I think sophomore year I had that security of, oh, everybody's coming back, and we're all going to just hang out. But the beginning of junior year I realized nobody's coming back. And it was kind of I needed to make an extra effort to maybe join orgs or get to know new friends. Make new friends and new connections. So that was different.

For juniors who will themselves study abroad, the prospect of leaving campus for half of the year or more heightens the experience of time in college as short and compressed. The usual rhythms of the academic year are interrupted, and first-semester juniors may feel that they are closer to being seniors than they had imagined: "Senior year. I'm studying abroad next semester, so I feel like, that's it for my junior year. Abroad is obviously going to count, but it's not going to be at [my college]. So I keep thinking I only have one more year. I feel like it went by so quick. It hasn't gone by yet, but it's going by so quick. In general I just feel like it's flying."

In virtually every sphere of their college experience, the junior year is one of anticipation, accompanied, for many, by preparation for their senior year and beyond. It's too early to apply to graduate or professional school, but not too early to prepare for those applications. It's too early to look for a job, but not too early to apply for summer internships that might be bridges to desirable jobs. It's too early to say goodbye to your classmates, but not too early to get a sense of what that will be like because your friends who are seniors are leaving. And your friends who are seniors might also be making you a little nervous about what it will be like to return to college as a senior in the fall.

The Senior Year: A Tug of War with Time

Time is much on the minds of college seniors. To those sophomores who began their second year thinking and worrying about life after college, restarting college as a senior recasts those earlier thoughts and worries as naive. Time really is running out *now,* and the time until graduation can be counted in months, not years. Even if college seniors wanted to focus on the present and postpone planning for the future, their families, friends, and professors will repeatedly ask: "So, what are you doing after graduation?"

When responding to the question about what was most on their minds as first-semester seniors, many students employed the analogy of being a senior in high school. The analogy is an imperfect one, as many students noted, because it fails to capture the uncertainties and ambiguities which confront seniors as they envision their lives as college graduates. As one senior succinctly put it, "At least in high school, senior year, I knew I'd be at college. I didn't know where, but I knew I'd be at college." Although some were headed directly to graduate or professional schools, most seniors were not, and their futures appeared uncertain and ambiguous on many fronts. For one student, the beginning of his senior year was focused on:

> What happens after graduation—not just like what job am I going to get, but where am I going to be living? Am I going to be near friends, or am I going to be in an entirely new town or near family? Or what will life look like? In high school you are waiting to graduate, and in middle school you are waiting to move up to high school. For all of our lives there has been this next step, and I think I am really worried about what the next step is going to be once I'm graduated, how I am going to create a long-term plan or something for myself.

The question of what "the next step is going to be" may also call into question whether college has prepared them to take that step. The liberal arts tradition has long eschewed preprofessional curricula, so it may not be clear to students how to translate what they have learned in college to what they will do afterward. A student who was beginning her senior year "just figuring out what I'm doing next" spoke to this issue using the high school senior analogy:

> I mean it's easy in high school because you know your goal is to go to a good college, but that's all. It's kind of abstract. But after college you have to be a lot more specific, and I still don't know what I want. I'm still just as lost as I was freshman year [of college], as far as what I like. I guess I know some things I don't like, but it doesn't really matter as far as getting a job. I know what major I might not have wanted to be, but I don't necessarily know what would have been the perfect major for me. And it's the same with the workforce. I just don't know yet, and I need to figure out a plan so I'm not just going home and sitting on a couch.

Seniors felt they were being pulled in two directions at various points during the year and that, in response to these countervailing pressures, they wished they could slow down time. On the one hand, seniors were preparing for life after college—sending out resumes, applying to graduate schools, seeking fellowships—with the hope of having a plan in place by the time they graduated. For some, these activities diminished their academic experience.

"School work definitely seems to be losing its priority in my mind," one student remarked. "It just seems to be less important, not that I am slacking off, but really, I have turned my focus ahead I think." On the other hand, seniors often became more academically engaged if they were writing a thesis or doing independent research. It was not uncommon for this group of students to define success in their senior year as getting good data, delving deeply into the literature of their discipline, or developing the skills necessary to write extended, complex arguments. Indeed, one of the goals of these types of capstone experiences is to anchor seniors in the present.

For a greater number of seniors, however, the desire to spend time with their friends was the major reason they focused on the here and now. The first-year students who were anxious to make good friends are now seniors seeking to cement and maintain those friendships. Even though he was thinking about career plans at the beginning of the year, one senior reflected the sentiments of many when he said that he wanted "to stray away from that because it's more of just . . . having fun [the] last year here. And connecting with friends. I think it's more of a social thing than an academic thing for my experience senior year." Another senior was "looking forward to enjoying the day-to-day things [like] hanging out with my friends" but also worried about "graduating and not being able to see my friends as often as I'm used to now."

But what about those students who were experiencing little social connection or academic engagement in their senior year? Although there were only a few, it is worth noting how their experience of time differed greatly from the vast majority of their peers. These students were not oriented toward the future because they were *planning* for being out of college; they were oriented toward the future because they *wanted* to be out of college. When asked what was most on her mind at the start of the year, one senior replied, "that I have, however many months, [before] graduating." She went on to elaborate on the bleak outlook she had for the coming year: "I'm just trying to stay open minded. Maybe I'm trying a little harder this year. I don't think it's getting anywhere. I guess before I graduate, I'd love to actually enjoy something here. Some constructive experience that [my college] has. I'd like to find something in it that I enjoy." In response to the same question, a student said:

[I've] kind of outgrown college, or more so, just [my college]. It's a nice environment, but it's really small, and I'm a people person, and I feel like

I've exhausted all of my "getting to know people" side of myself. There's not enough to go around. You've met everybody fifteen times. It's like, okay, I need graduation; I need to see my diploma and feel like I'm doing something important.

Lacking strong friendship networks, failing to feel at home in a rural environment or on a small campus—for these and other reasons—one's college can seem like "a bad fit" for a few students by the time they reach their senior year. For the vast majority, however, the offer of a second senior year would be quite appealing as they prepare to enter the "real world."[20]

Conclusion

Experiencing time as future-oriented and compressed is common and something that typically takes hold early on in college. This experience of time is in large part tied to a series of decisions that colleges ask students to make. Anticipating these decisions leads students to plan for and focus on the future. Many other factors, of course, also contribute to this temporal experience: a college search that takes up a lot of students' time in high school, the high cost of attending college, the avocational nature of liberal education, among others.

Given the potent combination of these cultural and structural forces, it is not surprising that college students find it difficult to "be in the moment." But some do, and their counternarratives suggest that swimming against these strong cultural and structural currents requires deliberation and purpose, self-awareness and vigilance. These students come to know they are different from most students and, throughout their time in college, they work hard at maintaining their oppositional stance. While the decision to focus on the present usually emerges after students have restarted college a few times, a very small number will start college with this goal in mind. Jason is one of these students.

Jason arrived at college excited about making new friends and learning new things. In his first interview, halfway into his first semester of college, Jason said that the most rewarding thing about college thus far was "learning a lot, which is definitely what I wanted." His mark of a successful first year was how much he has learned and how he learns. He wanted to develop his ability to learn independently by living with the uncertainties that accompany acquiring new knowledge:

> I don't have to go through the process of not knowing. Not understanding happens a lot, but perhaps I've gotten to the point where, if I don't understand, I'll wait until I [do], so I never have to wonder at the time if I don't understand. And if you do understand, then your classes are so much more meaningful. That's definitely the most rewarding, understanding, and I have understanding and control over my academic life.

Jason closed his first interview by stating that he was "excited to see what's coming in the future. It's not so much about success: it's the experience of learning and meeting new people and stepping out of my comfort zone. I'm definitely looking forward to the future."

The emphasis on learning and living in the present continued when Jason restarted college as a sophomore. Unlike many of his peers who were beginning to make plans for being out of college, he gave a very different answer to the question about what's most on his mind as his sophomore year got underway:

> Just learning as much as possible and getting as smart as I can. And just taking advantage of this place as much as I can. And by taking advantage, I mean just doing everything I can to get involved here and take advantage of the resources here, of the people ... this is just such a great opportunity to speak to people and learn about different ways of life. Just to learn. I just want to do that as much as I can.

By the beginning of the sophomore year, not having an answer to the question "What's your major?" proved stressful for many. In college, students "declare" majors, and this declaration signals something more than one's interests, skills, aptitudes, or passions. It signals something about the kind of person you are. Students often believe that those who voice their intended majors early on were more confident, embarked on a clear path through college and thinking ahead to life after college. By contrast, those still playing around with the major declaration could be viewed as clueless or at sea.[21] Jason gave voice to these perceptions when, as a first-semester sophomore, he was asked if he felt any external pressure to choose his major:

I definitely do. I mean the convention is that if you don't know your major then you don't have your act together and you don't know what you're going to do with your life and you're not ambitious. And even if you communicate to someone that you're ambitious but you don't have a major, that makes you disorganized. So I feel pressure, but it's something that I'm trying to notice and sort of ignore. Because what I realize is that my major is going to mean very little when I graduate from [college]. What's going to matter is how well I do here and the things I learn here.

These sentiments continued into the next year when Jason was looking forward to the opportunities afforded by restarting college as a junior: "I want to make the most of my experience here. It feels like a completely new year: different classes, different focus in my classes, completely new." As a senior he returned to the theme of how college students experience time in colleges as compressed, as an obstacle to the development of meaningful friendships, as promoting efficiency rather than creativity. Unlike Stephanie whose adherence to a rigid schedule made her in some ways a slave to time, Jason strove to be time's master:

I think it's very easy at [my college], and maybe this could be true among all colleges, it's very easy to be wrapped up in the productive mind-set here and to forget about the value of taking a walk in the quiet with someone . . . and no longer being a slave to time. Because we live by: today a meeting at 10:30, then lunch, and then classes and office hours. And being so regimented that we're always looking at our watches. So time is always at the forefront of our minds. I think that in trying to interact with people in the most meaningful way, you have to forget about time to a certain extent. I think that's a weakness of college life in general, and something that I hope senior students can find a way to combat on their own through having one day where they don't do any work or finding a friend that knows how to step away from this efficient mind-set at some point.

How would you use your time differently?

I would be much more selective with who and what I'm giving it to. I think it's really important to have the freedom to forget about time.

I think that one should always realize that time is a non-renewable resource and the ways that you use it; everything that we do, every way that we use our time is a choice to not use it in a million other ways. So there's only twenty-four hours in a day we have to just mentally think about using it in that way and giving people that we love, the activities that we love, the time they deserve. Yeah, I think that's important and it's something that I'm only learning this year.[22]

Time is indeed, for everyone, a "nonrenewable" resource. And college students, like most of us, wish that we had more (or less) of it at times, or that we could go back and make different decisions about how we spent time. We sometimes tell students that "college is the best four years of your life," but we don't often tell them that there is a rhythm and flow to those four years that will affect how they experience time in college. First-year students, who start college happy not to be applying for much of anything, are told they have a lot of time to explore their interests and to find their "passion." But it isn't long before they are back in the application saddle, focused on declaring a major or studying abroad. Because students view those decisions as the most important ones they will make in college, they might see their junior year as a brief respite from—and a time to prepare for—the application process that will reassert itself in their senior year. There are good reasons why college students are so future-oriented. They spend a lot of time in college planning their way into, through, and out of college. Given the student culture and the college practices that reinforce this experience of time in college, it is no wonder that it is a rare occurrence to run into a Jason at one of our schools.

THREE

∽ Connection

Where did you live freshman year?

DAN, SENIOR: In [my dorm], on the third floor. I feel like it was just a perfect storm of people. It was probably pretty cliquey, but I feel like most of my friendships and relationships are direct descendants, if you will, of the friends that I made freshman year. I'm living with half the people, or see on a regular basis, half the people that I lived with freshman year on that floor.

Would you say that your friendships have changed over time?

SONYA, SENIOR: Most definitely. Because you're friends with people who are mostly conveniently positioned to your room, the people on your floor. Then it takes about a year to discover that these people, although they're nice, might be really boring. I don't mean really boring but don't have the same values. And so you go through the phase of finding your-self and finding people that you actually go well with. But also I went through a reconciliation with the people in my dorm, I softened towards them this year. They're not boring. They're different, and it's worth exploring the differences.

O N THE FACE OF IT, one might question the wisdom of bringing to-gether hundreds of adolescents, housing them with one another in resi-dential dormitories, making parental supervision difficult if not impossible, and then asking them to make important life decisions and choices. It sounds more like a recipe for "Par-tay!" than learning. And the truth of the matter is that for many students having fun with their college friends is an important measure of college success. For example, when a fall semester sophomore was asked what would make her upcoming year a successful one, she responded: "Got to play basketball and not be one of those bench players, so I can play and then have a lot of fun with my friends." When students talked about their goals for the coming academic year, they were more likely to mention maintaining friendships with peers than exploring new academic areas. Nevertheless, the vast majority of students described working to achieve *both* academic and social goals. Rather than distracting them from a liberal education, making friends with fellow students and managing their social lives was an integral part of their college experience.

The social environment of college offers an opportunity for students to build lifelong social skills, such as getting along with others, making friends, working together in groups, and learning how to lead. Social experiences can also function as a respite from the chaotic, life-without-punctuation described in the Time chapter. If the academic lives of students are often stressful and focused on getting good grades, their social lives can be a welcome break from what seems like a never-ending series of papers, problem sets, and exams. Of course, not all students acquire stable, supportive, and drama-free college friendships. Some struggle to fit in with their peers, and still others come to feel betrayed by early friendships.[1] But for those who succeed in making friends—and the vast majority of students do in fact succeed—friendships and social experiences afford students cherished opportunities to take a break from their coursework and to find pleasure in "just hanging out."

Friendships influence how students think, how they feel, and how they act. Unhealthy college friendships can derail academic effort and lead to self-destructive behaviors like binge drinking.[2] Healthy college friendships and social interactions can invigorate academic motivation and inspire new directions and new commitments. When these healthier types of friendships and interactions occur between those who are racially, ethnically, or in some other way different, they can challenge students to examine their choices, evaluate why they believe and act the way they do, and help them appreciate perspectives informed by very different life experiences.[3] When students talk to their friends and acquaintances about what they learned in the classroom, or bring to the classroom ideas and knowledge anchored in their social experiences, they have an opportunity to develop a deeper understanding of not just the college curriculum but also themselves and others. Here's one female senior responding to a question asking about her most memorable social and residential experiences at the college:

> Another sort of big turning point [was when] my best friend in freshman year, my roommate, came out as gay and has now had a serious girlfriend

for about a year and a half. That really opened the door to a lot of great discussions for me, and everyone that I know. You can read about queer theory and whatever, but when you really know someone and they're your best friend, it really does change your perspective on the gay experience in America on and off campus.

In this chapter, we look at the ways in which students connect with their peers, their motivations for doing so, and the consequences of those connections. Classes, dormitories, theme housing (e.g., French House), roommates, varsity and intramural athletics, community service learning, study abroad programs, and student organizations and clubs are all part of the institutional structure of a residential college. This structure influences the kinds of social decisions students make. At times this influence broadens a student's academic interests, extracurricular interests, and social networks. But not always. Moreover, the ways in which our institutions tend to channel behavior and choices are just one part of the story. The other part of that story, of course, is the students themselves. Colleges can only provide, with varying degrees of success, the proverbial water for meaningful, possibly even transformative, social experiences. It is up to the student to drink. And though students vary in their definition of what it means to have friends, whatever the definition, most students make having them a priority. Once a few good friendships are established, some students show considerably less interest in making additional friends and exert minimal effort in meeting new people. Others actively cultivate new social connections throughout their four years of college. Although very different, both of these approaches to college friendships can help students develop some of the values, skills, and habits that a liberal education is all about.

First-Year Friendships

New students start college with a mix of apprehension, anxiety, and excitement. For most, it is a transition like no other they have experienced: living away from parents and siblings, friendless or virtually so, and confronting new and uncertain routines and expectations placed upon them by our colleges. Some enthusiastically welcome the change and are happy to replace their hometowns and high school experiences with the wider and more diverse pool of people they find at college: "I came from a very small, deathly Republican town and I'm more open here, and I can make friends a lot more easily here. In high school I was very outspoken and everyone hated it, they were like just 'Shut up and get out.' And here it's like, 'No, no, keep talking.'"

Regardless of their feelings for the places they are leaving behind, an immediate priority for new students is to make friends. When students were asked, shortly after they arrived on campus, to define a successful first year, their most common answers were "good grades" and "good friends."[4] Rarely did they cite only academic goals: "Doing well in my courses, of course, making a lot of friends, making lasting friendships with a lot of friends, really getting to know the school very in depth. So that way I can come back next year and really feel this is my school, this is my home, this where I belong. Not that I don't feel like that already."

First-year students feel a pressing need to adjust to college life and to validate their personal and social worth through friendships. Having friendships means having others to share the college experience, hang out with and have fun, and lean on for support. As one student put it, she liked her friends "because they're very supportive. My friends seem very healthy, and they make me happy when I'm with them. They help me adjust. We can talk about things." Establishing a social support network also means being able to concentrate more on academic work. A first-year student described his friendships with this in mind:

> I was able to meet and network with different people very quickly, which I think gave me an advantage over other incoming freshmen. You know, you need some place to take that deep breath and step away from it all. If you don't have that, if you don't have friends, if you don't have the support system around you, it's very hard to be focused and to be motivated and to do your work.

The vast majority of first-year students achieved their goal of making friends.[5] When asked in their first interview what was the best part of college, many were pleasantly surprised at the speed and ease with which they had found friends: "I think how fast I've made friends. We've only been here a couple weeks but they're definitely friends, that if I had a serious problem, I wouldn't have any issues coming to them with it immediately. I feel like we all bonded really fast and got close really fast, which is good." Many students shared this student's surprise with how quickly they made friends in the first few weeks after arriving on campus.

The Friendship Market

What accounts for the widespread success in making friends during the first few weeks of college? In late August and early September, a college campus becomes one big friendship market where new students come together for the purpose of conducting successful transactions—making friends. Students are simultaneously buyers and sellers of friendships. Those "selling" friendships are numerous and highly motivated to sell (i.e., they want friends) in the face of an exciting but uncertain experience looming before them. Those "buying" friendships find that they have a lot of options since few first-year students arrive on campus with any friends. One first-year student described it this way:

> The first day I went room-to-room to talk to people and met them that way. I met people in my classes; I met people in the student union. I just sat down and talked to them. So that's a nice way to meet a lot of people. And it's easy to meet people here because they don't have an immediate group of friends and you're not shut off from meeting, which is nice.

Thanks to the vetting process conducted by college admissions officers, the buyers and sellers typically have much in common.[6] Students have been selected with an eye toward difference and diversity but also with regard to similarities in academic ability, accomplishment in one or more endeavors (e.g., academics, music, theater, sports), future aspirations, and so on. In addition, as we saw in the Time chapter, students *self*-select into these colleges after an extensive college search process geared to finding and getting into the "right" college. For many students, the "right" college is not simply the most highly ranked of those that accept them but also the one that seems like a good fit socially as well as academically.

The admissions process enhances the prospects that a buyer and seller will want to make an exchange. The large supply of potential friendships, a substantial demand for friendships, and highly motivated buyers and sellers—students—means that the price of friendship will be relatively low and the volume of transactions high. Ample supply and large demand, however, are only part of the story when it comes to understanding the abundance of early college friendships. Buyers and sellers of friendship also need physical spaces and structured opportunities to meet face-to-face. The college provides those, and in the process, exerts additional leverage on the social lives and friendship networks of first-year students.

Orientation, Housing, Roommates, and Classes

Residential colleges welcome first-year students with camping trips, question-and-answer forums, first-year mixers, student organization fairs, residential hall meetings, and a host of other events and activities that bring them together, facilitate friendships, and promote social integration. These efforts are largely successful judging from the many students who described a college-planned activity as one of the more memorable bonding experiences of their first year. Wilderness outings and other group activities that take place before classes begin can be particularly effective in building friendship ties.[7] When asked where she had met her friends, one student answered:

> Pre-orientation was key. After pre-orientation ended we all gathered at the final dinner. That's when I started hanging out with the people that I'm hanging out with now, and we kind of just clicked and it was great and now I have my best friend and we do have a group that we hang out with and there's a bunch of them from pre-orientation.

Efforts by the college to bring students together, however, are not always appreciated. For a few students in our study, notably students of color and, to a lesser extent, international students, these efforts were seen as heavy-handed and presumptuous. Evelyn, an Asian American female, was annoyed by an invitation she received to a dinner for students of color: "And I got invited to this colored students dinner, which I thought was the stupidest thing I'd ever heard of. Because I just feel like they're trying aggressively to cater to the minorities by trying to make sure they fit in, and by trying so hard it feels like you stick out. And I just don't feel that it's necessary." Nina, an international student from East Asia, was offended by the college's assumption that same-race relationships would be a social priority of hers: "I'm Asian so I should be joining an Asian student organization? Why can't I join the black student organization on campus if I want to? The college makes it such a big deal that I'm yellow and you're white and you're black. Or like I'm gay and you're not so you shouldn't be joining organizations for gay students. It just boxes you."

These responses were two of the most poignant criticisms that first-year students directed at college efforts to help them make contacts and establish friendships. For Nina and Evelyn, well-intentioned institutional actions were perceived as placing them under the spotlight and diminishing their individuality. Although Nina and Evelyn were not the only students to feel this way, the majority of first-year international students and students of color tended to view their college's targeted social programming in a more favorable light:

What have you found to be most rewarding since you've been on campus?

International orientation. That was like the best experience so far.

What did you like about it?

Because we were a small group. We were all internationals, so we got along very well. It was a really cozy atmosphere. The leaders were nice. I mean the people that were working with us and showing us around. So it was just perfect.

This student valued the opportunity to meet other international students whereas Evelyn expressed disdain for an invitation to a similar event. Such polar opposite reactions are not surprising: it is hard to imagine any college-sponsored event that would please every student. With the goal of promoting campus diversity, colleges must balance their desire to help students establish themselves socially without simultaneously marking them as somehow in need of special treatment. They risk alienating students with broad outreach efforts based on presumed social identities that may in fact have little salience to students.

Efforts to foster connections among new students continue well beyond orientation programs and the first few weeks of the semester. Colleges place students with roommates and assign dormitories where they will live with other first-year as well as upperclass students. Most require first-year students to live on campus and to purchase a year-long meal plan in order to eat at a college dining hall where it is rare to find a table designed for just two diners, let alone one. Colleges also assign first-year roommates and, of course, require students to take classes, some of which are open only to first-year students. Residential colleges are designed in such a way that first-year students eat, sleep, and work in one confined setting. First-year students cannot escape one another's company even if they wanted to.

Residential arrangements for housing first-year students are key to understanding how friendships are formed within the first few months of college.[8] Dormitories and residential houses were, by a substantial margin, the most frequently cited venues for establishing first-year friendships. Most students did not even "walk five minutes across campus" to be with friends. They didn't have to. They tended to make friends in their dormitories and, more precisely, on their particular dormitory floor:

> I made some awesome friends within the first week of school. My floor, the freshman floor, is so close. We are all in each other's rooms all the time. We go out together, we have movie nights together, we stay in, everything we do we do together and I think that's definitely helped. I didn't expect that. I really hoped to get along really well with my roommate but I didn't expect that the floor would get so close so fast.

Another student highlighted the importance of proximity with the observation that the location of one's room on the floor can shape friendship choices:

> I really do think that they [friendships] are based on proximity. I live on the corner and basically the girls that are here and I hang out, and then the girls over there hang out. I was just thinking about that when you were asking and I was like, "Wow, it's kinda weird, but it's kind of out of convenience. You're right across from me, so we can hang out."

Even closer than students in adjoining rooms were college-assigned roommates. Sharing the close quarters of a dormitory room often led to friendships, even best friendships: "I get along really well with my roommate; she and I are inseparable so that helps a lot. That was probably one of the things that made this transition so much easier. You fear getting the worst roommate ever. That's every freshman's fear, not getting along well with your roommate. And I got a really good one so it helped out."[9]

It is a rare first-year student who does not nervously anticipate arriving on campus and living with a complete stranger. Many new students have never shared a room before and soon they will be sharing one that is probably smaller and less well-furnished than their home bedrooms. In preparation for that moment, many reach out to their soon-to-be roommates during the summer to get acquainted and talk about the college experience that is about to begin.

First-year students believed, with good reason, that establishing good friendships with their roommates would ease the transition to college. For many, an ideal outcome was a roommate who made them feel at home: "I didn't really have any roommate issues at all [this past year], which is just nice. I look forward to going back to my room in the same way that I look forward to going home." Others expressed a much less sentimental view of the perfect roommate. They considered respectful coexistence to be the gold standard of roommate relationships: "We all say that we're the only people that have the perfect roommates. We're all completely different, have completely different friends, but we never fight and we have the perfect room. We're clean, everyone likes everyone. It's fine."

Of course, some roommates struggled to live with one another and sharing a small room created tension and even hostility between them. When this happened, students encountered one of the more challenging social situations of residential colleges. Some students simply suffered through it and spent as much time as possible away from each other, maybe even away from their rooms. Others drew lines down the middle of their rooms and lived on their own halves. Reconciliations were possible when students were willing and able to talk about their differences: "[With my] roommates, it was bad, really, really bad at one point and it got a lot better. Just a different culture or way of living or whatever. But we came to a common ground and so it's actually better now. And it's probably a good thing that we went through what we did so we could have a better understanding and respect for one another." Regardless of the nature of the relationships, first-year roommate assignments require students to make many decisions—big and small—about how they are going to live together and how they will work out differences and disagreement if, or when, they arise.

Extracurricular activities and classes were also venues for meeting people and making friends but were not as important, at least initially, as dormitories and room assignments. Student clubs and organizations produced fewer first-year friendship ties than dormitories in part because many first-year students have relatively limited involvement in them at this early stage in their college careers.[10] Some students were feeling a little overwhelmed with their courses and not ready to add more to their plates by committing to one or more extracurricular activities.

Classes would seem to be ideal venues for making friends because all students are required to take classes and each course brings together the same group of students two to three times per week. Course-based friendships, however, were not common among first-year students. The following response from a first-year student was typical: "The key I think to friendship is talking to people and seeing them. If you only see them in class for a few minutes afterwards, that's not really going to work. And they live far away, and they're not going to come see me, and I'm not going to go see them because it's a hike, and so I only see them in class."

The introductory lecture courses taken by many first-year students present formidable barriers to social interaction. These courses tend to have large enrollments and classroom seating arrangements that direct eyes to the front of the room rather than to other classmates. The lecturer's voice monopolizes, or at least dominates, class time and students rarely speak except to ask or answer questions. The large enrollments and limited student-to-student interactions of lecture courses can also contribute to an atmosphere that feels more competitive than collaborative. While many colleges, including those in our study, offer small seminar courses—typically no more than twelve to sixteen students—open only to first-year students, students enrolled in these courses did not make many friendships in them.[11] Perhaps this is because the total amount of class time in a typical college class, including first-year seminars, amounts to less than four hours per week. Furthermore, a small class size is no guarantee that professors necessarily will talk less or students will engage more with one another in collaborative group activities.[12]

Two groups of students—athletes and international students—were exceptions to the dominance of dorm-based friendships. First-year students who participate in sports tend to make friends with other teammates.[13] This is not so much an exception to the proximity rule as it is an extension of it, given the enormous amount of time athletes spend in the company of their teammates. Similarly, the friends of international students tend to be, from the very start of college, other international students. For this group, the power of residential proximity is partially overridden by their desire to connect with other international students undergoing the same dual transition—one to college and one to a new culture. Colleges largely succeed in promoting friendship ties among international students with the help of advisors, student centers, student organizations, and events specifically targeting this group of students. Collectively, these efforts simulate a lesser version of the "routinized proximity" found in residential halls.[14]

We expected to find proximity to be less salient in the early friendship choices of Asian American, African American, and Latino/a students. Like international students, students of color often confront additional challenges in transitioning to historically white institutions, such as developing a sense of belonging that we will discuss in the Home chapter. Such challenges might create a preference for "supportive alliances"[15] with same-race peers and, given their limited numbers, require students of color to look for them beyond the confines of their residential halls and dormitory floors. At least in the first year of college, that turned out not to be the case. Dorm-based friendships, some with students of the same race but others not, were nearly as common among students of color as they were among white students.

This finding surprised us, but perhaps it shouldn't have. As previously noted, many first-year students, including students of color, did not find time to join extracurricular activities like cultural or ethnic clubs that would bring them into contact with other students of color. The following response comes from a first-year African American female when asked if she had joined any clubs, organizations, or teams on campus: "I signed up for some but then I felt like I couldn't really manage my time well enough yet to actually commit to them. I didn't want to disappoint anyone or like be an inconvenience to anyone, so I didn't really want to stay in a club or a team and make a commitment. So I might do one next semester."

This may be a small part of the story. We suspect a bigger part is that many students of color, unlike international students, have been navigating white-majority American institutions and interacting with white American peers for most of their lives and have become comfortable and adept at doing so. The students of color who apply to and then attend a white-majority college may be those who feel particularly comfortable in such a setting or consider themselves at least somewhat prepared to deal with the challenges that they present. Whatever the explanation, proximity-based friendships were prevalent among first-year American students regardless of race or ethnicity.

Diversity in the First Year

One of the social highlights for many first-year students was living and learning at a place more diverse than their high schools. This was particularly true for white students.[16] First-year students were typically excited by the "completely different" experiences and perspectives of their new college connections:

> I really like the people. I think that's the best part. Everyone comes from so many different places and some have experienced what I have; yet others have completely different experiences. I think it's important to open up my mind to different types of people and different types of situations, which I definitely have, and not be ignorant to people's values and backgrounds.

Interacting with students from different family backgrounds, ethnicities, nationalities, and religions was an important by-product of the proximity rule governing the social lives of first-year students.[17] By not venturing far from their dormitories in search of a social life, many first-year students found themselves discovering shared interests and socializing with roommates and dormmates who, under different circumstances, might be perceived as too different to approach. One first-year student had this to say about making friends in her dorm:

> It's so inconvenient to be picky about your friends here. I felt like I had to make friends with the people on my [dorm] floor and that was really great. That was really, really good because it meant that I socialized with different people that had different priorities and different social preferences. Definitely not the kind of people I hung around with in high school.

Although interactions in first-year residential settings did not always culminate in long-lasting college friendships between students of different races, they did represent the most prolonged period of time that the typical student engaged regularly with other students who were racially and ethnically different.[18] Interactions with diverse others could lead to "self-discovery," which is how Molly described her residential experiences in the middle of her first year: "I don't think I've realized how white, New England, Catholic, Irish I really was until I came here, and I was with people who were not. That's been really interesting, kind of a self-discovery-type of situation." Molly and her roommate, an international student from Korea, struggled in the beginning to overcome their differences. Most of their disagreements centered on academic choices and interests, but they were rooted in cultural differences as well. Molly favored courses in the humanities and tended to have a narrow, parochial view of the sciences: "Chemistry ends with a periodic table [but] religion is a huge, open spectrum that has no end." Her roommate was pursuing a premed track and taking a lot of science courses. She considered Molly's courses, such as Greek and religion, to be impractical. Giving voice to these differences, Molly said:

> So that's been my closest encounter with diversity, living with this person and understanding why my academic choices are a complete joke in her perspective. And then thinking it absolutely ridiculous she's taking two science courses. I never would have expected that to be an issue until it became apparent that it was almost resentment that I was writing papers and reading things when she was doing lab reports. So it's been interesting. It's been an adventure.

This difference in perspective made interactions between them awkward and tense for several weeks. The awkwardness and tension were difficult but, at the same time, something that Molly could frame as an "adventure" afterward. Her openness to learning from her situation, to stand back and look at it in a detached manner, helped the two of them to move beyond mutual resentment to mutual respect. Molly learned to appreciate how growing up in Korea shaped her roommate's academic choices and broader social perspectives. Molly also realized how much growing up in the United States had influenced hers. It was a lesson that seems unlikely to have occurred had Molly interacted with only her best friends, who she described as "white, Christian girls with very similar family situations and economic backgrounds." In the first year at least, colleges are able to capitalize on the power of proximity by using first-year housing assignments to promote social interactions among students of different backgrounds.[19]

Social Challenges and Social Restarts

Although many students are able to find friends—even good friends—in the first year, the first-year friendship market does not work for everyone. Some students struggle with shyness and are uncomfortable when meeting new people, particularly at the large social gatherings that take place during new student orientation and the first semester of college. Others find it difficult to make friends because of their own high expectations. For example, when Garrett was asked in the spring semester of his first year if he had developed close friendships, he responded: "I really haven't developed this close relationship with anyone as of yet. I'm occupied with things. I know a lot of people, I talk to people, they're good people but I wouldn't say they're close friends. It takes a while for me to call anyone my friend or consider anyone my close friend. It takes a lot of trust."

Unlike most first-year students eager to make friends, Garrett showed more restraint and set the bar high for calling someone a friend. Garrett didn't just want someone with whom to eat dinner or hang out; he wanted a true confidant. His high standard for friendship was incompatible with the "make friends quickly" ethos driving the first-year friendship market.

It wasn't just shy students or those with high expectations who faced difficulties making friends. Some students who made friends relatively easily when they arrived on campus eventually started having the kinds of reservations about expediently formed friendships that Garrett had from the start. By the second semester, some students felt socially confined by a group of dorm friends with whom they spent too much time:

We've been discussing that maybe we want to explore more friendships because we feel like this group of friends is just too much together now. So we're trying to go out and discover new things. Because first semester we wanted to just stick together, but then second semester it just came by, we weren't sick of each other but, you know, we're living in a dorm and it's just so much time together.

Others expressed disappointment with "superficial" relationships established in their first few months of college:

> I realized that there are a few friends that I had first semester that I don't really talk to anymore, and I feel like that's because first semester you just want to meet people so that you can have people to go to the dining hall with and not feel alone, and people you can hang out with on the weekend. But you don't really take the time to make or create meaningful relationships with them. I just created lots of superficial relationships. Now I have a few people that I really care about and value.

Winter break and several weeks at home gave this student time to reflect on her campus friendships from a distance. For her and others like her, restarting college in the spring semester of the first year meant letting go of questionable friendships and investing more deeply in others.

A number of first-year athletes also felt socially hemmed in by early friendships formed with team members. As a varsity athlete, Amy expressed considerable ambivalence about the time she was dedicating to soccer and her teammates. While she appreciated upper-class teammates who offered helpful advice, she found participating in a sport to be a socially greedy activity that was preventing her from meeting other students:

> I've mainly become friends with people on the soccer team, and I think it's good and bad, because I feel like I'm not great friends with people on my hall, not because I don't like them but just because I'm never there. My roommate's really good friends with them and they're always off doing things, and I'm off doing things with my soccer friends, so it's not a bad thing. So the season's about to end and I'm actually interested to see what happens. Because I eat dinner with my soccer team every night. Maybe I'll start eating with people from my hall or maybe I'll stick to the people I'm closest with on the team. But I don't mind, I like having close friends, but I think I need to branch out maybe a little bit more.

Amy clearly felt something was lacking in even her closest friendships on the soccer team. Her opportunity to take action came at the end of the soccer season when she was faced with a decision—continue to devote all of her social life to teammates or explore other possibilities for friendship. Amy chose the latter option and not long into the spring semester restart she made several non-soccer friends. These new friends became her closest friends for the next three years.

The most common and at times most dramatic limitations to early college friendships occur when roommate friendships sour. When this happens, a social tie that is typically a valuable asset in the college transition process can quickly transform into a serious liability.[20] At the very least, students who have invested heavily in roommate friendships at the expense of developing other friendships will find themselves temporarily friendless. For one student in this predicament, a new semester became an opportune time to find new friends:

> Last semester I was really close with my roommates, which was good. But it was also bad in a way because it didn't force me to go out and meet other people. Because I know there were a lot of kids who weren't happy with their roommate situation who met other friends outside, which was nice for them. But since I didn't have to do that, I really didn't make the effort to. But now for some reason, there's all this tension in my room between two of my other roommates and another one. So these two gang up on the other one. It's this really bizarre, catty, girl, middle school kind of situation, it's pathetic. So now it's like forced me to go out and make some other friends.

Dealing with roommates who had different political and social views, conflicting sleeping schedules, boyfriends or girlfriends sharing the room—the list goes on—tested students' patience, coping skills, and resilience. One student, irked by her roommate's snoring as well as her belief that poor people should not have children, had a creative idea for dealing with her: "Oh my God, she engenders a desire in me to plant things she's mildly allergic to at her bed, because I don't want to kill her but I would really like to annoy her. So maybe just something she's mildly allergic to."

By and large students did not resort to toxic flora to resolve roommate problems. They found ways to co-exist with their roommates even if their relationships did not evolve into lasting friendships. In dealing with roommate issues, some students turned frustrating situations into opportunities for learning how to resolve, or at least cope with, interpersonal conflict. And they could always look forward to a restart in the sophomore year, as many did, when they would be living with roommates of their own choosing.

The Enduring Nature of First-Year Friendships

Despite the limitations of first-year friendships keenly felt by some first-year students, it was striking how many described their new friends as close friends and even best friends. Many fully expected some of these early friendships to last the duration of college, an expectation that was often fulfilled. Students in their senior year referred to these friends with adjectives like "core" and "closest" and expressed strong feelings for them:

> My core of people has always been there, but I've also had other people who've come in and out. Here, it's easy to have what I call acquaintances. People who are convenient in the moment, who you're friends with because it's convenient. But then when you don't have that class together, or you don't have that common upperclassman who you hang out with anymore, you're not friends anymore. I never really thought of them as friends, like true friends, because there really is no deep relationship. So I've had people who I hung out with, but it wasn't a close friendship. My real friends I've had since freshman year.

There was a widely held belief among students that friendships formed in the first year were the strongest and most meaningful friendships. Students who failed to make close friends in their first year felt they had lost an opportunity for something special:

> For a lot of people, your first semester is the time when you meet a lot of people. And actually it turned out for most students here that their best friends in their senior year are actually people that they either roomed with or the friends they made in their freshman year. So sometimes I felt that because I was just being weird my first semester I lost the opportunity to actually get to know a lot of people who can potentially be my best friends.

Why are first-year friendships so prominent and enduring for many college students? First-year students experience "liminality" as they enter the phase of emerging adulthood, a transition between the two roles of dependent adolescent and (quasi) independent adult.[21] They find themselves leaving behind their former lives and facing the largely unknown role of college student that lies ahead of them:

> I think there is definitely something special that happens freshman year when you depart from everything that is comfortable to you and you are thrown into a new environment and you become startlingly close with a few people who you eat every meal with and live with. I certainly made friends since then but when it comes to closest friends it's certainly the people that I lived with my freshman year and have continued to live with all four years.

When this senior described his first year as "definitely something special . . . when you depart from everything that is comfortable to you and you are thrown into a new environment," he was articulating his own experience of liminality and his uncertainty about how to navigate a new institution and a new role. Not surprisingly, the friendships he made during the emotionally charged start of college became invested with deep meaning and inspired enduring loyalty.

Liminality, however, is not the only reason behind the power and persistence of first-year friendships. These friendships possess another distinct advantage when compared to connections formed later in college—first-year connections have more time to grow and deepen as friendships. When asked to describe her closest friends at the end of her sophomore year, Maria said:

> We've been together longer, so we've gone through ups and downs. So I think our friendships are a bit stronger. Like being there for the other person. Like them seeing me absolutely miserable when I applied to all of these programs and I only got into two. So they've been there for that. My grandfather passed away and they were there. And then you always plan things for their birthdays and you go out of your way. Just things like that strengthen the friendship.

It is somewhat striking that many close college friendships were based on our institutions sorting of students into residence halls and rooms. It seems only a slight exaggeration to conclude that a great number of such friendships were the predictable consequences of the first-year housing assignments decided on by college administrators.

Friendships after the First Year

Restarting college as a sophomore, junior, or senior differs in important ways from starting college as a first-year student. The majority of upperclass students return to campus with established friendships and roommates they have selected. For them the anxiety about finding friends and sharing a room with a stranger is a thing of the past. The motivation to make new friends is not nearly as intense as it was when they arrived on campus at the start of their first year. It's no longer the marketplace of their first year. Gone too are orientation week and other activities organized by the college to help socially unconnected first-year students become socially connected. With one or more years of college under their belts, upperclass students have a much better idea about what it means to be a college student and, as we will see in the Home chapter, feel much more comfortable at college.

The sheer volume of friendship-making decreases after the first year and so too does the role of proximate living arrangements for friendship formation.[22] When new college friendships are made after the first year, they tend to be the result of attending the same classes, pursuing similar interests, participating in the same activities (e.g., student organizations and athletic teams), or having friends in common. After the first year, residential living spaces typically become less a place for establishing new friendships and more a place for hanging out with roommates and friends one already knows.

Each upperclass year shares in common various types of restarts and new beginnings—new classes, new living arrangements, and new extracurricular activities. But each year also presents its own particular set of social dynamics and issues. Sophomores winnow their first-year connections to a smaller group of friends and close friends. Juniors face the social opportunities and challenges presented by study abroad, either when they leave campus or when they decide to stay. Seniors reconnect—or not—with friends from whom they were separated during junior year and try to maximize the time spent with close friends before graduation.

Sophomore Year: Solidifying Friendship Circles

Most students restarting college as sophomores have already-established friendship networks which may now require some pruning. With the anxiety of being socially unconnected mostly gone, many sophomores find themselves reexamining existing friendships and making decisions about which friends to keep, which ones to let go of, and whether to make new friends:

> Last year was meeting as many people as you could and not really having a deep connection with them but at least knowing them. And this year it was kind of interesting. I just took from those acquaintances and chose people who I wanted to have deeper relationships with and I went with that. But I didn't actually go out of my way to make new friends this year. Just because I am happy with the friends that I have right now so I don't need to.

Two features shared by most residential colleges can prompt even the most unreflective student to reflect upon his or her friendships in this manner. First, students get to choose for themselves, typically in a housing lottery, where and with whom they would like to room in their sophomore, junior, and senior years. This lottery system for allocating rooms motivates many students, at least once every year, to contemplate their friendships and roommate possibilities: Do I want a roommate or should I live alone? Is it a good idea to room with my best friend or could that strain our friendship? Do I want to live in a really cool room or do I stick with Jim and suffer the consequences of his very low lottery number? The uncertainty surrounding the housing lottery can be stressful and some friendships have crashed on the rocks of low lottery numbers.

Second, with the breakup of first-year living arrangements, friends who were just across the hall from one another in the first year may find themselves at opposite ends of campus in the sophomore year. That can be a fortuitous separation when friendships are no longer desired or a difficult one when they are. For some students, restarting college as a sophomore meant deciding whether spatially distant friendships were worth the effort required to maintain them: "The people who I lived with last year that I was really close with are living in different dorms [this year] and I never see them. And they were such close friends last year, but because I don't live with them or live near them at all, it's hard."

Some sophomores viewed this separation as a good test of their commitment and their friends' commitment to the relationship: "People told me that sophomore year you sort of realize who your friends are, and who they aren't, because you see who will make the effort to come see you wherever you live, and who you want to make the effort to go see." At the start of sophomore year, many students were testing and reevaluating friendships that were no longer conveniently located on the same floor or in the same dormitory.

While most sophomores were making friendship decisions about which first-year friends to keep and which ones to let go, a smaller group of sophomores who did not make close friends in their first year were taking advantage of the college restart to do so. One who did was Michelle. Like other new students, she had minimal expectations for friendships and connected with those around her, specifically with other students in her dormitory. Despite sincere intentions, Michelle developed very little commitment to these early friendships and, by the beginning of her sophomore year, was casting about for new ones. Classes and extracurricular activities were her salvation: "In your first year, you're kind of just thrown together with people in your dorms and those are who you think your friends will be. For some people it works out that way, but for a lot it doesn't and you meet more people in your classes and by being more involved in organizations." By the end of her sophomore year, Michelle had "really good friendships" thanks to her involvement with the Spanish Club and her staff position with the college newspaper. For Michelle, restarting college as a sophomore helped her to find more meaningful friendships.

As they moved beyond the first year of college, students typically expressed more comfort in their social surroundings and found it easier to strike up conversations with other students. They also enjoyed the benefit of the exponential growth in the number of friends of friends. Initial conversations became much easier once new acquaintances discovered having friends in common:

Last year, I was good friends with people who lived all around me and it was easy [to make friends] in that sense because everyone was there. But now everyone's sort of spread out in dorms and houses and all over the campus, so that makes it a little more difficult. But [it's also] easier in the sense that I'm finding that as I'm meeting people we already have a lot of friends in common and we know a lot of the same people.

Despite the social opportunities created by wider-ranging social networks, classes, and extracurricular activities, many sophomores expressed less motivation to make new friends than they did as first-year students, in part, because they were satisfied with the friends they had:

I think in a way it's harder because when you're a freshman you are kind of open, you feel an open mind to everything. But once you're a sophomore you're a lot more comfortable with the environment that you have and the people that you know. So you don't have the incentive to go out and meet people, unless you have a really extroverted personality. I do see people from my class but I've already made friends. I already chose the kind of group of friends I have. So you just don't really go out of the way to meet more people.

Many students felt that the organization of upperclass students into friendship groups—students often referred to these as "cliques"—reduced the motivation to make new friends. Meeting people in an environment where most had friends changed the dynamics of interactions and made it more difficult to become friends: "I think it's easier to make the kind of friends you'll say 'hi' to every day and be friendly with, but it feels a little harder to make the genuine friendships because you've kind of already got those friends now." Friendship groups also created expectations of loyalty and exclusivity that emotionally complicated efforts to make new friends: "Every time I hang out with my new friends, I feel like I'm betraying the other people. Like I'm not spending as much time with them. Plus, these people have their other friends so it's hard to break in." The webs of social ties that connect students into friendship groups and exclude them from others also shed light on why many students, when asked if they had made new friends in their sophomore year, reported doing so with socially unattached and uncommitted first-year students:

I feel like I only talk to the people that I established friendships with last year, and I think that whole let's go out and make new friends thing has ended. Not so much for me. I felt that at first but then I met all these new first years, they introduced me to their friends so it kept going. But I felt like from a sophomore point of view, I haven't really made any more sophomore friends. I've made more first year friends but I've basically maintained or met a couple new sophomores.

Cliques, limited time, comfortable routines, and diminished motivation were the major factors behind the solidifying of many friendship circles in the sophomore year. The social closure that some students resisted in their first year (recall Amy's experience with her soccer teammates) became more acceptable, even desirable, in subsequent college years. Upperclass students often viewed social closure as inevitable and "natural" as they committed what time they could to their closest friends.

Decline in Diversity Interactions

One casualty of social closure in the sophomore year is a decrease in interactions among students of different races, despite the fact that many students regard meeting students from different backgrounds to be one of the highlights of the first year.[23] As sophomores become less dependent on residential halls for a social life and more focused on cultivating close friendships, a good number of them drift away from cross-race interactions and friendships and gravitate towards same-race ones.[24]

Among African American, Latino/a, and, to a lesser extent, Asian American students, a desire for same-race connections sprang from many sources. Some students, many of whom grew up in neighborhoods and attended schools with little racial diversity, were drawn to same-race friendships because of their familiarity. Conversely, other students actively cultivated same-race friendships because of their relative novelty and perceived potential for greater closeness and mutual understanding. Stephanie, the African American student whose struggles with time management were described in the "Time" chapter, fell into this group: "My high school was mostly Latino in a very white community. It was nice to come here and find people that I could relate to. I mean I wanted black friends so it was nice to join a cultural organization with students who had some of the same aspirations and stuff. Because in high school it was really limited."

Another student, also African American, saw interacting with her same-race peers as a way of connecting with the cultural heritage of her father. When asked why she joined the Caribbean Student Association, she responded "Because my dad's from Jamaica, so I figure I should join some clubs that revolve around Caribbean students and activities." Like Stephanie, this student joined a campus cultural organization to be around others who were racially and, in her case, ethnically similar. The more time students of color devoted to these organizations after the first year, the more likely it became that their same-race interactions increased and their cross-race interactions decreased.[25] Not surprisingly, these changes often meant that new friendships with students of different races became less common as students devoted more and more of their social lives to cultural organizations.[26]

White students had a similar experience, although some framed it less as a matter of choice and more the result of "natural" forces. Here's Michelle again reflecting on the social sorting that took place in her sophomore year:

> I think that in college, even if the place is really diverse, like unconsciously a lot of the time you end up gravitating towards a group of people with whom you feel comfortable. So they're more similar. So we like the same music you know. The majority of the people working on the newspaper I would say are mostly white which I didn't think about too much before but that's true. And coming from a similar middle-class socioeconomic background. Not so much really affluent people. And then also most of the people that I'm close friends with in that group are also agnostic I would say.

Michelle's comments are particularly striking because they illustrate how racial self-segregation is not always intentional. In her account, the homogeneity of her friendship group was a by-product of her decision to join a student organization—the college newspaper—that lacked both racial and class diversity. On the surface at least, she did not join the newspaper because of a preference for same-race and same-class friends. Michelle did wonder, however, whether such a preference might have "unconsciously" played a role.

Essentially, the decline of diversity interactions and friendships results from "contexts of placement" yielding ground to "contexts of choice."[27] Colleges place first-year students in particular contexts (e.g., orientation programs and residential halls) that are often designed to maximize student diversity. Over time, these contexts of placement give way to contexts of student choice (e.g., sophomore-year roommate and extracurricular activities) and racially segregated patterns of mixing and mingling tend to increase. Friendship networks do not necessarily become entirely segregated by race nor do interactions among students of different races entirely disappear. But after the first year, cross-race interactions are more and more likely to occur in venues like classrooms rather than in social settings like dormitories.

As Michelle's story suggests, racially homogeneous friendship networks are not driven exclusively by students acting on their social preferences. More subtle forces are also at work. A common one, transitivity, is the tendency for friends of friends to become friends, as this sophomore noted: "It's easier to make new friends because my friends have new friends and they just introduce me to new people." Transitivity occurs because it is socially and psychologically advantageous to form new friendships with those who are already friends of friends.[28] Transitivity and same-race preference are two distinct mechanisms leading to friendship ties. Nevertheless, when working in tandem, transitivity can substantially amplify the effects of a few same-race friendship choices and transform moderately segregated friendship groups into even more segregated ones. Social dynamics like this suggest that we must be careful not to attribute the homogeneity of some friendship groups entirely to a presumed desire among students for racially similar friends. Students can be, to varying degrees, unwitting participants in the creation of their segregated social networks.[29]

Colleges struggle to find ways to stem the growing segregation of friendship circles and the declining number of diversity interactions after the first year. Some commentators argue that colleges should abolish ethnic and cultural organizations because they facilitate racially-segregated social networks that heighten feelings of ethnic victimization and decrease a sense of common identity.[30] Responses from a number of students in our study could be seen as sympathetic to this argument. While they believed that group-specific organizations undermined a broader sense of community, they all fell short of endorsing their elimination. One white student, for example, described feeling left out because she did not have a cultural organization of her own:

> Sometimes, as just a white girl from Pennsylvania, I feel like—that might be silly—but I feel like I don't fit in at my college in terms of having a group to go to. Like I'm 50% Scottish and my dad's 100%. I have a lot of Scottish pride, but there's no Scottish club. So I guess sometimes I just feel like I don't have any group while some girls have [the African American student organization]. Sometimes I feel left out or I don't feel like I have a culture because my family has been in the U.S. for so long. Because you're not diverse enough, you don't have a place to go to.

Another student, an African American female, strongly criticized "her" cultural organization for failing to be more inclusive:

> I have a strong distaste for the black student organization because I've never been a believer in diversity being formed in separation. I feel like you have to not assimilate, but integrate. But how are they supposed to learn about you if you sequester yourself off? I understand the need for social organizations based on like region and ethnicity or whatever. But I believe that there has to be a big opening. Like you have to tell everyone you're welcome. Come to us. Come to our meetings. Join our organization.

Negative attitudes about ethnic and cultural organizations, however, were vastly outnumbered by enthusiastic praise. Many students of color found a purpose and camaraderie in their cultural organizations that were missing in other parts of their college experience. White students talked about a greater racial awareness and appreciation after attending an event organized by a cultural organization. A few even joined one of the cultural organizations on their campuses. Clearly, any college wanting to eliminate these organizations would face stiff opposition from the many students who benefit from their presence.

Regardless of whether they do more harm than good to the college community, cultural organizations on college campuses play a prominent role in the racial and ethnic sorting of the student body that becomes more and more apparent after the first year. So did other organizations like the student newspaper and Ultimate Frisbee. Many students viewed such sorting as unsurprising and natural. They were more divided on whether it was desirable.[31]

Junior and Senior Years: Study Abroad and Preparing to Leave

If a good deal of social decision-making in the sophomore year centers on the solidification of friendship circles, many social decisions in the junior and senior years are precipitated by disruptions to those friendship circles because of study abroad programs. The percentage of juniors who spent one or two semesters studying at another university, either in the United States or abroad, exceeded 40% at all of the colleges in our study.[32] The national study abroad participation rate has grown steadily over the last two decades as colleges have worked to make these experiences more affordable to all students and not just those from higher-income families.[33] Colleges pitch study abroad as a way for students to pursue various interests like learning a foreign language, experiencing a different culture, or living in an urban environment (for those schools not already in an urban environment). Loftier goals include giving students an "experience that will challenge you and provide you with the opportunity to grow as a global citizen."[34]

When students speak of the sophomore slump, it is partly a reference to the growing predictability and regularity of college life. Spending a semester or year in an entirely different place presents an opportunity to restart, to break out of academic and social routines and habits that have become, for some students, stultifying and boring. One junior compared life at her home college to her new, study-abroad life at a European university:

> I'm really, really excited to be here. At my college, it's easy to get stuck in a rut and into a daily habit of seeing the same people all the time and doing the same things all the time, getting tired and just wanting to get everything over with and go to bed. But over here there is so much to do and there's so much to see and to discover. I feel like I'm more up for getting out of the house and doing other things outside of just schoolwork.

Study abroad programs dramatically lower the predictability of college life and offer a partial remedy to social closure and the loss of diversity in social interactions. This was true for the following student when asked what she liked best about her study abroad experience:

> Well obviously the classes have been a really important factor for me because I really do like what I'm studying. But also I've been hanging around with people who spend more time socializing than people at my college. Just sitting around and talking to people about their lives and where they come from and their political views and things like that. I've actually learned a lot from a few people who I've met here that has opened my eyes a little bit to how people see the world differently or what it's like to come from a different background and how it's affected them and how they see the world. To spend more time just like talking with people who are different from you, which I didn't do as much at my college.

Many described their study abroad experience as a time of greater independence and personal growth during which they practiced interpersonal skills, made new social connections, and acquired a deeper appreciation and understanding of worldviews different from their own. Study abroad succeeds as an experience of deliberate and reflective decision-making in large part because students confront new situations without the crutch of their close college friendships. Study abroad is a college restart that creatively disrupts routines, social ties, and, on a deeper psychological level, a sense of order and continuity in one's life.[35]

With so many students spending part or all of junior year away from campus, those who do not go away also find themselves restarting college as juniors in a different social scene. As early as the spring of their sophomore year, some "stayers" are concerned about the upcoming departure of their friends: "A lot of people are going abroad and I don't know how that's going to work. I'm just like oh, everyone's gone and I don't really know many people from the year below me or above me. So I guess that might be a slight worry." Others fear that it will be more difficult to concentrate on their classes and coursework absent their friends: "A lot of my friends are leaving so I guess I'm worried about that. About being less focused because people aren't always around." In the absence of close friends, some juniors simply resign themselves to a junior year that will be less socially and academically fulfilling.

What is a lonely year for some "stayers" is quite the opposite for others. Study abroad pokes holes in the social closure and cliques that characterized the social life of sophomore year and opens up new possibilities for friendships. Some stayers discovered extracurricular opportunities that likely would not have been available to them had they been away in their junior year: "I actually joined an a cappella group this year, and I don't think I would have if I was studying abroad junior year and tried out senior year. I don't think they would have taken me just because usually these kinds of orgs don't take seniors. I think that's an experience I wouldn't have been able to obtain if I was away."

When students who studied abroad returned for their senior year, they encountered many unfamiliar faces. The first-year students and sophomores were all new to them, many juniors were studying abroad, and their older friends, with a rare exception here and there, had all graduated. Returning to campus felt like restarting college as a first-year student: "Everyone says this, but it's like being a freshman but not having the cons of being a freshman. It's kind of like you're in this freshman limbo, but you don't have the benefits nor the negativity of it. In some sense, you're like fresh meat, but in some sense you're the wise old guru on campus."

Friends separated in their junior year by study abroad enjoyed reconnecting as seniors. It was one of the highlights of senior year: "Seeing my friends for sure. A year without seeing any of my friends was kind of hard as well." Reunions, however, did not always go as expected and some friendships were unable to withstand the personal changes and new friendships that occurred during the time apart:

> For me it was really hard missing a full year. It was harder to connect again. Like students tend to connect with people that didn't go abroad at all. I had a couple of good friends that didn't go abroad. And I'm not saying that's the only reason, I'm saying it was just harder. I don't know exactly why. I had a really good friend and we're not really friends anymore

Seniors returning to campus after studying abroad sometimes feel like they are reliving the start of sophomore year when they came back to campus after summer break and found many of their first-year friends dispersed across campus. Time away from campus and the college restarts that follow them create fertile conditions for students to reexamine their friendships and to chart new directions for themselves. Some seniors once again found themselves in the familiar mode of negotiating new friendship ties and maintaining—or not maintaining—old ones: "You come back and it's a different dynamic, there are new people around and so you become friends with different people. So I'd say that's how my relationships have changed. I'm [still] really good friends with my best friend at this college and we've been good friends through the four years."

As discussed in the Time chapter, other seniors see their shrinking number of friends as a sign that college is coming to an end: "If I go to the café, I don't know as many people anymore. I'm like, 'Oh, yes. Now I feel like it's time to leave.' But it's not necessarily a bad thing, because I feel like the college is renewing itself and it's always an ever-changing sort of dynamic. Which is good." Before they graduated, many seniors resolved to invest more in their existing friendships:

> I guess senior year is just a very different environment for me because, you know, you're getting out soon and you have a pretty clear purpose or goal after you graduate. So I feel that when I'm trying to enjoy my life I will think more about doing more things with my friends who I know rather than trying to get to know more underclass students.

Nevertheless, college's "ever-changing sort of dynamic" continued to generate new opportunities for those seniors open to meeting other students and making new college friends: "I made a lot of close friends this year. That is a significant thing in my life because I have learned that I can become very close and open towards people that I normally would not be. That is a personality change and high point of this year." Some seniors also began to contemplate the need to make new non-college friends. As they got ready to leave campus, many were thinking about their social connections beyond campus:

> Socially, I would like to think I've branched out a lot more. Although this year I feel like I've been branching out less because, for example, all the seniors I got to know last year graduated. But in a way it's also been widening because throughout the networking and job searching process

I got to know a lot more of people outside my college. And it's also been nice to say in the fall I actually got to visit some of my friends in Boston who were alums.

In many ways, college has been prepping these students for the social challenges and opportunities that await them after graduation. They have restarted their social lives many times over the last four years, making friends, losing friends, and relying on friends along the way. Many have done so with the security and stability of some close friendships established in their first year. By the time they graduate, they have acquired a toolkit of social skills for making new connections and a group of college friends that they can call on in the months and years ahead.

Going Deep or Going Broad

How do college friendships help students acquire the decision-making skills that lie at the core of a successful liberal education? The answer to this question centers on the two dominant approaches to college friendships: "going deep" and "going broad."[36] The two approaches are not mutually exclusive. Most students engage in both but often with a proclivity for one. A junior eloquently described the difference between these two approaches. When asked if she identified with a particular group of fellow students, she responded:

> I like hanging out with the same people all the time because I know where we left off yesterday and we're going to pick up from there and keep going. Whereas hanging out with different people all the time is a bit confusing to me and I don't like that style. I like smaller groups and constancy. One of my good friends keeps telling me that I need to diversify more, but I just said this is what I like and that's what I'm going to do. I guess what surprises them is the fact that we most often eat together, we don't change. But then again, I have this other friend who every time is with a different group of people, and she stays in the student union for like two hours and makes sure she meets everyone. I can't be like that.

Going deep and going broad are linked to intrinsic features of the residential college experience. Going deep is partly the result of the first-year college transition when many deep and enduring friendships are formed. First-year friendships have remarkable staying power and stability. Going broad, on the other hand, is linked to the ubiquitous academic and social restarts of college life and the social opportunities they create. Restarts are the impermanent and disruptive counterpart to the stability of first-year friendships. Restarts make it difficult for a going-deep approach to be practiced exclusively. Going broad does not necessarily mean interacting with students of different backgrounds but, when it does, going broad can significantly impact a student's intellectual development, social ability and civic interest.[37]

Dan, whom we quoted at the beginning of this chapter, exemplified the going deep approach. He committed to close friends early in his first year and counted on them throughout his college years. Dan described his friends as inspiring and motivating. They were a memorable part of his college experience, not just because of the good times he shared with them, but because their friendship furthered his intellectual and personal growth in ways not matched by his academic experiences:

Which person in the college community has had the most influence on you?

Probably my friends. There are professors that I really respect and have learned a lot from. But I don't think anybody [has influenced me] as much as the people that I've stayed up with late talking to about what I learned in class that day.

In what ways have they influenced you?

Just helping, just being there to slowly change their world view, as I did, and go to the lecture on Thursday night with me, and then talk about it afterwards. All those little things. I mean just becoming adults with me.

Deep friendships like Dan's add both continuity and stability to the overall college experience. Going deep attaches students to their colleges, sustains their motivation, and buoys their spirits during difficult times. Close friendships are both a resource for college success and an indicator of it.

Sonya, whom we also quoted at the start of this chapter, embraced the social fluidity of college life. Her going broad approach defied the forces of social closure. Friends and an openness to new social connections were a priority for all four years, and she successfully navigated social barriers that others found formidable. Like most students, Sonya established close friendships. Unlike other students, however, she did not feel socially constrained by them.

Sonya arrived at college with a desire to be the center of attention and a tendency to choose extracurricular activities based on whether they would elevate her stature on campus: "I just wanted to participate in everything and not because I really was interested in the thing. It was because I wanted to be visible and wanted to have a certain type of power over some other people." She was also judgmental of others: "Then it takes about a year to discover that these people, although they're nice, might be really boring." By her senior year, Sonya had become much more thoughtful and open-minded about others: "I went through a reconciliation with the people in my dorm, I softened towards them this year. They're not boring. They're just different, and it's worth exploring the differences."

During her four years of college, Sonya excelled in her courses, won numerous awards for her scholastic achievements, developed a close personal and professional relationship with her faculty advisor, studied abroad in her junior year, and captained a varsity athletic team. By any measure, Sonya was an exceptionally successful and well-rounded college student. Despite many impressive academic accomplishments, she chose to highlight her social relationships when asked how and why she had changed in college: "I wouldn't say that just college is the reason why I did [change]. It is because I also met people that [showed] me the way to learn these things. I went to a study abroad program that helped too, and my roommate did too, you know, so in that way, yes, college did help me to have a turning point."

Regardless of their approach to friends—going deep or going broad—many students from the very beginning of college viewed their friends and fellow students as central to the pursuit of new possibilities and new directions in their lives. Some students, like Dan and Sonya, referred specifically to their close friends and roommates when discussing how college had changed them. Others referred to the wider community of their peers—both close friends and acquaintances—that created an atmosphere, a set of social norms and expectations, conducive to becoming a better person:

What has been the most rewarding thing about coming to college so far?

I guess just the opportunity to actually be a student and a complete change of atmosphere. An atmosphere where people do their work. It's an atmosphere where you are expected to come to class. I guess the most rewarding part has been this challenge of doing well in my classes and getting to my classes. I have been looking forward to being a student for eighteen years. I appreciate the opportunity to basically change everything to become a more serious person. Or pretend to become a more serious person.

For this first-year student, college represented a welcomed transition—a new start—in her life, particularly after a summer during which she "partied every night from about eleven to seven in the morning." She was grateful to find herself in a place where "people do their work," a place where friends and peers were serious about their classes and who expected the same of others. She hoped their example would help her to become more serious too but she also realized that social connections alone could only motivate new choices and directions; they could not guarantee them. The hard work of becoming a new person and not just pretending to be a new person was up to her.

Conclusion

Most students establish meaningful friendships soon after they arrive at college. Some of these friendships will endure not only for the next four years but also long into their post-college lives. Friends are a sustaining and supportive force for students as they confront the restarts and uncertainties of college. Friends are what students miss most when they are away from college and reconnecting with them is what they most look forward to when they return. Whether students choose to go deep or go broad in their friendships, both approaches have the potential to foster intellectual and personal growth in ways academic pursuits alone cannot.

Friendships, nonetheless, exist in a continually changing social environment punctuated by interruptions and restarts: new classes, new semesters, new living arrangements, new extracurricular activities, and study abroad programs. College presents many opportunities for students to pause and think about their social priorities and friendships. First-year students anxiously connect with other students, sophomores reexamine their first-year friendships, juniors have a chance to broaden their social horizons in study abroad programs or to pursue new friendships and extracurricular activities if they stay on campus, and seniors reconnect—or sometimes don't reconnect—with friends after being separated in their junior year. Recurring opportunities throughout the four years of college provide students with practice at making connections, maintaining connections, and defining what they want those connections to mean. Residential colleges help students to develop critical social skills and habits that they will carry with them into their adult lives.

FOUR

∾ Home

Do you feel at home in college?

CHARLIE, FIRST YEAR: Do I feel at home? I feel very accepted, and I know
a bunch of people now. I don't know, home is a very complicated word
and can have many meanings. But home in the sense of acceptance and
feeling as a community—kind of—definitely my college is that. But
home being where I grew up and having memories, that's my home at
home. But here is definitely "home-ly."

SHORTLY BEFORE HE BECAME PRESIDENT of Yale, Bart Giamatti wrote
about using the iconic patterns of baseball to set order to his days. During
a game, the batter starts at home many times and, if lucky or skilled, gets to
go around the diamond, touching all the bases, until he is home again. This
is what students in residential colleges go through. They start at home, leave
to experience an unknown set of circumstances, and then return home many
times in their college years. They leave their childhood homes to navigate
uncertain experiences that are shaped by rules and traditions but also by their
own decisions, and then return home. Unlike baseball players who return to
the same home plate that they left, though, students may return to homes
that are quite different or fit them differently than the ones they left.[1]

Leaving home and then constructing a new home is a major ritual of
adulthood that students entering residential colleges undertake, often for the
first time. Residential colleges make much of the fact that they are living and
learning environments where students learn not only from courses but also
from the array of experiences living with peers provides. For many students
who arrive at college, "home" has had an ascribed status. They didn't choose
their birthplaces; they were given them. For most students, going to a residential college will be the first opportunity to realize that home has the potential
to be an achieved status, something they create and will have to recreate in

their future. No one wants to be "homeless" after they leave their birthplace, although they may remain tethered to it throughout their lives.

Maybe one of the greatest, yet least often realized, gifts that residential colleges give to students is a structure within which to create homes away from home. Attempting to ease students in their efforts, colleges use the rhetoric of home to describe what life will be like on campus. Many colleges refer to their residential programs as house systems in which students live in houses instead of dorms. Dorms themselves have shared communal space, often stocked with living room furniture—couches, easy chairs, fireplaces, and pianos. Admissions publications tell entering students that they will become part of the "college family," and alumni return for homecomings. But students come to college from different kinds of homes and may have different perspectives on what their new home at college should be like. How do students deal with differences in geography, opulence, and culture between their college home and family home? How do they construct the many physical spaces they will call "home" at college? And how does all of this happen when students know that college is at best only a temporary home?

People moving to a new location find a sense of home in a variety of ways. They get to know people and make friends. They decorate their living spaces with familiar objects and images. They develop a fondness for the climate, the type of community, or natural environment of the new place. They become familiar with the geography or perhaps they already associate the new place with positive previous experiences, like summer camp or vacations. They come to value the work they do in the new place.[2] Their new home may be more supportive than their family home. All of these differences may help students create new homes at college but also suggest why it might be harder for some than others. For instance, some students chose to attend a college in Maine because they loved the state based on their summer camp experiences. They wanted to return to a place in which they had fond memories. But students from other regions of the country or from urban areas found both Maine's climate and rural setting alienating.

We examine students' construction and reconstruction of college as home—as a place where they belong—throughout their time in college.[3] As Charlie acknowledged in the quote with which we began this chapter, home is a complicated concept. It is both a physical space where we live, and an emotional or psychological space where we feel a sense of comfort or belonging.

Every year in our interviews we asked students, "Do you feel at home in college?" If they answered "yes," we asked when they began to feel this way and why. If they answered "no," we asked what they thought would help them feel at home. Their responses helped us better understand what "home" meant to them, whether they saw college as a place where they could create a new home and then whether they felt as if they had. In their first year, we asked these questions shortly after students returned to college from winter break, the first time many students had spent an extended period of time in their family homes since starting college. We asked these questions every year thereafter, often at times when students were making key decisions about where and with whom they might live. Feeling at home in college is complex because students not only move between their family homes and college numerous times, but they also make many decisions about the physical spaces in college in which they will live. The choices of where to live in college, the changes students make in the physical places they inhabit, and the ways they feel about those spaces all serve as opportunities to reexamine what home means to them. They are excellent examples of the starts and restarts that students experience in college.

Students chose to attend their college, in part, because they believed it would be a "good fit," or they talked about it "feeling right." The vast majority used language that suggested that they had high expectations for feeling at home in college, and we found that almost all students' expectations were eventually met. Yet, when and how—not to mention if—college felt like home varied greatly. Some students relished the fact that they felt at home quite quickly, whereas others, at least initially, saw it as unnecessary and not particularly important. For most, feeling at home in college was dependent on their ability to find friends and develop a social network. Others, though, felt at home when they got to know faculty or when they figured out the expectations and structure of college courses and how to be successful in them.

The structural restarts of college—going home between semesters and at the end of each year, moving into new living spaces, studying abroad— affected students' understanding of what home meant and where it was. Developing a sense of home became an exercise in comparison. College often seemed more like home when home with family increasingly felt less like a comfortable fit. College also seemed more like home when students had to create a new "home" while studying abroad. Students rewrote their college narratives as they deepened their understanding about who they were and what home meant to them.

Although leaving family homes and establishing new homes is a transition that most young adults make,[4] making this transition in a residential college differs from other environments. Oma and Adam illustrate this complex process. They are middle-class, African American students from southern cities. Although their backgrounds were similar in several respects, their transitions to college and their paths to finding home were quite different.

Oma: Outside Her Comfort Zone

Oma did not quickly think of her college as home. Coming to a predominantly white liberal arts college in a small New England town was, as Oma said, "outside of her comfort zone." In the first semester, she called her parents and high school friends daily. She sought counseling to deal with homesickness. People she met at college seemed quite different from her old friends. Back home, she would spend time talking to people, finding out how they were doing, but at college "people are not that way . . . I mean, they'll say hi and just keep going." The large drinking parties that seemed to make up the social scene for many first-year students particularly horrified her. When asked in her first interview how she found social life at college, she said, "I don't think there is a social life here . . . I have been to the parties and, where I'm from, those are not parties. I mean, people are just getting drunk. That's not a party."

Although Oma found her transition to college challenging, she was not surprised by this nor did she expect college to feel homey: "I wish I were more social, like I wish this social life here would consider people from other backgrounds. Stuff like that. But it doesn't." Rather than trying to fit into an alienating social scene, Oma chose to develop connections to students through other venues. With a fellow student, she started an organization for students who identified as being African. This organization met regularly and got Oma connected to peers with whom she felt she had something in common. Although she made this effort to find a sense of belonging in her first semester at college, Oma still was eager to return during winter break to her family and the town where she went to high school. But when she got there, she felt different and people told her she had become more judgmental and opinionated:

Last semester I missed home a lot. I actually was seeing a counselor because I missed home so bad. And you know, I went back home and in two weeks it was like, "Okay, I'm ready to come back to school now." It's very funny because I was mad and complaining every day that I want to go home. So I don't know. I guess I thought I miss home, but then when I got home, like, "Okay, I want to go back to school now."

Oma's social life and her sense of fitting in improved in her second semester, but she was still acutely aware of her difference as a black woman on a predominantly white campus. When asked, shortly before the end of her first year, if college felt like home, she said:

It's better, but it's still not home. As time goes on you get to see a few people who actually have the same background as you, and it feels a little good to know that there's someone here that knows what I'm thinking or someone knows what I'm saying. But I have to say it took awhile to get to know that there are those people here, which is kind of bad.

Oma thought that much of the challenge of fitting in her first year stemmed from her minority status: "I feel like, not only am I a minority here, but I feel like most of the stuff that's done here is done for the majority to fit in here. And I've had conversations with a lot of people who feel the same way." Nonetheless, there was one respite for Oma. She said she felt at home when she and other students with African parents cooked a meal together: "We cooked a traditional meal together and just invited a couple of people to come and join us. I felt really good personally, because I thought it smelled like home. It just felt like home for once."

Going home for the summer produced the same sense of dissonance that Oma felt during winter break. At the start of her sophomore year, she felt more comfortable and was eager to dig into her courses. She still felt at odds with what she saw as the dominant culture on campus, but restarting college as a sophomore had its benefits: "It feels like you're familiar with things. Like you know what you're doing, sort of. Sometimes you have a lot of work to do, but because you've had that last year you know that it's going to get done. That's just this feeling that, 'Oh yeah, I know what I'm doing.'" By now, she had decided to major in history with a concentration in African history. One of her history professors became her academic advisor as well as an important mentor both academically and personally. She referred to him as a "father figure": "He's probably the only person I can go and cry to on this campus. He's very helpful to me. We've talked about things ranging from nothing to a lot of things. After a while, you just get really comfortable dealing with the same person." She also made new friends, some of whom she met through an interest she developed in African music.

Oma's engagement with her academic interests, and finding an academic advisor with whom she developed a meaningful personal relationship, were foundational to her beginning to create a home at college. Nonetheless, at the end of her sophomore year, she was still doubtful about ever calling college "home": "It's just not home for me, because it's very different. It's not anything that I can say, 'Well, if you make this better, I'll feel at home.' It's just not going to be."

Despite not feeling entirely at home at college, Oma did not want to be away from campus for an entire year because she wanted to take certain courses being taught at her college. She decided to study abroad for a semester at a program in a large, diverse European city. She found the program and urban life stimulating, but her time away made her think more positively about life at college, particularly living near friends and working closely with faculty. Senior year she lived with friends in an off-campus apartment where she could cook and "be herself." She continued her close relationships with faculty in the history department, did an honors project, and was admitted to an excellent graduate school. When asked at the end of her senior year whether college felt like home, Oma replied, "It's not the same as home. Definitely not. But it's been good."

In her four years at college, Oma navigated an environment that didn't feel particularly welcoming to her but one in which she learned to thrive. Oma never called college home, but she developed a sense of belonging when she found peers who shared an interest in Africa, developed a relationship with an academic advisor, and became passionate about a course of study. College became more of a home for her than the home in which she grew up, a home from which she increasingly felt alienated. Although by most accounts, Oma was a success in college, she was not without regrets. She thought she may have focused too much on her coursework in response to her ambivalence about how she fit into the social life at college. When asked what advice she would give an incoming student, she said:

It's not just four years of school. It's four years of everything, and I would advise people to do things outside of courses. Because, I mean it is college, you're supposed to be doing work, blah, blah, blah, but it's also like you're 22 or 21 by the time you get out of here and *you should be getting a lot more out of this than just academics—which I didn't do* [italics added]. So, I mean, that's something that I would advise people.

Despite feeling regret for not attending to more things outside of academics, what Oma was most worried about when she thought of going to graduate school on the West Coast the next fall wasn't her academic ability or background but moving far away from her friends on the East Coast: "I'm a little worried that, I mean I hope it doesn't happen, but I'm really worried that I might not be in touch with all of my friends as I should be."

Adam: Fitting in from the Start

Like Oma, Adam came from a predominantly African American community in a large southern city. He chose his college because, when he visited it as a high school senior, he saw it as "a very friendly environment." Whereas Oma saw her college choice as going outside of her comfort zone, Adam described college as "comfortable": "Just walking on campus, I felt like I could be a part of this." Like Oma, though, he didn't minimize the differences between where he came from and college:

There's a gap in like the cultural diversity here. I knew that coming in so I was not shocked. It was something that I was aware of. Like six percent black diversity or something like that. Twenty percent overall diversity. But, yeah, you kind of feel it more. It's not bad because it teaches you how to deal with other people. But at the same time, being from the South I'm used to so many more multicultural surroundings and stuff. That was probably the biggest thing.

Unlike Oma, Adam dug in socially and became very involved in student organizations. He joined the African American student organization and a Christian fellowship group, and sang with the choir. For his college jobs, he did housekeeping and worked in the library, becoming close to the staff with whom he worked. When asked whether college felt like home at the end of his first year, Adam responded:

> I do feel some sense of it at this point. I wasn't expecting it to come so early, but now a lot of my insecurities and things are kind of mellowed, kind of evened out or whatever. It's becoming less and less of a struggle, day by day. And certain things that were kind of important to me before are not that important anymore. So it's becoming a place where it's not necessarily a struggle to be at. It's awesome.

Adam was eager to go back home for the summer, but when he restarted college as a sophomore, he talked about how home had felt different: "Well you just appreciate school; you appreciate the difference in culture. Because when you go back home, it's like you are reinserted into your culture, but it's funny because you don't fit quite the same way as you did before you left."

Adam chose a major in political science and enjoyed his courses, although he struggled to achieve average grades. He made some connections with faculty in his department but formed closer relationships with staff in student affairs and admissions. When asked at the end of his sophomore year what he meant when he said he felt at home, Adam answered:

> I don't feel like there's an aspect of [my college] that I'm closed out from or don't feel welcome to. I feel like that in terms of community, we're all involved and we all look out for one another, in some sense. Even if we don't necessarily like each other. There's certain things that we come together on, regardless. So it's just community.

As a junior, Adam chose not to study abroad. When asked why, he said he was too involved with things on campus to take a break, but he also wanted to improve his grade point average and the grades he would receive while studying at other institutions wouldn't be "counted." When asked as a senior whether he felt at home, he more emphatically said yes:

> When I'm at home too long, I'm ready to go home which would be here [college]. I don't know if that's [because I am] so much attached to my things like my personal possessions or, I mean, I do enjoy seeing people

I've met over the last four years. I have a rapport with different faculty, different staff. I know so many of the facilities people. Like we stop, we have random conversations. People have named children after me. A staff member in the library whom I work with named a grandchild's middle name after me. You know, so, and that's not a requirement to feel a part of it. But it's just that you build these relationships and like your reputation precedes you. Those kinds of things, just a sense of knowing and a sense of belonging and a sense of responsibility, make me feel like something is my home.

At the same time that Adam expressed a deep sense of belonging in college, he also expressed a desire to leave by the time he was a senior. After graduation, Adam wanted to return to "someplace warm" and a more urban environment, similar to where he grew up. He felt as though he had "used up" all the opportunities that were available to him:

Graduation cannot get here soon enough. I am ready, yesterday . . . I'm always looking for that next thing. And I've done almost everything I can do at [my college] without like running it. You know, I've done the student government, I've done the judicial board, I've done classes, everything except maybe languages because I did that in high school. I've done everything. So it's kind of like the sense that you have maxed out at a place.

Oma's and Adam's home-making at college is a study in contrast. Although both entered school aware of the disjuncture between their backgrounds and their college environments, shortly after arriving they made different decisions about how to handle whatever dissonance they felt. Adam joined lots of clubs, continuously sought out new friends, and became heavily involved in campus life. He created social connections early on and through these developed a sense of belonging at college. As Adam recognized that he no longer "fit quite as well" into his family home, he embraced college as his new home. But after four years, Adam was ready to leave home once again. As he experienced growing out of his family home once he went to college, he experienced growing out of his college home; he was ready to move on. Adam practiced home-making by embracing a variety of opportunities that allowed him to broadly sample where and with whom he fit in his environment. Then he felt he used it up and wanted to start the process over again.

Oma was much more reluctant to see college as her new home and spent her first semester overwhelmed by feeling alienated and homesick. Like Adam, when she went back to her family home, she felt like she no longer fit there either but, unlike Adam, stayed "in-between" homes—neither totally belonging at college nor in her family home. Oma only seriously began to develop a sense of home at college when she became engaged with her academic program. She established close ties to a valued mentor, and even though she found her history courses difficult, she pursued a history major, studied abroad, and completed an honors project. As a senior, she didn't feel as though she had outgrown college, but was in fact worried about moving far away from it and from the friends that she had made there. Unlike Adam, Oma hadn't outgrown her college home; she wasn't ready to move on. Her practice at home-making was also characterized by embracing opportunities but she did so more selectively and cautiously than Adam. She didn't feel as though she had used up college by the time she left. She regretted not doing more.

Leaving Home and Finding Home in the First Year

Oma's and Adam's stories are not atypical. All of the students in this study, even first-generation students like Oma, expected to attend a residential college. As we previously described, most students, with the help of parents, guidance counselors, teachers, or community organizations, had elaborate college searches, applied to many schools, and were admitted to many of them. Although some had more options than others, most *chose* to attend the schools they did and talked about their positive anticipation of attending college. The differences between their family homes and their college homes are only more obvious than most. Even though most students entered their colleges willingly and with high expectations, the degree of comfort and familiarity that they felt once on campus differed quickly and dramatically. Some reported feeling at home almost immediately. One student replied that she felt at home "actually, probably the first week." She thought it was because "it's such a small campus, you kind of know everybody by their faces so it doesn't feel like you're totally in a strange land." Another student said he started to think of college as home within the first month: "I mean just as soon as I got used to it. Got used to, you know, the college life."

In the first year, friendships (or lack of them) were the most commonly cited influence in determining how and if students felt at home in college. One student who found a social network quickly said: "I feel like I connected with a lot of people, which is really nice, and I've gained really good relationships with a lot of my friends on my floor which is good. And I've gotten to know a lot more people in my house. It's a very family place." Another student had the opposite experience: "I know I've met a lot of good people and I click with a lot of them, but it's just like you don't really have that core group or something that you can always go to, or you can just be like, 'Hey, you know, let's hang out.' So, it's probably just that that doesn't make it feel like home much."

It is not surprising that finding friends was of great importance to students' sense of home. For many, coming to college was the first time they had lived away from family and long-standing social supports, so finding new friends to give support was an essential piece to creating a new home at college. Getting used to living in a communal situation also was an important factor in students' feeling at home. Many of our students not only had never lived with strangers but also had never shared a bedroom, so having roommates and unfamiliar people in the dorm made them anxious. "I started out the year really nervous, because I've never shared a room with anyone," one student recalled. "I've never shared a bathroom with anyone. I was like, what am I going to do, like you're brushing your teeth and someone walks in, like what do you do?"

And for some, college felt like home because their family homes no longer did. This was true for both Oma and Adam, who felt less like they fit in at their old homes after going to college, but it was also the case for students who literally lost space in their homes. "I don't have a bed at home, at my house," said one displaced student. "It's a whole big long complicated thing that happened with my father over the summer, and I don't have a bed. So when I'm here and there's a bed it's like, 'Oh, it feels so good to be home.' But it's not really home. It's just kind of home."

Like Oma, some students said they began to feel at home when they gained greater control over their academic experiences. One said knowing "how to navigate the campus and my courses" was a key factor in coming to feel at home while another referred to the increased predictability of her coursework: "I guess just having a routine, like a set routine that I have every day. I don't know. Like knowing what I have to do in order to succeed. I feel like I have a better grasp on that now." And finally, some students began to feel at home when they received a good grade or when they found themselves having conversations with faculty outside of class. For these students, having their academic lives under control was critical to making college feel more familiar.[5] They remind us that there are other ways to craft a college home than developing a strong social network in the first year.

Going Home and Returning Home

In addition to difficulties in finding friends and in feeling comfort with their academic experiences, students often cited discontinuities between their family home and college as reasons why they did not feel at home in college. Some lived in very different regions of the country or types of communities than their college—the South versus the Northeast, urban versus rural. A number of students of color and international students echoed Oma's sentiments about ethnic or cultural disconnects as a reason why college did not feel like home. A Latina sophomore from Texas said: "[It's] culture shock for me, because I live in a place where 80 percent of the people are Latino, mostly Mexican. For me, it's not been hard to assimilate but, well, there are so many cultures here. So yeah, culture shock mostly." An Asian American sophomore who had lived in a large city commented:

> I can't eat certain foods. I can't have real rice, I can't have Asian food, because Asian food here just is not Asian food, and it's not home. And then it gets really cold. But other than that, it's pretty. I think the biggest shock I've ever encountered here was the racial thing. Being a majority back home, and then coming here and being minority, that was the hardest thing.

These students often mentioned factors like food, weather, or the size of the town when asked what would need to change to make college feel more like home—"Probably a change in weather, more students, and public transportation"—but their comments suggested a bigger issue: the need to craft an identity as someone different from a majority culture, something they may have not have needed to do in the schools and neighborhoods of their pasts.[6]

For all students, though, returning from school breaks served as opportunities to restart college. Many students came back from winter, spring, or summer breaks resolved to tackle the challenges that plagued them before they left or develop new perspectives on what they wanted to accomplish. College began to feel less foreign than their family homes because it better accommodated the new selves they were developing.[7] Articulating this change well, a sophomore said that being at home in the summer between her first and second year forced her to "be who I've always been for the last 18 years," whereas college allowed her "the freedom to change and not have the pressure to stay the same":

> You know there was definitely an evolution I could see from the first year. The first time I went home to my parents' house that was still home. And then by summer of that year, when I came back to college, college really felt more like home to me. It was a place where I could be who I wanted to be and with my room, I could make whatever decisions I wanted and it was just really a nice place to crash if I needed to crash, or to be really happy when I needed to be really happy.

Shortly before leaving school at the end of her first year, another sophomore commented: "I catch myself calling college home. And then when I'm at home I'm like, 'Okay, I need you to drive me home now Mom.' Home being college." An international student expressed a similar sentiment in her sophomore year:

> I think it's interesting because once when I went back for winter break and my mom asked me, she said, "Oh, so do you feel when you go back to China, do you feel you're going home or do you feel you are coming to China for a temporary stay and then you're going home to college?" And I feel like, yeah, it's actually the latter. And my mom's like, "Oh."

When students left college for breaks, the homes they went back to frequently felt like different places from those they left. As Adam said about returning home, "you just don't quite fit." Soon after returning from winter break, first-year students often commented on how their relationships with their high school friends had changed:

> I don't know what they thought about me but . . . it was really weird. They didn't seem to have changed as much as I thought they would have from going to college. And I felt that I had changed a little more. Just because of my experiences while I am here. So it was kind of, it was fun hanging out with them, but still, they didn't seem to have gotten past high school mentality.

Another first-year student mentioned chafing under her parents' control: "Because my parents were always like, 'Where you going? What are you doing? Who are you going to be with? What time are you coming home? That's kind of late, you should come home earlier. Be careful.' It was just like, 'I'm independent now. Leave me alone' . . . It's very inconvenient and frustrating."[8]

That these types of responses were common was not surprising. Being more independent, trying out new social networks, and developing different academic and extracurricular interests—all things that happen in the first year of college—change students so that their old environments and relationships may no longer feel as comfortable or familiar. As one first-year student commented, "It wasn't that home changed. It was more me changing, and home being too much of the same."

For all students a changing sense of home can be a difficult yet expected "growing-up" experience, an important part of emerging adulthood. Yet, for some students of color the change between who they were prior to attending college and who they were becoming was particularly dramatic. Oma is a good example. She felt different from most of the people she met in her first year at college but when she went home during school and summer break between her first and second year, she also felt quite different from her peers back home. Another African American student described her experience of going home for winter break in her first year as feeling like "a visitor in my own state." A Latina student expanded on these sentiments. She was looking forward to seeing her family and friends during her first winter break but, when she got home, her friends told her she "was very white, culturally." When asked what she thought people meant by this, she replied:

Like the way I talk. The way I present myself at times. Vocabulary I use. Things like that, you know. It's just the way I talk and just how fast I talk, and they kind of think, "Oh, you're conceited now. It's like you want to be uptight, like uptight white girl." No, not at all. It's just, I hang around with people that talk like this and it's, you know, not on purpose . . . It was more like, "You're becoming white. You need to be more Mexican. You need be in touch with your culture."

Similarly, a first-year African American student talked about an exchange he had over Christmas dinner with members of his extended family that ended in "an eruption." He described, in particular, one cousin's reactions:

He thought that this school had changed me and made me into some, you know, this crazy fool about things. I said "No, it's just my classes have opened my eyes." I learned a whole lot about African American studies in terms of reparations, homosexuality, and other issues. These are things I probably felt somewhat worried about before, but I became more exposed and more knowledge[able] about the subject to the point in which I was able to form my own opinion on it. And so yeah, I think my family did notice a difference, and they started to notice more of an activism in me and sort of a different consciousness when it came to social issues.

The dissonance that some students of color feel when they return to their communities and families can be troubling. College changes them, or their sense of who they are, but it may not yet be their new home. And although researchers differ about the effects that strong ties to their previous communities have on students' persistence in college, most agree that family support is a vital component of students' sense of well-being and growth.[9] Feeling as though they no longer "fit" in their family home *nor* in college may result in students feeling stuck somewhere in between who they have been and an only partially articulated idea of who they are becoming. Oma weathered her "in-betweenness" but the struggle wasn't easy.

Some students who initially did not feel a sense of home in their first year talked of transferring to other schools, but few actually did. The retention rates at our colleges are very high, even for students from underrepresented groups. Most stayed because things got better. They found a group of friends, connected with a faculty member, or felt some success in courses. They often shed what might have been unrealistic initial expectations for college being constantly wonderful or "the best years of their lives" and realized they can do okay even if college is not always a place of comfort.

Finding and Leaving Home in the Last Three Years

A unique feature of residential colleges is that they routinely require students to change their living arrangements. They change dorms, rooms, or room-mates. They move to new places to take summer internships. They decide to study abroad. Thus, home-making in college is unique; not only is college a temporary home lasting only as long as they are students, but the places students call home during college are also temporary, lasting often only for a year at a time. Students' decisions about where and with whom they will live can disrupt not only their physical space, but their emotional and psychologi-cal space which can, in turn, disrupt their academic lives. At the very least, their decisions serve as opportunities to reflect on what home means.

Restarts with Changes in Residences and Roommates

One of the most anxiety-producing times in residential colleges is when students have to decide where and with whom to live the following year. As we've seen, many students talked about the housing lottery as a time of stress. Did someone with whom they wanted to live want to live with them? Would they be lonely if they lived alone? Would living off campus with friends give them a greater sense of being at home? These decisions also made them confront their own needs for companionship or solitude and for physical spaces that would give them comfort or support their academic needs. In the past, either growing up in their families or in their first year at college, they had little choice over their living environments. In their last three years of college, however, students have many choices about where and with whom home will be.

When we asked upperclass students what would help college feel like home, they most often mentioned the importance of moving in with a group of friends. A senior said the following about finally feeling at home:

Freshman year, not at all. Sophomore year, it got better. Junior year I was gone, and then now I think, yeah . . . Because this year I'm living in a suite with my friends, whereas before I was just kind of by myself for the freshman and sophomore years. So senior year, actually being with friends, so I see them all the time and can hang out in the suite in the main room and things like that, so definitely more [at home].

Another student felt at home her first year when she had friends who lived on her dorm floor but did not feel at home her sophomore year when she ended up not getting along with her chosen roommate and sleeping on the couch in the dorm lounge much of the time. By her junior year she again felt at home when she moved into a suite with three other friends.

For other students, particular places made a difference in whether they felt at home. One student described her dorm as "family room like." Another reported that the residential hall she moved into as a junior felt like "sitting in my living room." "It's a comfortable place to be when I want to get back and away from the stresses of everything else. So it's like home." For other students moving into an off-campus house helped create a home, as the senior quoted below described:

I live off-campus with people whom I really care about. And there's definitely like a family there, a living arrangement that I haven't had before. I just love the idea of having a house to ourselves. We have a backyard. We have a campfire in the back. We have our own laundry. The school bus drives down the street in the morning. It's a very residential [neighborhood] and it's almost like the best of both worlds. I feel like it's more home than [other places].

Finally, for some students creating home was tied to having a space of their own. At the end of her sophomore year, when asked why she felt at home at college, a student who was living in a single room responded: "I like going to my room at the end of the night. I feel like that's my personal, private space. It's just mine. I mean it's only mine for eight months, but the overall atmosphere in the room is mine to create."

These students' stories about how their living arrangements shaped their sense of belonging remind us that students don't just come to college; they come to particular spaces and people that change over time. Students who felt at home in their first year when their social networks were tied to others who lived nearby may have to restart their home-making when, as upperclass students, their friends live further away or when their core group of friends are studying abroad. Each decision they make about where and with whom to live is an opportunity for them to reexamine what "home" means and how they want to create that home. These decisions serve as practice for the adult task of "home-making" that they will do after they graduate.

Restarts with Study Abroad

For many juniors, a major consideration about their homes was connected to the decision of whether to study abroad. Those who planned to study abroad needed to decide when and where they wanted to go, as well as what they believed they would need in order to feel at home in those new places. Students who decided to remain on campus worried about with whom they would live. Would college still feel like home without their close friends? Leaving a place in which they now felt at home and having to reestablish that feeling in another country or at another college was too daunting for some to consider. For others, somewhat oddly, studying abroad provided an opportunity to find home for the first time. Laura is a good example.

Laura was not exuberant about attending her college. Growing up in a white, suburban, upper-middle-class family, Laura wanted to go to a college located in a different kind of place, but her parents encouraged her to base her college choice on financial aid and the prestige of the college. A few high school friends attended a nearby college, so Laura somewhat reluctantly matriculated at her college. When asked in her first year if she thought of college as home, she responded with a qualified yes: "I don't know, I wouldn't say home is where the heart is. I wouldn't say I love it here. I mean I consider my house where my family is my home, but I don't consider anywhere else except here my home, besides my actual home. So yes, by default I guess."

She spent much of her time on her friends' campus and liked the atmosphere there better than at her own college. By sophomore year, Laura was resigned to staying at her college, but when asked if she felt at home, Laura responded with the same ambivalence she did her first year: "Yeah, probably just because I've been here longer, so I'm more used to it."

Laura studied in Paris her junior year and had a great experience. She enjoyed living in a city and felt as though she became more independent and resourceful than she had been in the past. Ironically, she became close friends with other students from her college who, when they all returned the following year, became the social network that Laura previously lacked. When asked while she was still in Paris whether her study abroad experience had made her think differently about her college, Laura said, "It's made me appreciate various aspects of it. Just like, the campus is so pretty and the professors are really, really friendly."

When she returned to campus her senior year, Laura realized that compared to Paris, college felt much more like home: "I don't know if Paris changed things for me, but *everything* has changed. I've made new friends, because I had none here before, and it's like my whole world has been turned on its head . . . Suddenly I realize like, oh my god, I really do love [my college] and there are a lot of great things about it." Part of Laura's joy at being back involved her realization of how supportive her college had been of her development. She talked about how college allowed her to develop her intellectual curiosities and become "more verbally nimble." She described her college as a place where she had "come into her own."

After graduation Laura went to China to teach English for a year. She missed the "intellectual energy" of her college years and reflected on how she didn't fully appreciate college until after she left. It was a place that taught her "patience and bravery" and made her more resilient. In China, she talked about coming "home," by which she meant returning to her college.

Laura's experience was not unusual. Another student who was mostly alienated from college before studying abroad remarked after returning: "I definitely wanted to come back and take advantage of everything college had to offer . . . I'm really happy to be back in a place where everyone's kind of the same age. Everyone's an undergrad student here and going through the same things." A third student described herself as "definitely feeling at home here academically" something she "didn't realize until now." Leaving their college "homes" to study abroad gave these students the opportunity to reexamine and then restart their relationships with their colleges, and to see their home in college in a whole new light. In comparing their college home to where they were living while studying abroad, many realized, some for the first time, how important their colleges had been to their development and construction of their new selves.

Whereas these students might previously have said they did not feel at home at college, when away from their colleges they longed for them. There was poignancy in these restarts in which students acknowledged their newfound sense of college as home, while at the same time realizing how soon they would be leaving again. As one student put it: "It scares me having to move again and do the whole transition thing, like figure out where to go if I want really good Pad Thai or pizza. Just having to re-do everything again, meet new people, find my new place. Like you realize that's because you do feel at home here."

Most students shared the above sentiment. They crafted homes at college, recognized the value, and, somewhat regretfully, realized that they soon would have to do the whole process of home-making again in a new place. Laura and Oma are examples of students who, even though college did not feel like home quickly, or perhaps never fully, were reluctant to leave. Less common were students who had felt at home in college but were ready to leave. Adam is a good example. Even though he felt as though he very much belonged at his college, graduation couldn't come quickly enough for him because he had "maxed out" the place and wished he were gone "yesterday." A senior who also felt at home throughout her four years at college said she was ready to leave so that she could go "back home": "I think maybe just in my last year, certain things have become more important to me—like realizing that even though college was really fun and being away from home was fine, like maybe I want to move closer to my family, things like that."

Colin exemplifies how a student's sense of home can waver throughout college. As a first-year student, he thought of college as home because "it's a small community and everybody knows everybody." But the longer he stayed at college, the more this "small community" quality alienated him. Colin missed the diversity, sunshine, and excitement of the large southern city in which he grew up. He had a large group of friends at college but didn't anticipate staying in touch with them after graduation: "I'm very excited about finishing at [my college]. I'm ready to move on. I'm ready to be done with small town type living. I'm more of a city person. I'm ready to be an adult."

Conclusion

In the beginning of this chapter we stated that home-making for students in residential colleges is often a comparative exercise. Where they perceive themselves being at home changes as they change and as they decide what it is that makes a home in which they want to live, a home that provides comfort and support as they undertake new challenges. Developing a sense of home plays a critical role in supporting students' ability to fully engage academically. Home at college can be a refuge from the stress students often feel, and family homes in which they grew up may seem less "homey" as students develop new interests, ideas, and needs. Every new home provides a new perspective on previous homes. Emerging adulthood is characterized by this exploration of identity—figuring out who you are, whom you want to be around, and what you want to do with your life. And emerging adults move for work, love, or education a great deal more often than other age groups.[10] So is the practice students in residential colleges receive in home-making "good" practice?

It may seem counterintuitive to suggest that the process of creating a home at college is good practice for adult life. The process at college is easily trivialized because the structure of coming and going between home and college, and switching roommates and/or residences every year, is so ingrained in our portrait of college life that it is often not examined. Of course, when you go to college you move residences often, jockey between your family home and college home, and get used to living with a variety of roommates. The process may also be trivialized because living in a college residence doesn't require the host of logistics that other adults face when they move into new homes. College students don't have to remember to get their electricity turned on, find the nearest grocery store, or figure out which bus will get them to work.

Residential colleges do simplify students' home-making, particularly in their first year when most of the decisions about where and with whom to live are made for them by the college. Roommates are assigned. Planned activities require a degree of community among residents on the same dorm floor or in the same house. Students can try things out, think about what they might need to feel at home, and reflect on what works and what doesn't without making long-term commitments either to the people or place they live. There is also a large support network—dorm advisors, residential life counselors, deans of students—who can offer advice and mediate tensions. Colin suggests that what he has done at college is a "schoolboy" exercise at creating a home and not as practice for a task he would need as an older adult. Perhaps this is why Colin felt like he wasn't going to be a real adult until after graduation.

But ironically, rather than infantilizing and constraining students in their home-making efforts, the structure that residential colleges provide may actually make students' efforts more difficult. First, home-making is challenging because residential college requires students to make a bundle of decisions about home, many more than their counterparts who may move into apartments or other non-college residencies. Housing lotteries that ask students to pick new roommates and new rooms every year often become critical moments when students reevaluate—or feel like they are being reevaluated by—their social networks. Study abroad can disrupt friendships when students leave campus during different semesters. These disruptions and changes mean that the process of home-making in college is one with many restarts, and although these restarts provide opportunities for students to learn from and reflect on the decisions they make about what is important to them in creating a home, they also are challenging.

Second, decisions about home-making happen in the context of all the other decisions they make—about friends, work, relationships to faculty and advisors, time—and all of these decisions shape each other. Unlike other young adults who move away from home and find new places to live, students at residential colleges live, work, and play in the same space and with the same people over a number of years. College felt more like home to Oma when it helped her explore an academic passion. College felt less like home for Adam when, both academically and socially, it felt like there was nothing else of interest to do. Home in college is the accumulation of the variety of decisions students make and, in this way, attending a residential college is excellent practice for reflecting on what home means and finding home as an emerging adult.

FIVE

∾ Advice

What makes for an ideal advisor?

KEERA, SENIOR: Somebody who listens and gives me constructive advice, [and] who is honest with you and doesn't sugar coat things. They tell you when you're doing well; they tell you when you should step it up. Somebody who's making sure you're successful in whatever you want to do. I got really lucky in finding the advisor I have now.

PAIGE, SENIOR: Someone that is open-minded and in tune with what you want, but also will give you guidance. And also someone that cares about what you're doing and will use their experiences to help you with that. In terms of my advisors here, I find that in them. I haven't spent as much time with my advisors as I should, but I think that's on my side. They're not supposed to be like, "Oh, come meet with me every day." I'm supposed to be the one initiating that, and I haven't as much as I should.

ZARI, SENIOR: Well, I don't know. I'm not going to my advisors that often. I don't look to them that often so I don't really know. Maybe I should look to them more often.

A T MOST OF OUR COLLEGES, the first faculty member that students meet for substantive, one-on-one interactions is their academic advisor. Their advisor is responsible for helping them with the transition to college, answering questions about the academic program and college requirements, helping with academic planning, and connecting them to key college resources and services. These early advising experiences have the potential to provide students with practice in how to interact with faculty in ways that aid academic decision-making, and with greater insight into how to identify potential mentors. Much as colleges assign first-year students roommates to jump-start peer interactions and friendships, they assign first-year students faculty advisors to jump-start student-faculty interactions. And while the former jump-start can be remarkably successful, the ambiguity inherent in faculty-student advising relationships can impede the effectiveness of the latter. For the vast majority of new college students, the roles of teacher and student are not new, and the main expectations for these roles are relatively well defined for both. However, the roles of advisor and advisee are less clear, and the expectations for these roles may not be shared among or across faculty and students. Not only will individual student-faculty pairs need to work together to define the nature of this partnership, but its effectiveness will depend heavily on the student's and the advisor's commitment to, and investment in, developing a meaningful one.[1]

The first-year advising relationships described by Gabriella and Sara provide contrasting examples of how these early advising jump-starts can develop into meaningful student-faculty relationships or simply stall out. When asked to describe her interaction with her first-year advisor, Gabriella responded: "We had a bunch of conferences just to talk, to catch up on my life and see how I was doing in my classes and stuff. It's mostly just like hanging out for a half hour and talking about stuff that we've been doing or stuff that I've been doing mostly. I like the fact that I can go and talk to her, and [she] can give me mini-advice."

Gabriella, like many students, chose to attend a liberal arts college because she wanted to make strong connections with faculty. In her sophomore year, she explained why this was important to her:

> You have someone to go to besides the people in your home or your close friends from [my college]. You have higher authorities to go to— someone who can actually give you real tips on how to do something: "You should do this" or "Other students of mine have done this." And that kind of helps a lot more than "I think you should do this, because you know it's good for you."

Gabriella believed that her advisor would play an important role in her college life, but only if they developed a level of comfort with each other that would allow them to step outside of the hierarchical professor and student roles. Although students expect (and want) teachers to take the lead and to some extent dominate in the classroom, that is not necessarily what they expect (or want) from their faculty advisors. In the fall of her sophomore year, Gabriella described how close she had gotten to her faculty advisor:

> It's very relaxing, and it's not like professor to student. It's more like two people having a conversation, which I think is very valuable because it puts aside a lot of discomfort when you're talking to someone that you

see above you. I still see them as my professors, but when we're talking one-on-one about advice and things, we put that aside, and it becomes a lot more comfortable to talk about things.

Learning how to interact with faculty and staff, particularly a faculty advisor, increases students' opportunities to obtain relevant, personalized advice—advice that can promote competence and growth, and aid in decision-making.[2] However, establishing these relationships is challenging; it takes time, effort, and, most importantly, self-initiative. For students like Sara, these first-year faculty relationships seemed difficult to establish due, in part, to a lack of face-to-face interactions. When asked to describe her first-year advisor, Sara commented:

He doesn't really advise. I met him once [at] the beginning of the year and then after that I just emailed him and asked for my [registration code]. He emailed [it] back to me, and I can just take the classes I choose or drop the classes I choose. Which is kind of nice, because I don't have to do anything. But, at the same time, I wish someone would tell me something, you know, like any type of guidance.

Although Sara was frustrated by the lack of guidance she received from her advisor, she also enjoyed being left alone—not having to justify her decisions to her advisor. Because she didn't meet face-to-face with her advisor, she never gave him the opportunity to provide her with feedback or to ask her to reflect upon her decisions. In fact, Sara did not believe that her advisor could provide her with useful information because of a perceived mismatch between her own academic interests and the expertise of her advisor: "They put me with a really strange advisor . . . someone in the philosophy department. I have no idea why. I mean he's nobody who I would probably want to take any of the classes that he teaches. And so it wasn't really applicable to ask him advice." When asked to elaborate on why her advisor couldn't help, she explained, "I didn't really try. I didn't make a huge effort to utilize him." Acknowledging her own lack of initiative and effort, she also pointed out that her advisor didn't reach out to her: "He wasn't forthcoming, like I want to help you." Sara seemed unsure about whether her advisor was interested in helping her, and this may have discouraged her from reaching out to him.[3]

Students will need advice about a wide variety of academic decisions and, as we described earlier, making these decisions is a complex and messy process. Most students start college with relatively limited information about courses, professors, requirements, and available resources. Even seemingly simple decisions—Which math course should I take? Which course will challenge but not overwhelm me?—can involve substantial risk. Using a faculty advisor as a principal resource helps to reduce the uncertainty and risk inherent in these decisions because even if their faculty advisors cannot answer all of their questions, they can direct them to those who can.

To understand how seeking and responding to advice evolves during college—from the first year through the last—we asked students whom they consulted about key academic decisions. Not surprisingly, the individuals with whom students consulted changed over the four years of college. Although most students entered college relying on their parents for all types of advice, most quickly came to recognize the value of consulting with faculty or staff about their academic decisions in college. The relationships students develop with these adults change as students' experiences shape and reshape who they are and what they want out of college. Students are given multiple opportunities to decide from whom to seek advice as well as to reflect upon the advice they are given.

High School Advising: The College Search

In the first interview we asked, "Who was most influential in your college search and decision-making processes?" Virtually all students described parents as pivotal advisors and only half mentioned consulting with guidance counselors. Prior to starting college, many students had limited opportunities to practice consulting with adults who weren't their parents, and consequently hadn't yet learned to seek advice from professionals as a way to help manage the uncertainty, risk, and ambiguity in decision-making.

Parents

From the student's perspective, a parent—that person who has known them the longest and arguably the best—is well-positioned to help them articulate their needs and interests when they are applying to college.[4] Parents who have attended college are especially able to guide their children's search process and help them identify a set of colleges that will match their needs and interests.[5] It's not surprising then that some of these parents "drove" the search process. As one student described:

> My dad was my partner in this whole exploring colleges thing. My way of looking at colleges was to read whatever information there was and then take a bunch of notes, look at those notes, and then make a list of the colleges I liked . . . He had a different way of looking at colleges. He got me to make a list of questions that I wanted some answers about. So like one of the questions was, "Is there bicycle parking." And he got all this information and put it on a spreadsheet, [for] all the colleges that I was interested in, plus one that he made up that he called Hardvinceton, the averages of Harvard, Yale, and Princeton for a comparison of all the colleges I wanted to actually go to.

But not all parents drove the college search. Eve described that although her parents "helped a lot when I needed them," they otherwise let her manage her college search: "They weren't the kind of stressful parents who were hounding me all the time. They just let me do everything, and then if I needed help they would help."

Parents played a minor role for only a few students. Many of these counterexamples were first generation[6] or international students who often talked about their parents' lack of experience and expertise when it came to applying to college.[7] One international student commented: "My parents are not familiar with the system of U.S. education. So I just told them I am applying, I told them the names of the institutions, then that was it." A first-generation student shared:

> My parents left the decision wholly up to me. They were like, "Wherever you want to go we'll support that," so that was pretty much it. It's something that was very important. My parents didn't have the opportunity to go to college, so they really wanted me to be able to have things that they didn't get to have. And they weren't trying to live through me, but they wanted me to be able to experience everything.

Finally, some international students who had spent many of their high school years at boarding schools described parents who no longer knew them well: "I don't have much [of a] relationship with my parents. I see them about a month out of the year. [My father] didn't know I was going to [my college] until maybe a month ago when I said to my father, 'I am going to [my college].' My parents care a lot, but just they don't have the time."

Nonetheless, most students—no matter whether their parents played a strong role or a more limited one during the college search—felt that their parents cared for them, were concerned for their future, and wanted them to find a college where they could be happy. Students felt strongly supported in their goal to attend college. Parents, even highly involved ones, typically left the decision about which college to attend solely to the student. As the student of one such parent described: "They felt I had a good sense of what I wanted so they trusted me [to decide]." As we will see, the parents of the students in our study were much less interfering and less overly involved, on average, than the popular image of helicopter parents would suggest.

Guidance Counselors

Guidance counselors were mentioned as being influential in the college search about half of the time, typically in addition to parents.[8] Students from under-resourced high schools were less likely to mention guidance counselors as helpful advisors because they were often one of hundreds of students with whom the counselor worked:

> If you go to a public school and your class is 350 students, you don't really get a chance to know your counselor, or they don't get a chance to know you as well as you would have liked, because they just have an incredible amount of students they need to take care of. So, you'd just drop by for a couple [of] minutes and talk to them, and they try to help, but it's not a one-on-one thing.

By contrast, those attending well-resourced high schools, typically private high schools, were more likely to develop the kinds of close relationships that allowed for personalized advice; their counselors were less overburdened and had time for one-on-one meetings:[9]

My college counselor was so helpful. She was so organized, and I guess it's a lot easier coming from [a private] high school. She only has to help 41 girls versus a huge public school; you know you [can only] take care of so many girls. We all became so close. We hung out in her office. Her door was always open.

Even for students who mentioned guidance counselors, though, some only helped manage the application process, serving a more bureaucratic role rather than the more expansive role described above: "My guidance counselor really didn't even do much. She just took care of the paperwork and everything." Others gave advice that students didn't want to hear. Sam, whom we will hear more about later in this chapter, did not appreciate his counselors' advice about the colleges to which he should apply. He wanted someone to support his choices rather than question them. When asked if his counselors were to blame for the fact that he was only accepted to two of the eighteen colleges to which he applied, Sam responded:

It would be easy for me to say, "Yes," a part of me wants to say [yes], but I don't think that's true. I think that's just a way of saying, "It's not my fault." And I realized afterwards [that] I was kind of upset with [my counselors], because they were very dismissive. I don't want to say they were like, "You're not getting in." Maybe [they were] more realistic than anything, but I think maybe, at that point, I wanted someone [to be] more of cheerleader than a college counselor . . . Maybe I'm a little bit bitter about that.

Getting advice from parents and guidance counselors makes sense to students—parents know them well and their guidance counselor's job is to help them get into college. These advising relationships harbor little ambiguity. When they arrive at college, though, not only will they be seeking advice from strangers, but how much and what type of advice they can expect from these strangers is often unclear. In addition, one might anticipate that students coming from high schools with strong support from guidance counselors might arrive at college with clearer expectations about what constitutes effective advising and an increased ability to develop meaningful relationships with their faculty advisors; however, this wasn't always the case.

Obtaining Advice in the First Year

Although most students begin college with parents as their primary advice-givers, in a short time, the majority of students will broaden that network to include faculty advisors.[10] Students typically meet their faculty advisors (called "premajor" or "first-year" advisors) during the first week of college and work with them until they declare a major. This first advising relationship sets the stage, for good or for ill, for future advising relationships as well as for relationships with other faculty. In addition to a faculty advisor, many students will include other college staff in their advising networks.[11] The variety of advising resources available to students allows for multiple perspectives on the many decisions they will be called upon to make in their first year: what courses to take, which activities to join, learning how to live collectively, among others.[12]

Although most students sought advice and guidance from their faculty advisors, there were vast differences in the kinds of relationships they developed with them.[13] Some students, like Gabriella, quickly established a meaningful partnership with their advisors; while others, like Sara, failed to turn to their faculty advisors for much of anything—perceiving them to be more of an obstacle to course registration than useful consultants. Most students were more like Gabriella, reporting that their faculty advisors provided helpful advice. Eve, whose parents helped but did not micromanage her college search, described her advisor as "helpful and available" and "really good at helping me choose my classes":

> He was helpful because [as] I was stressing out about having to fulfill my requirements he sort of said, "No, this semester take it easy. Take what you want, and then we can deal with your science next semester." I thought I would take environmental science to fulfill my science, and he said, "If you're not planning on majoring in that, then don't take it."

Marianna's advisor also provided helpful insight into classes that might be a good fit:

> My advisor e-mails me, "We need to talk about this." So it's a lot of both of us talking to one another, like, "I need help with my course selections,

are you available?" She's been great, and really has good insight into my strengths and weaknesses and which teachers would be best for me, and the classes that would be best.

But even for students who found their advisors helpful, most limited their expectations to advice on course selection.[14] Brad, whom we will hear from again, is an example:

> I only really see her when I am [registering for] courses, but when I do see her I am always happy I do because she's really caring and interested in what I'm doing. And she's always very helpful. Still, I only see her when we're choosing classes. But it's always worthwhile. So I think it's a good relationship. I'm definitely not complaining. She's very nice.

Students often described their advisors as "nice," even if they did not find them to be helpful or did not agree with the advice they were receiving. But for some students, "nice" advisors only included those who did not challenge them to rethink their decisions. As Sam's comments about his high school guidance counselors suggested, "nice" advisors were "cheerleaders" rather than critics.[15]

It's not surprising that many students have limited expectations for advisors. By scheduling the initial meetings of advisors and students around course registration, we imply that the primary goal of advising is to help students make decisions about courses. We suspect this may be why a large majority of students found their interactions with their faculty advisors helpful—they only expected advice on a narrow range of academic topics. For both students and advisors, limiting expectations to routine academic choices is a way to manage the ambiguity or unfamiliarity of their relationship. Students may limit their early conversations with this stranger to academic rather than personal topics because doing so feels safer. Faculty may do so because they actively resist the in loco parentis role, or at the very least feel unsure about how that would play out with students they just met. So while both students and faculty know what they don't want to do (students don't want to overshare nor overstep appropriate expectations of an advisor; faculty don't want to take on more than they should), neither has clear expectations about what they should do. Thus, limiting conversations to a precise yet limited set of familiar academic topics may help both students and faculty begin to resolve the ambiguous nature of this relationship.

Students who defined their relationship with their advisor in this limited, help-me-find-courses manner can be divided into two groups. The first group viewed their faculty advisors as a "general practitioners" who had broad useful knowledge of the college curriculum. These students were, for the most part, quite receptive to the "well-roundedness" and "balance" their advisors urged upon them. The advisor for one student urged him to select a balanced curriculum: "I was pretty much set on [a political science major], so I really wanted to take [political science] courses, but she wasn't willing to let me take so many courses in [political science], because she said that part of the liberal arts education was to shop around for courses." Another student's advisor encouraged her to balance her curricular and extracurricular activities: "He also advised me to actually try to do outside activities as opposed to just concentrating on class, which I would have done anyways, but it was nice to have someone to tell me to do that anyways."

Students in the second group, however, resisted their advisors' attempts to insert balance into their course schedule:

> [My advisor is] really nice. It's just [that] we're very different. I'm very black and white; I needed a plan for the four years. She's like, "Why don't you explore and see how you feel?" And I'm not quite like that. So it was really hard when I was trying to pick out my classes for this fall because she's like, "Why don't you spread your econ classes out and take things for fun?" And I'm like, "No, I just want to get these things done"—so that I can later, perhaps in France, do the fun [stuff]. And she's just a firm believer [that] you need a little bit of everything. Which is good, I agree, but not when I'm trying to get something done.

This student, and others like her, were less interested in advice about exploring the curriculum and more concerned with achieving their own particular curricular goals (e.g., completing the requirements for their intended major or studying abroad), and were especially frustrated if their assigned first-year advisor was not a professor in the discipline in which they intended to major.[16] They had little use for an advisor with broad knowledge of their college and its curriculum, but limited knowledge about courses in their intended major. From the outset, they only wanted to see someone who was a "specialist" in their intended major:

> I mean she's really nice. She just can't help me with what I'm interested in. Which is really rough, because I don't know what to do. I feel completely lost all [of] the time when it comes to scheduling and what classes I'm taking. I get nervous [that] I'm not going to be on the right track for completing what I want to complete on time.

These students arrived at college having already decided on a particular major and had trouble seeing the value of an advisor who could only provide them with general advice about how to navigate their college's curriculum. They failed to see their interactions with their non-major advisors as opportunities to learn about other disciplines, hear different perspectives on their course choices, discover alternative paths through the curriculum, and, perhaps most importantly, practice interacting with faculty so that in subsequent years they might use those much-desired "specialists" more productively. For these students, a decision made prior to entering college limited them. Instead of recognizing the benefits inherent in forming any kind of tie to their advisors, they formed no ties. Forming even weak connections to advisors can provide students with access to important people, information, and resources outside of their own social networks through the connections of their advisor.[17]

The majority of students failed to move beyond course selection in their early conversations with their advisors. By late fall, Eve still described her advisor as "a really nice guy," but she had only talked with him a few times and only about her courses. However, other students' initial conversations about courses and balance evolved into deeper, more expansive conversations. By the end of the first year, these students had developed relationships with their advisors conducive to self-reflection and personalized advice. Jessica, the student profiled in the Time chapter who sought balance through self-reflection, had an advisor who encouraged "reflective conversations" or conversations that focus "on engaging students in talking about their most significant experiences; exploring how they have been affected by those experiences; and making sense of the effects for their view of the world, themselves, and their relationships." By meeting regularly to talk about successes and challenges, an advisor can use such reflective conversations to "help students frame academic and career choices."[18] Jessica may have been particularly open to an advising style that encouraged self-reflection:

> I think we have a really good relationship. If I can't make a meeting, because we schedule meetings every week or every other week, then we'll talk on the phone for maybe 30 to 45 minutes. Or I'll go over to her office, and we'll sit and talk. Usually it starts with, "Like how's class? What are you struggling with? What do you feel that needs to be improved upon?" And afterwards it will go into, "So what are your plans this weekend?" and then it just goes on to anything else. But being with her and having her ask me questions and sometimes probe me to think about things a bit more, I think it's really helpful.

We probably shouldn't be surprised that the majority of students expressed hesitation or ambivalence about developing deeper relationships with their first-year advisors. At most of our colleges, students don't choose their first-year faculty advisor; it is someone to whom they are assigned—that jump-start that we mentioned earlier—and students rarely ask to be reassigned.[19] Although they recognized that their advisors were supportive and "nice," they rarely took responsibility for initiating interactions with them. One student reflected that "taking the initiative to meet with her [advisor] was a bigger step" than she was ready to take. Another said that her advisor "gave the impression that he was always there should I need him" but she never visited him during office hours.

For others, infrequent contact, stemming from the absence of mandatory meetings or the routines of everyday life, contributed to their failure to develop a relationship with their advisor. For one student, her expectation of frequent contact with her advisor came from her private high school experience; she never had to "seek out" her advisor there (he lived in her dorm), so she was not prepared to do so in college:

> I think I saw [my college advisor] at the beginning of the year, for me to pick courses and then I, for some reason, figured that there'd be like little advisor/advisee meetings that he would set up with all of us and maybe like meet at lunch one day, but that never happened. I guess that

was just [my] expectation, because my advisor from high school lived in the same dorm, so when I went downstairs, I'd walk by the door to his office. If he was there, the door would be open, and you could just stop in and say hi. I'd see him and stay and talk to him almost every day. So I was used to that. I never took the time to go and seek out my advisor here because I never had to do that before. And then it came [to] the end of the term, and I hadn't really talked to him. So I need to visit him more. He's nice.

We often think of well-resourced high schools as providing students with experiences and practices that advantage them when they start college, but this student wasn't able or willing to translate her practice at talking to advisors in high school. Ironically, private high school experiences may handicap rather than help some students in college. Not only is it easy for private high school students to meet with their guidance counselors, but they also develop close relationships, perhaps making the transition to a more limited advising relationship more challenging.

Some students failed to develop a close relationship with their advisor because they didn't carve out time to meet with them.[20] Sometimes they decided that other tasks took priority; meeting with their advisor just never made it to their to-do list:

I [was] slammed by work when we registered for classes. So I really didn't have time to go around talking to people, and my friend had to call me at 3:00 in the morning and be like, "Hey, did you pick out classes? Because registration's like in five hours." And I was like, "Oh yeah. I should really do that." I was [working on a class] presentation, and it was like, "Okay, I've got to find classes." So I made a quick run through the course catalog, and I was like, "Oh, that sounds good. Sure, why not?"

This student went on to explain that she hadn't been able to consult with her advisor because they were both "really, really busy" and their "schedules didn't match up."[21]

Finally, students may decide to keep their distance because getting close is risky, especially if their advisor is, or could become, their teacher. In order to take full advantage of faculty advisors, students must be willing to share themselves—warts and all—with someone who is not only a near-stranger but may also be one of their instructors, grading their academic work or challenging their beliefs and knowledge in the classroom. This can feel especially risky for students struggling academically or for those not engaged in their advisor's course. For Sam, the tension created by his advisor's dual teacher/advisor role was a direct source of his reluctance to deepen their relationship:[22]

> I think it had started off not so great just because of how the first-year seminar was and what I expected it to be. I expected it to be a little bit more engaging than it ended up being. That kind of turned me off to soliciting her advice. I'm not going to assume that it's good advice or bad advice but [that] prevented me from soliciting it. That initial negative experience kind of blocked me from initiating too much. I mean she made an effort to talk about registering and so on. I'm sure she's a resource that I could potentially use, and maybe I should, but I haven't really gone to see her during office hours to discuss in detail what I should be doing. Maybe I should do that, but I don't know if I will.

In the first year, most students had a limited conception of the range of academic topics for which they could turn to their faculty advisor for advice. For some, this limited role worked fairly well in that they received helpful advice about their academic plans. Others, however, were frustrated when their advisor was unable to provide them with specific advice about courses in their intended major. Students who failed to connect with their assigned advisor rarely took the initiative to request another one. They saw *advising* as an obstacle rather than an opportunity, and as such, made little effort to restart by seeking a new advisor. By limiting their interactions with their faculty advisor, they failed to practice the adult task of advice seeking. Most students did not break out of this limited conception of advising during their first year, but those who did benefited by getting advice that cut across many aspects of their first-year experience.

Finally, what about parents? Not surprisingly, given that most students began college using parents as their primary sounding board, we found that students continued to share their experiences with their parents and found those conversations helpful.[23] As one student described, "I would just let out my frustration to my parents. I like to keep in touch with them and tell them what's going on. So that was always helpful. It's always good to have listeners that are not within our college." When students sought advice from their parents, we found that it was less alarming than helicopter-parent stories might suggest.[24] Although students frequently asked their parents about how best to manage their time and take care of themselves, they rarely sought academic advice.[25] For example, Marianna consulted her faculty advisor about academic issues, but turned to her parents for advice about work and sleep habits:

> And then also the time management thing . . . There wouldn't be times when I would just flat out ask them certain questions, but just telling them about like, "Oh, I pulled an all-nighter last night," and my mom would kind of advise me. Like, "You need to make sure you stay on top of things. Talk to your professors." So just advising me on my well-being, being able to go to bed early and that sort of thing.

Thus, the first year of college can be viewed as a restart of advising from high school. Students transition from relying on parents for academic, social, and personal advice to a more bifurcated conception of advising. They turn to parents for advice around personal issues, such as time management and coping, and to their faculty advisor for advice around academic issues, particularly course selection. That said, a significant minority of first-year students made a more expansive transition in advice-seeking in which they turned to their faculty advisors for advice about academic, social, and personal issues.

The Sophomore Year: Another Restart?

As discussed in the Time chapter, students reach an important turning point in their sophomore year, one in which a number of significant academic decisions will be made—deciding about study abroad, declaring a major, and for many, selecting a new advisor. The press of these upcoming decisions increases the need for an advisor, and students recognize that restarting their relationship with their first-year faculty advisor provides a valuable opportunity to gain helpful, personalized advice about these decisions. About two-thirds of the students in our study—both those who had made deep connections in the first year and those who had more limited, help-me-find-courses relationships—sought advice from faculty advisors for these key academic decisions. But the development of these more expanded advising relationships took time, effort, and initiative.

Restarting a Key Advising Relationship

At the start of the sophomore year, most students remain assigned to their first-year advisor and, when they return to campus after the long summer break, they need to restart those relationships.[26] A number of factors helped with this restart. First, and perhaps foremost, was having developed what many students described as a "comfortable" relationship with their advisor during their first year of college.[27] Gabriella, whom we met at the start of this chapter, described how much less "discomfort" there was in conversations with her advisor once they were able to move beyond the typical hierarchical roles of professor and student, and able to interact on a personal level rather than solely on an academic one. Others felt "comfortable" when a level of closeness was achieved that was not necessarily familial but a melding of family and school:

> I feel more comfortable [talking] to her rather than [to] my friends or my mom, because she's kind of close but not [too] close. Because she's a teacher she can help me, and I can take her seriously. And since she's a teacher, I can rely on her and know that she's not going to tell anyone. She's kind of like a third mom.

For other students, "comfort" did not necessarily require a personal relationship. Instead, it grew out of the belief that their advisors wanted them to flourish. These relationships were characterized by mutual trust and respect. Students often mentioned that their advisor provided them with feedback about their decisions in a straightforward, non-condescending manner. As students grew and matured, they sought out and accepted advice from faculty even when it was not always positive. No longer looking for cheerleaders, they wanted advisors who would be honest critics:

> [My relationship with my advisor is] just really comfortable. We're not all personal with each other necessarily, but I really feel like he thinks highly

of me. And I think that he wants the best for me, which is something I really want in an academic advisor. I don't feel like there's a stupid question that I couldn't ask him. I think that he doesn't patronize me, which is something I've experienced with a lot of teachers. He's just very straight with me, and he'll tell me when he likes an idea I have, [and] he'll tell me when he doesn't.

For some students, restarting relationships with advisors was facilitated when they perceived that their advisors were willing to invest substantial time and energy in advising them:

My advisor was someone who was prepared to invest enough time in me to say, "You know what? I don't agree with you. This is why I don't agree with you. This is why I don't think you should do this." I don't think anyone has ever had as much trouble trying to take a course pass/fail as I have had. In the first semester, he did as much as talk to my professor. And in the second semester, he said, "Okay, you should talk to your professor, and then think about it." In both cases I chose not to take [the course] pass/fail on his advice. He spent a lot of time [with me]. He was patient enough to sit down and say, "This is why this is not a good idea."

Some students recognized that even when their advisor's feedback was delivered in a rather blunt manner, it was grounded in a concern for their well-being. Although the advice Gabriella described appears harsh, she recognized that her advisor was talking to her more as an equal than as a professor: "She's really funny, and she pretty much wants to be more of a friend than just your advisor. So she will just talk to me like, 'Are you dumb? Why are you going to take another political science class? You know you didn't enjoy it.' And it's pretty funny to hear her say that."

For others, reestablishing their relationship with their advisor occurred when there was a reason for crossing paths on a regular basis, such has having a job in the professor's department: "I work [in her department], so I'm always able to keep her up to date on what's going on, so we're close. She's a great advisor, and when I declare [a major] and change advisors officially, she will be my advisor unofficially. She'll be the person to talk to about problems."[28]

Finally, a shared academic interest was another important route to restarting by establishing a common base from which to develop and then sustain a relationship. For about a third of students, their first-year advisor became their major (or minor) advisor. Nileen planned to stay with her first-year advisor when she declared her major, in part because of their common academic interests:

> I might actually stick with her [as my major advisor] because she gives some really constructive advice. I honestly can't think of anybody else ... and since my first-year advisor is in [my major] department, it would just be convenient for me to take her as an advisor. So it definitely feels good to have somebody that you think is supporting you. And it's not that I'm going to get a better grade, but she's definitely helping me out. I think somebody has to show interest in my extracurricular life and stuff like that, and that's what she shows. She was very warm and she wanted to know how I was doing and stuff like that.

However, having an advisor with whom the student did not share an academic interest did not necessarily create an obstacle to a long-term relationship. Some students planned to continue to seek advice from their first-year advisor (even after they transitioned to a new major advisor) because they valued the strong relationship they had established and recognized the benefits of continuing it. These students valued the "general-practitioner" qualities of that first advising relationship and recognized the benefits of having multiple advisors:

> My relationship with my current advisor is very good. We really connected last year. I always see her around, [and] just stop and talk to her, even if I don't need academic counseling. She's always going to be my secondary advisor, because there's just stuff that maybe the science teachers won't be able to help me with, like maybe the humanities. She has a lot of knowledge about scholarships and fellowships and general grants and that whole side of it, the application kind of side of stuff, so I feel like she'll be a really good resource for that going into junior-senior year.

Thus, by the fall of the sophomore year, most students were well-positioned to acquire personalized advice over the next year. They had moved beyond solely seeking advice about course selection and had established a "comfortable" relationship with a faculty member who could support them as they made other important academic and, in some cases, personal decisions. The number of academic decisions that must be made in the sophomore year, and the perceived importance of those decisions, may push some—but not all—students toward more meaningful interactions with advisors.[29] These students and faculty successfully reduced the ambiguity inherent in the advising relationship by establishing a common set of expectations for the relationship that allowed the students' advising needs to be met.

Lost in Limbo

Although the majority of students successfully reestablished a relationship with their faculty advisor when they restarted college as sophomores, about a third failed to do so.[30] The majority of these students claimed to make decisions on their own without seeking advice from others.[31] In a sense, these students had neither formal nor informal advisors. For a small minority, this occurred because their first-year advisor was no longer on campus when they returned to college in the fall. One such student described himself as an "advisorless child." By mid-fall, most of these students had yet to find a new advisor. When faced with the unexpected loss of an advisor, students often didn't take the initiative to acquire a new one.[32]

Other students in this group failed to restart relationships with their advisors for reasons related to the structural nature of advising at our colleges. Some students voiced ambiguity about the role of a *first-year* advisor in the *sophomore* year. As they attempted to disambiguate the nature of this relationship (Who is this person to me now, in my sophomore year?) some turned to the institutionally supplied label as a clue.[33] When asked if she had an advisor, one sophomore described her confusion: "We had first-year advisors, but I don't think we obviously have the same ones because we're not first years. So I don't think we're going to have an advisor until we declare a major." Another wondered, "He's a first-year advisor, so I don't know if we can still talk to them. But I guess we could. I don't know." Brad, who found his advisor "nice" and met with her sporadically in his first year, was unclear as to what he should expect from her in the fall of his sophomore year: "I would assume that I shouldn't really be expecting much because we're supposed to be choosing a major and getting an advisor from them." Because his advisor hadn't "emailed or anything," he decided "that this is kind of in my hands now."

Other students who believed that their first-year advisor lacked the expertise to give them useful advice continued to voice their desire for a "specialist" as they narrowed their search for a major. As a sophomore, Sara still saw little value in consulting her first-year advisor: "My premajor advisor is kind of useless because he was in a department that I would have never wanted to take a class in, and he really wanted me to take math and science that I never would have wanted to do. So my interaction with him was mostly, this is what I'm doing, give me my code. And it was kind of ridiculous." Another sophomore commented that it was "useless to have an advisor, especially if she's in another department than the one I want to study, since I don't feel she's well prepared to help me with my questions about my [major's] requirements." He also noted that by avoiding meeting with her, he could also avoid interacting with someone who doesn't just "encourage you [but] pushes you to explore other fields" when he "pretty much [had his] mind set on government." For students like this one, interacting with their old advisor was seen as more of an obstacle to achieving their goals than an opportunity to reflectively question those goals.

For the remaining students, it was difficult to restart an advising relationship that was never established in the first year. Some remained unsure as to whether their advisor was truly interested or invested in advising them: "A lot of students don't feel like they have [an] advisor, but I don't feel like they actually think that the person is there to really help them. I think it's more just a name on a paper at this point at least like at the beginning of the sophomore year." But others often acknowledged their own role in failing to reestablish a relationship with their advisors. As one student commented, "I had no qualms with her. She's a fine person. We don't really have a bunch of communication, but that's not her fault. It's not like I've really tried to see her." Sometimes both parties failed to take the initiative and this was occasionally attributed to the absence of a shared academic interest:

Maybe he's someone I could really talk to, but neither of us took the initiative last year or this year to really speak to each other. And because he's a computer science professor, I really feel like he can only help me so much. I actually don't think he could help me that much because I want to major in something in the humanities, and he's a computer science professor. But, he's a great guy, and I wish that I would have spoken to him more last year.

Finally, we found that those sophomores who failed to restart their relationships with their first-year faculty advisors were also less likely to meet with *any* faculty outside of class and more likely to say that establishing close relationships with faculty was not important to them.[34] As one student said, professors are there to "teach [in the classroom], and that's about it." Although another voiced the opinion that "it makes the class more fun sometimes when you can relate to your teacher," he didn't see any other advantages to establishing close relationships with faculty. Another student agreed about the limited benefits of getting close to faculty:[35]

I think a lot of times it's just because the student's gone in to ask for help and they're trying to make a good grade in class, and I think the teacher will see that. But I don't know if it helps them in terms of grading. Maybe they get a better grade because they see the teacher more [often]. I think [that's] more likely the answer than anything else. And I think the professor sees that they're trying and I think [the professor] would be more willing to give them the benefit of the doubt, but I don't think it's any more beneficial. I mean it might be a little bit more beneficial but I don't think there's necessarily a gap between the kids who do get a personal relationship and the kids who don't.

In contrast, students who valued close relationships with faculty described both the more instrumental benefits that came from knowing someone well (e.g., letters of recommendation, summer internships, jobs after graduation), and the less tangible benefits of receiving personalized advice. As one student related, "It's important to be close to them because they won't be able to help you if they don't know who you are." Another student commented on the many opportunities afforded by developing meaningful faculty relationships:

I think it's very important, because it builds up your character. I guess it puts in a good name for you, if anything ever comes up . . . whether it's work or just volunteering. You made that chance to actually stay in contact with a former professor or you became really good friends, and you're one of the people who they think of when something comes up. Yeah, I think it's a really smart thing. And also even when it comes to class work, they know who you are and they know your potential. It's a more open friendship relationship. My mother also said, if all else fails, make sure you and your professor have at least that connection.

Junior and Senior Years: Finding the Ideal Advisor

As students begin their junior year, all have declared a major and acquired a new advisor. Somewhat surprisingly, even students who started out "lost in limbo" often went on to establish valuable relationships with their major advisors:[36]

> My first-year seminar advisor wasn't an advisor really. I think I met with him twice to tell him what classes I was taking, but that was all. But I didn't really have any academic interest in his field or anything, so we haven't seen each other in a while. So I felt like I had very little advising as a freshman and sophomore. And then I've known [a social science professor] since second semester sophomore year, and he's been very helpful with everything. He's very approachable and really enjoys talking about what you're doing which I appreciate, and always has good ideas.

The advising restart afforded by the major declaration allowed those students who had failed to connect with their first-year advisors (and perhaps with any faculty) to establish a new advising relationship with someone with whom they shared a strong academic interest. Only a minority of juniors and seniors continued to "go it alone,"[37] and about half readily admitted that they hadn't taken advantage of opportunities to make that happen.[38] One senior explained, "I guess it's kind of like my fault. In terms of professors, I never really went out to get to know them or sought them out as much as I should have." Another senior said: "I feel like, coming here, I knew what I wanted to do. For the most part, what I wanted to do was mathematics, so I was just following this path that I already knew. I sort of just don't feel like they were helpful, or that I really needed them in any way."

By the time they were seniors, many students described their current faculty advisor as "ideal."[39] The ideal advisor was available, supportive, caring, interested, knowledgeable, and gave constructive advice.[40] In some cases, ideal advisors were those with whom students had a strong personal link: "I think that one of the things that really shows that—or like makes me keep on wanting to go and talk to them—is that they have shown an interest in me personally. They've reached out and spoken to me, they support me, they want to talk to me, [and that] I think is a big thing." In other cases it wasn't a personal connection that made advisors ideal, but the expansive academic and career issues they discussed:[41] "I don't think that to be an ideal advisor you have to have necessarily a personal other than academic relationship. I'd say [my advisor] is pretty ideal, but we don't necessarily talk about things outside of academics or future plans or whatever. But I guess it's just the connection."

Most juniors and seniors experienced a deepening of their relationships with their advisors while at the same time expanding their advising networks. Nileen commented, "You can't depend on one person to be your guru. Like [it] just doesn't work that way."[42] Another student appreciated her major advisor because even though she was "very professional and very understanding, . . . she's not going to lie to you if you do something wrong"; she also liked keeping in touch with her minor advisor because "talking [with] him I can just forget about all the worries that I have because I know that someone is still there and listening to me."

Seniors were future-oriented—busy preparing for life after college—so their advising networks often included people who could help them with their next steps. If it was graduate or medical school, then faculty advisors were important resources. If law school or the corporate world were next, then seniors worked to establish alumni/ae contacts, often through their college's career planning center. They also sought advice from family and friends as they contemplated moving to another city, state, or even country. When we asked Jessica to whom she turned for advice regarding her post-graduation plans, she described a broad advising network:

Who have I talked to? I've talked to my advisor. I've talked to the medical professions advisor. I talked to a lot of alumna. My parents. People who are in the position [that] I'd like to be [in]. Asking them, not necessarily "What I should do" but "What did you do." Getting a feel if there's a trend [that] maybe I should be following.

Establishing Effective Advising Relationships: Three Case Studies

Reducing the ambiguity inherent in the advising relationship involves multiple conditions. Not only must students and faculty be willing to meet often, get to know one another, and establish shared expectations for the relationship, but they must move beyond the typical student-teacher relationship to establish a "comfortable" relationship conducive to meeting the student's need for personalized advice. The establishment of such meaningful relationships can be facilitated when both faculty and student share common academic interests. The experiences of three students further illustrate the student's role in the establishment of an effective advising relationship. Students who decide to "go it alone"—often viewing their advisors as obstacles to be avoided—miss out on numerous opportunities for self-reflection, advice, and support. However, students who commit to establishing strong ties with their advisors have a trusted guide who can help them navigate the many decisions surrounding their goals in college and post-graduation.

Sam: Going It Alone, Missed Opportunities

We met Sam earlier: his high school guidance counselors were not the "cheerleaders" he wanted them to be. We also learned about Sam's relationship with his first-year faculty advisor. Even though he took her course because it "was a political science course" and he wanted "to establish [a] connection now" with someone in his intended major, their relationship quickly stalled because the course was not what he expected. Sam only met with her for course registration and, even then, it was only to *tell* her which courses he was going to take rather than to *ask for advice.* Sam later reflected that if he had "had a better relationship with her, I probably would have sought her help more." Sam decided pretty early on that he couldn't benefit from his advisor, even though their shared academic interest was what originally drew him to her.

In the spring of his sophomore year, Sam declared his major, a decision (from his point of view) that harbored neither uncertainty nor ambiguity:

"It's been clear since high school that this is the thing." Interestingly though, in the same semester he declared his major, Sam expressed ambivalence about sticking to his prescribed path: "Sometimes I think [maybe] it would be more interesting if I didn't know what I wanted to do. Maybe college would be a more interesting thing, basically where you kind of feel everything out, just kind of come to what you do."

For his major advisor, Sam chose a professor he had never met, and wouldn't meet until well into the fall of his junior year. When asked around this time if he wanted to have close relationships with his professors, Sam responded that he thought it *should* be important but didn't think that it necessarily had been important to him. He recognized that he might have gotten more out of advising if he had tried to get to know his professors:

> I guess somewhere within me I feel like I need something to justify talking to the professor, but that isn't the case. I mean you should go to strike up a relationship with them so that you see each other as people as opposed to the professor and the student . . . so you better understand each other. And I haven't taken advantage of that and it's not good.

By the end of his junior year, Sam had only met with his advisor twice, and only to talk about "logistical stuff, like my [general education] requirements . . . I always e-mail him like 12 hours before the deadline. Here are the classes I want to take. This is why I want to take the class. Please remove my hold so I can register."

For many students, the junior year is an important time for setting up research opportunities or summer internships. When we asked Sam about any potential research opportunities, he said that he wasn't entirely sure: "Maybe if I went to office hours I would know this a little bit better, if they are doing active research right now. I imagine if I heard about anything that they were doing that really intrigued me, I would pursue it, but I'm not really aware of anything going on right now." The summer before senior year, Sam had neither a job nor an internship.

As Sam started his senior year, he was most excited about "getting [his thesis] over with." Sam's meetings with his major advisor about his thesis started off rather bumpy: "I haven't had the most open communication in terms of what [his advisor's] expectations are and what I'm providing. I feel a lot of times it's like we're talking on different radio waves." Although Sam and his advisor met weekly, they never developed a strong relationship and Sam said, after he finished his thesis, that he regretted "never feeling that sense of attachment toward" it that he knew other students had. For Sam, having an advisor with whom he shared an academic interest was never enough to facilitate the development of any sort of meaningful relationship. Even though he selected his first-year seminar precisely because he wanted to establish a connection to someone in his intended major, his disappointment in the course derailed that plan. Perhaps his lack of attachment to his senior thesis derailed that relationship as well.

Sam also regretted that he never developed an ongoing relationship with a professor even though he saw that as something quite possible at his college: "[I have] never been particularly good about following up with professors after a class . . . that is something I really like about [my college], there isn't this hard definition of the professor-student relationship. You can see yourselves outside the classroom and you're just people and you can engage like that." But Sam never made the effort to break out of the limited student and teacher roles.

Despite his regrets and his infrequent encounters with faculty, Sam loved college: "I wouldn't trade the experience I've had for anything" even if he nonetheless recognized that "it would have been a different experience" had he made different choices or, in some cases, actually made choices rather than steadfastly following a self-prescribed path to achieve his career goals. Sam might have had a "different experience," perhaps a better experience, if he had gotten to know his professors (especially his advisors), and if he had sought advice, or any kind of feedback, from adults. "One professor said that I was impervious to criticism," Sam declared as a senior. "I don't know if she meant it as a compliment or not, but I'd like to think it was a compliment." It is hard to tell if Sam's reluctance to consult with faculty was because he didn't want to hear what they had to say (recall his experience with his high school guidance counselors) or because he didn't believe they had anything important to offer him. In either case, it was a missed opportunity.

Brad: Finding the Specialist and Finally Getting Close

Similar to Sam, Brad didn't develop strong ties to his first-year advisor. Although Brad appreciated his advisor and found her helpful, he met with her infrequently and only about course selection. By the spring of his sopho-more year, Brad no longer met with her: "She was an art history teacher, and I'm not interested in art history at all. We haven't really had that much con-tact this year, which is fine. If I did contact her and I wanted to meet, I know she would right away. But we don't have the same academic interests."

In general, Brad valued close relationships with his professors: "If I de-cide to go to grad school, you're going to need to have really good recom-mendations." He also recognized that such relationships could provide other benefits, even if he did not articulate what those might be: "But still, more than that, I think it's good to have a close relationship with your professors, because we're at such a small school, and we're privileged to actually have that opportunity." Brad listed having "a good relationship with at least one faculty member" as a goal of his sophomore year, acknowledging that it would re-quire "a little bit more effort on my part."

By the end of his sophomore year, Brad was well on his way to achieving that goal. He was meeting with his professors "definitely a lot more this year," in part because "there's been a lot of things to work out like majoring and minoring and study abroad" but also because he found

> teachers that I've liked better this year which has made me approach them more. Any professor that I feel comfortable with, [then] I feel comfortable talking to them about anything academic [or] social. They're people to look up to, but they're also very approachable which makes it less like a teacher-student relationship and more like a mentor.

For Brad to "feel comfortable" with his professors, he needed to become en-gaged in their class or to relate to them on a personal level: "I love my English class; he's an amazing teacher. It's just the way we analyze things. It's inspired me to minor in English. I came to college wanting to be an English major, and I kind of abandoned it. But he's gotten me back into it." The personal connec-tion Brad felt to another professor led him to ask that professor to be one of his major advisors: "I haven't had him for a teacher, but he's just so friendly and so welcoming, and he's so easy to access, and he's just so helpful. I could tell that he'd be a great advisor. And I know he's an amazing, brilliant man."

As a junior, Brad talked about how he got to know his teachers as he took more classes with them: "Professors that know you, someone you're comfortable with. Obviously fitting more with the field you're interested in" were the ones with whom he developed strong ties. Yet when asked if there was anything he wanted to improve upon as a junior, he still noted that his professors needed to "get to know me better. I've never been one to go to professors' houses and what not. I wish I would do that. Maybe I will."

Brad's senior year began with a critical decision as he debated whether attending law school immediately after graduation was still the best path for him:

> I was one of those people who was very much on the law school path right after graduation. And dealing with the fact that I wasn't sure about that and didn't really want to do that right away, it made me not really sure if that's good for me. Learning that, and going to senior year where it seemed like a lot of people had things figured out, it was hard for me personally. It was almost, not like it was a quarter-life crisis, but a precursor to that sort of thing. It was an important time.

Brad applied for a number of jobs and received multiple offers. In the end, however, he accepted a prestigious fellowship to spend the year in Africa working for a nonprofit organization. For Brad, this was a chance "to really explore and learn about myself. If I had taken a job at [prestigious company] I would have been making good money, but I wouldn't have been working towards what I wanted. And I would have felt like a lot of what I've done at college was sort of bullshit in a way."

To make this difficult decision, Brad turned to friends and family as well as to faculty and staff who knew him well and who had the relevant "life experience to give advice. A person that knows me well here is going to give me the best advice. And there are certain people that I trust really here, and I wasn't hesitant." As Brad went on to explain, his college community provided a "safe place" for him to resolve this crisis:

> In so many different ways the community is so important. Like the classroom and connecting with your professors and being able to go to their office hours and talk about whatever you want to talk about. Feeling like you're not going to fall through the cracks. That's not going to happen anywhere else. No one cares about you like this. [My college]

provides a really safe place, the community here, for people to grow and to feel like they can take risks and still feel like they have a safe net to fall back on. There are so many people that care about you here, and so many people to get advice from.

One of the few regrets Brad had about his college experience was his inability to connect with certain faculty, such as a professor who "isn't teaching the way I really click with." He wished that he had been "willing to accept a different style or different method of teaching and take that for what it's worth," recognizing that those classes "could have been a little bit more fulfilling and rewarding if I had just taken a step back and said, 'Okay, this isn't my favorite professor, but I'm going to learn as much as I can from him or her.'"

Nileen: Staying Close

Unlike Sam and Brad, Nileen developed a strong relationship with her first-year advisor. Developing close relationships with faculty was something she valued and acted on from the start. Nileen had great affection for her advisor and described her as a "mother figure on campus" who provided support and advice about all aspects of her first-year college experience. She talked to Nileen about her friends and social life: "She told me that now is the time to decide who I wanted to interact with and who I didn't want to interact with. And it was completely fine if I found people annoying." And she talked to Nileen about her fall grades, which were not as strong as those of her friends: "I think I was a little like, 'What's wrong with me?' And she just told me to take my time and to realize that I'm coming from a different academic school, and so it would take me some time."

While Nileen's first-year advisor became her major advisor, and they remained close throughout college, Nileen selected a different advisor for her honors thesis in order to work with someone who had greater expertise relating to her project. She described the risk involved in this decision:

I went against my [heritage] code of propriety and decided that I was going to possibly offend [my major advisor] who I care about but didn't think that she really had enough experience in the kind of things that I was interested in. And so I decided to go with this [new] professor. I've never worked with her before. We really didn't know each other that well. But I knew that she knew [my research area] and I was willing to take that gamble.

Nileen described the relationship they developed over her senior year:

She's my rock. I really feel like sending her flowers on Valentine's Day because every time I'm feeling down she just says the right things. And the fact that she speaks [my native language] means the world to me. The fact that she can tell me in my own language that it's going to be okay is just incredible . . . And then I can write to her about things like "Oh, I [found] myself looking at pictures of ex-boyfriends yesterday. What's wrong with me?" And she'll write back and say a line of poetry, like something my mother would say. It's something from home. It's nothing that anyone else here who didn't know [my native language] would have been able to come back with. I feel like I really have a really strong connection with her.

This strong tie was not something that Nileen expected. She met her thesis advisor, briefly, the year before at a talk she was giving. After the talk, Nileen introduced herself, not something she usually did because she "can be paralyzed with fear in situations like that." But they had a friendly conversation and remained in contact over the summer. Nileen recalled there was "a little bit of awkwardness" in their initial interactions in the fall "because you don't know the person. You don't know what's okay and what's not okay." They had yet to establish a shared set of expectations for their relationship. By the spring, this had all changed:

I know I can swear in front of her. I know I could throw up in front of her or cry in front of her, and it would be fine. I never thought that I would be this close to anyone that wasn't my age. She feels like a big sister to me. We write to each other two or three times a day. She's a good friend of mine at this point.

Nileen had meaningful relationships with multiple faculty because she recognized early on that "you can't depend on one person to be your guru." She described not one but three mentors: her major advisor, her thesis advisor, and her poetry professor. When asked to describe her relationship with her poetry professor, she responded: "He's not my advisor, but he is more my informal mentor. And also [it's] a very casual relationship. I go to him when I'm feeling down, and I need to talk about something."

Nileen's advising experience was typical in that she had found an advisor with whom she was quite "comfortable." In other ways though, Nileen's experiences were not at all typical. She had a sustained, meaningful relationship with a faculty advisor from her first to her senior year, and her relationships with faculty and staff seemed stronger than her relationships with peers. One year after graduation, Nileen said that she missed faculty more anything else:

> I miss my [major] department a lot. A lot. A lot. I don't miss dorm life. I miss [my thesis advisor]. I miss [my thesis advisor]. I miss [my thesis advisor]. I miss going to department events and being treated like a family member. Just having new students come up to me and say, "Oh, [your professor] said I should talk to you about this." I mean they really gave me so much respect and I just miss them dearly.

The strong relationships Nileen developed with her faculty advisors in college provided her with the practice she needed to successfully restart advising in graduate school. In her senior year, Nileen visited the PhD program that she would attend and described her soon-to-be graduate advisor as "a complete genius and I respect him so much as an academic. But I heard from every single person that I talked to that he's really difficult to work with." Nileen set aside these reservations and decided to attend this program, as it was the best fit for her research interests. Describing the relationship with her new advisor in her first year of graduate school, Nileen said:

> I'm really pleased with it. He was described as a bit of a monster and a drama queen. Not a drama queen. Sorry. I should say a diva. And he is to some extent. He's a bit of a rock star in this department. But [we] got off to a really good start and I think it's still going pretty well. He's one of those people who really understands when a student is working and when they're not working. And I feel that I can't fake it on some level. So as long as I keep working hard I feel like my relationship with him will be good.

Sam, Brad, and Nileen made different decisions about how to interact with advisors, those assigned to them as well as those whom they sought out. Our advising systems would work best if more students were like Nileen, working from their first year to their last year to establish deep and meaningful relationships with more than one faculty advisor. Their college experiences would be richer and they would also get *practice* at developing these types of mentoring relationships—a valuable skill that they would benefit from as adults. Most students though are not like Nileen. They more closely resemble Brad, Sam, or someone in between the two. What would help more students move closer to Nileen's experience? What would colleges have to ask of both their faculty and students to make such a change? These are questions to which we will return in the conclusion of the book.

Conclusion

The advisor-student relationship is inherently ambiguous. Successfully reducing this ambiguity to establish an effective relationship requires both parties to not only share expectations but also commit to, and nurture, the relationship. For many, this can happen via a common shared academic interest. And although sharing such an interest can facilitate the establishment of a "comfortable" relationship, it will take much more. Unlike the roles of teacher and student—which are well defined for faculty and students—the roles of advisor and advisee are less clear. Students expect hierarchy in the classroom. They expect teachers to lead and provide commentary, and are often frustrated if their classes are dominated by student discussion. Although many students expect their advisor to take the lead, they most enjoyed advising relationships that downplayed the typical student-professor hierarchy—often describing them as "comfortable" relationships when they were "less like a teacher-student relationship." Students also expect teachers to challenge their beliefs and assumptions in the classroom. Some students, like Nileen and Jessica, appreciated advisors who provided opportunities for self-reflection and criticism by asking "questions and sometimes prob[ing] me to think about things a bit more." But others, like Sam, saw these types of conversations as obstacles to be avoided—wanting instead just to be cheered on.

The expectations that both students and faculty have for advising relationships vary. Students variously referred to their advisor as their "mentor," "personal counselor," "mother figure," "teacher," "friend," and "buddy," with each of these labels having different implications for students' expectations for their advisors. Additionally, these labels are most likely not the ones that faculty advisors would use to label themselves. Only by working together and sharing their expectations can the faculty advisor and the student advisee resolve this ambiguity to facilitate the development of a "comfortable" relationship—one that supports student decision-making.

Several factors facilitate developing "comfortable" relationships with faculty—relationships that allow students multiple opportunities to seek personalized advice about important academic decisions. First, students must be willing to seek advice. Students who use mandatory meetings for course registration as opportunities to seek advice about choosing courses and get to know their advisors are more likely to develop a level of comfort with their advisors than those who see these meetings as obstacles to avoid. Moreover, students who meet with their advisors regularly, perhaps even taking the initiative themselves to set up these meetings, develop more meaningful partnerships with faculty that allow them to seek advice about a broader range of topics. Being willing to take risks by reaching out to faculty on a more personal level often pays dividends by helping to reduce the hierarchy that characterizes traditional teacher-student interactions.

Second, students must have an advisor who is also engaged in the relationship. Those who perceive an advisor as caring, supportive, and interested in them (at least academically) feel more comfortable asking them for advice. As students mature, they come to appreciate an advisor who is more than a cheerleader (or validator); they value constructive feedback delivered in a respectful manner. Advisors who spend time with their advisees—are available and accessible—and who actively seek contact with their advisees develop and maintain meaningful relationships with them.

Third, students and faculty are more likely to develop a strong advising relationship when they share similar academic interests. A shared academic interest provides a common ground for initial conversations, but is neither necessary nor sufficient for the development of a strong advising relationship. Although some students are able to see the benefits of developing relationships with faculty whose disciplinary interests are different from their own—such as having an advisor who encourages balance and exploration and provides a more holistic perspective on their education—many others develop important relationships with their major advisor because both parties are perhaps more willing to invest time and energy when they share a common interest.

Finally, students commonly describe their ideal advisor as someone who is willing to get to know them as a person. Although Eve only met with her first-year faculty advisor episodically for course registration, in her senior year she described her major advisor as being "pretty ideal":

> Obviously someone who sort of has the same interest that you do in terms of academics. But also someone who understands you more as a person and understands more of what you do on campus and just doesn't see you in class or something. Someone who understands you're on a team or you also do this, or you are an RA or you do that. So they sort of see you as more of a whole person.

However, not all faculty want student-faculty relationships that go beyond academics. One senior remarked that it was "hard to find an advisor who really takes an interest in your future, because they are so overwhelmed with what they are doing with their classes and their own students." And not all students want more personal student-faculty relationships. One senior was "very happy" with her major advisor, who was her ideal advisor. She described him as "awesome," and as someone who offered "great career advice" and "shed light on things" that she had not considered, which helped her make better decisions. Yet when asked if she wished for a more personal relationship with him, she responded:

> Not really, just because I think that would be really awkward. I think there's a line, or boundary I guess, between a professor and a student that shouldn't be crossed. I know other people are a little bit more gray, I guess, when it comes to that issue, but for me it's academic stuff only and that's about it. Academic/career stuff, that's fine, but social things, that's just my problem. I don't really need to talk to him about it.

The variety of relationships students form with faculty advisors and mentors highlights the dynamic nature of advising. The multiple opportunities students are given to restart advising—by starting over or by deepening connections to faculty—denotes the extent to which this relationship is continually evolving. First-year students and sophomores who fail to make connections with their "premajor" advisors often establish meaningful connections with their major advisors. Perhaps this happens because students finally get what they want when they declare a major: an advisor in their own area of academic interest. Sam's experiences with faculty provided a counterexample, and suggests that this is too simplistic an explanation. Perhaps the jump-start into advising provided in the first year pays off precisely because students learn—through practice—how to get advice from faculty, as well as the consequences of not seeking advice. By senior year, many have found ideal advisors because they've become not only seekers of advice but better seekers of advice.

SIX

❧ Engagement

Denise, how are your classes going this semester?

DENISE: I'm really frustrated with my math class. I loved calculus last
semester, and I just really understood the way my professor lectured.
This semester I have another professor, and I'm not getting what's going
on in that course at all, which is really frustrating because I know math
is something that I'm good at. Because it has rules and structures, and
I can figure it out. But the way that it's presented is very fast, and she
frequently references previous examples. And it's like, "Oh, you should
know this." Like you should know that same random thing that we did
once three years ago? Really?

I love organic chemistry, because I get to play with these model sets,
which are basically like Tinker Toys for big kids. And they're very amazing. You can see them. They're colorful and I get to build things and
visualize it and spin it and hold two molecules up to each other and see
how they react and why. I'm crazy, but I really like organic chemistry.

My social justice class is frustrating because nothing's due. I don't do
things unless there's a deadline, and I need to get on a journal. But I'm
really liking the course and the readings are all very interesting. And we
have lunches every week, which is something that I really value because it's
just like a smaller group and we get to talk with the professor and it's really
good. But I need to, we're supposed to journal, and I haven't done that.

BASED ON THE DESCRIPTIONS ABOVE, would it be fair to say that
Denise was academically engaged in the courses she was taking in the
fall of her sophomore year? Perhaps the best answer to this question is "Yes
and no." Denise responded positively to some instructors, assignments,
and teaching methods but not to others. Sometimes her positive or negative responses were associated with an entire course (organic chemistry
and calculus), but she also could see both the positive and negative aspects
of a single course (social justice). When asked to name her best class, she
refused to select just one:

Organic chemistry and social justice—and for totally different reasons. One, because I'm passionate about the subject matter, and the other because it just really fits with the way my mind works and it's coming so easily, which feels really good, because it's something that's supposed to be really hard. And the professors are fantastic in both cases. And I just really look forward to going to class.

Denise's answers to "How are your classes going?" highlight the complexity of defining and studying engagement among college students. Scholars of higher education have been interested in student engagement because it is positively correlated with a number of outcomes colleges hope their students will experience—persistence, personal development, learning, and satisfaction.[1] Among the many measures that have been developed to define and assess engagement, the National Survey of Student Engagement (NSSE) is among the best known and most frequently administered and analyzed. It defines engagement as "the amount of time and effort students put into their studies and other educationally purposeful activities," and examines, for example, students' perceived level of academic challenge, the extent to which they are active learners, and whether their institution provides enriching educational experiences.[2]

Although analyses of the NSSE and similar studies have significantly advanced our understanding of student engagement, they provide a partial and inherently limited picture of how students define and experience engagement in college. In large part, the limitations of these large-scale surveys stem from asking students to describe their academic experience in broad, general terms devoid of context and curriculum. How should a student answer a question about how frequently she "asked questions or contributed to course discussions in other ways" if she does so in one of her classes (a small seminar in history) but doesn't in three others (large lecture classes in economics, biology, and sociology)? What if a student has rarely "prepared two or more drafts of a paper or assignment before turning it in" because he is enrolled in courses which rely heavily on in-class examinations? And should a student provide a low rating to the global question, "During the school year, to what extent have your courses challenged you to do your best work?" if only one course fits this description, but her experience in it made her significantly question several long-held beliefs and values?[3]

We did not define academic engagement a priori, but instead derived indicators of it from how students described their academic and intellectual experiences. When students talked about specific courses or general disciplinary interests as "loving" or being "excited about" them, as "really interesting" or fueling their "passion," we took these to be signs of engagement. This love for and excitement about courses or disciplines often meant that students devoted more time to these classes and talked more about them with friends or family. Evidence of deliberateness in course selection (based on topical interest or perceived challenge) also seemed to us to indicate engagement.[4] In addition, we were interested in how students' descriptions of faculty as challenging teachers or intellectual role models might enhance their engagement. In short, emerging from our data, academic engagement occurred when students focused on acquiring or creating new knowledge, were intrinsically motivated to learn, and derived pleasure from doing so.[5]

Because we asked students to talk about *each* of their courses and various other academic experiences *every semester,* we quickly came to realize that the defining element of engagement is its *particularistic nature.* Engagement is linked to specific classes, assignments, professors, pedagogies, subjects, and methodologies. As a consequence, it isn't possible to describe students as being "engaged" or "unengaged" in global terms. They have engaging and unengaging experiences throughout their time in college. This is clear from Denise's descriptions of her courses with which we began this chapter. One wouldn't expect students to be equally engaged in all of the courses they are taking in a given term, and they rarely are. Similarly, students may be engaged by some elements of an individual course—for example, Denise's interest in the readings and small group discussions in her social justice class—but find other aspects of the course (such as the lack of deadlines) troublesome. Professors teach differently, some subjects will be more appealing than others, and expectations for courses will sometimes be met, exceeded, or fall short. For these reasons and others, students often define and experience engagement through a comparative exercise in which they view other experiences as less engaging or unengaging.[6]

Students are especially likely to be caught up in this comparative exercise when they start college. Tyler's experience was typical in this regard. He was "pretty satisfied" with the courses he selected during registration but, after classes started, he changed his mind:

I haven't been that happy that I took some of them. Like my first-year seminar, because it's mostly anthropology. I was psyched at first, and then I've been, I'm just like, it's not what I want to do. So maybe that's a good thing, you know, I'm narrowing it down for my major. Calculus, I don't really like math, but I think I have to take it just to get it over with. Economics has been hard, but I do like German. I was glad I took German.

In his second semester Tyler enrolled in geology, music, and history classes. Looking back on the previous semester, he said:

I think I had to go through a period where I thought I had good classes but they didn't turn out to be everything I wanted . . . I definitely like these classes more than last semester because they cater more to [my interests]. Like I just decided, enough with just getting the gen eds [general education requirements] out of the way. I want to do classes that I like.

After his first semester in which he found some courses comparatively more engaging than others, Tyler "restarts" college in his second semester planning to choose courses based on interest rather than fulfilling requirements. If more students did this in their first semester, it is likely that they would find themselves academically engaged in something earlier on.[7]

How Do Students Become Engaged?

Engagement is always linked to either curriculum—the subjects that are taught—or pedagogy—how these subjects are taught. Often it is a product of both. But the ways in which curriculum and pedagogy interact to shape engagement vary considerably among students. For example, while students often major in disciplines that they find generally interesting, few are equally engaged in all of the courses they must take to complete their majors. This is especially the case in fields where students are required to take a broad range of courses within the discipline. Recall that Oma, whose sense of home was tied to her passion for African history, was not at all engaged by the U.S. history courses required for her major or the Russian history seminar she took in her sophomore year. Similarly, a student majoring in economics and math talked about how she arrived at her interest in microeconomics (rather than macroeconomics):

> I took statistics in my freshman year, and now I'm the grader so I really am into that . . . I really like that type of thing, just modeling and math. I think the overall experience in my majors has led me to decide that I don't really want to do the macro theory thing. I want to do the statistical modeling, math type of thing.

Because college offers students the opportunity to study new subjects or to delve more deeply into subjects familiar to them from high school, individual courses may prompt engagement, often leading to further study within a discipline. As a first-year student, Michael said that his most interesting courses were in physics and computer science because:

> There's a lot of interesting stuff in [my physics class]. There's like a lot of new kinds of physical things that I'm learning about . . . So there's a lot of things that I didn't know that I'm learning. That's really interesting. And then [my computer science course] is interesting too, because I've never learned how to do any programming and stuff, so I'm learning that. We do a lot of really fun programming labs where we usually have to program a game. So it's pretty fun.

For other students, engagement stems from the way courses are structured and the types of assignments.[8] One student talked about how her history course was unlike others she had taken because of its topical focus, an experience that led her, in the next semester, to do an independent research project on Martin Luther King Jr.'s march in Chicago:

> I'm very content with all of my classes right now, but if I had to pick one that I was really excited about, I'd pick this history class [on the civil rights movement]. It's really the first history class that I've had that hasn't been a survey course of a country or of a whole bunch of ideas. Well, really a little simplistic, but focused around a specific movement, so the ideas are focused, and it's an in-depth study of things which is, I think, a really nice experience. So I'm very excited about that.

Another student described how a novel assignment in his political science class deepened his understanding of his major:

> I've definitely done different things that I haven't done before, which obviously causes you to have questions. Like we had to make a campaign commercial where you had to do a poll the other day. So those things are new to me. And actually getting hands-on experience with my major, so I think it's pretty cool.

Students also become engaged by courses that connected to their personal lives or extracurricular interests.[9] Oma chose African history, in part, to understand better her family's cultural heritage. A South Asian student who enrolled in a course on Urdu literature while studying away experienced a similar type of engagement when she connected her family life to her academic interests. In response to a question about why she is excited by her study of Urdu, she replied:

> I guess it's just something that I always wanted to do and it is my native language. And I have kind of a longing for it. I miss speaking it. There are all these songs that I listen to that I never really understood properly. And now that I'm reading about that culture, it just helps me understand a lot about what my parents think and my family thinks. I mean it has a lot to do with my family.

Given the priority our colleges place on effective classroom teaching, faculty were a frequent source of engagement, even when students enrolled in courses which they did not expect to find particularly interesting.[10] This was true of a student taking her first class in art history, a subject in which she would go on to major. She described her instructor as "a great professor" for the following reasons:

> She really makes the whole class feel very continuous. It's not like we're starting this in a vacuum, and then this in a vacuum. She really makes impressionism lead into cubism and everything. So she's a great professor, and she's just so interesting and so smart . . . I want to take every class with her now.

Another had similar praise for his English professor:

> I mean he's unbelievable. He's the goofiest, most eccentric man ever . . . He's just really, really engaging. He can turn the stupidest comments that kids make into something that sounds intelligent, which is pretty incredible. And I mean his knowledge of everything, of English, of England, of literature, you know, it's just unbelievable. Before this class I hated when people would overanalyze things. But the way we do it, it makes sense and that's really encouraged me with English because I'm starting to understand these deep levels of analysis.[11]

For many students, challenging course material may prompt engagement.[12] Often this happens in courses that students perceive as "risk-taking"—courses in subjects they have never taken before or in which they have not previously done well. One student, for example, was surprised to find that chemistry was her favorite class despite being the most challenging. This experience departed from her high school mode of thinking where "normally I like the easier classes . . . but here the class I liked is the class that I had to work the hardest. And I only got a mediocre grade." Another student commented on the risk that her comparative literature course posed, not because of the subject but because of the professor's pedagogy: "It's challenging in a different way. Like I'm not a touchy-feely person and I don't like writing about how I feel about this or that. I don't really want to explore those feelings, [but] it forces you to do that and that's a challenge for me."

Just as students could be engaged by challenge, many described being engaged in courses in which they could connect what they were learning to the "real world" or to future career goals.[13] Jim provided good examples of both of these types of connections. He was engaged by a sociology methods course that was structured around a research project on student and faculty perspectives on campus climate. "It's actually been a good class," he says, "because we're learning stuff, and we're able to apply what we've learned to something throughout the whole semester." This was one of the few courses that interested him enough to talk to friends about outside of class. Jim was also engaged by courses that taught him how to do things that he believed would be useful in his future life, especially his sociology courses that helped him learn how people interact with each other and how to be a better communicator.

Similarly, a physics major said that he liked to take classes in which he could research new technologies—"like the latest in gadgets and whatnots"—to see "how the world works and how really interesting things that you might see on TV or in the movies, how those work."

Other students commented on their engagement in community-based courses.[14] One student who normally talked much more about his athletic interests than his academic ones became very engaged with an education course that focused on male development. For this class, he went to a local middle school and conducted focus groups with boys. Unlike any of his other courses, he talked about this course with his parents and his basketball coach. When asked why it was so engaging to him, he said:

> Because it allows you to see what you're talking about in class first-hand. Like we're always talking about the boy code and stuff like that and the stereotypes of boys. You can get a sense of that in YouTube clips or documentaries and stuff, but actually being involved in [focus] groups allows you to see first-hand their reactions to things and how they act in certain situations.

That curriculum and pedagogy can promote engagement in many ways is good news for college students.[15] Every year, every semester, every course, every class meeting offers opportunities for restarts that might foster engage-ment.[16] Many of these opportunities will be serendipitous and surprising; others, especially for students who have restarted college many times, will be deliberate and based on thoughtful self-reflection. But regardless of how students become engaged in their courses, how—and to what extent—does engagement become a regular feature of their academic landscape?

Patterns of Engagement: Episodic, Sustained, and Cumulative

Just as students are likely to be engaged in a given semester by different as-pects of the pedagogy and curriculum, they also exhibit different patterns of engagement over time. For many students, engagement will be *episodic,* something they experience only in some semesters in college. For others, engagement will be *sustained*—experienced to some extent most every se-mester in college—and some sustained engagement may even be *cumulative*

in the sense that engaging experiences may be linked and build on one another. And, as the patterns of their engagement vary, so do the paths by which
students arrive at engagement. Some will become engaged because they dig
deeply into the substance and methods of a particular discipline, whereas
others will find engagement by broadly exploring the curriculum and multiple pedagogies. What do these different patterns of engagement look like?
How do they follow from the decisions students make about their academic
program, and what consequences do they have? The academic experiences of
Adam, Michael, and Dan suggest some answers to these questions.

Adam: Episodic Engagement

Adam's decision-making about his academic program was essentially complete before coming to college. Given that he wanted to go to law school after
graduation, he thought he had little choice but to major in political science.
Fortunately, he liked the American politics course he took his first semester
because it examined multiple perspectives on current issues. He also liked
a political theory class he took the next semester because there were many
debates and they talked about the nature of love in class, something he didn't
expect to find in a political science course. But even though he had positive experiences in these courses, Adam's real enthusiasm for political science
emerged in the second semester of his sophomore year in a course focused
on legal case studies:

> I like [this course] because you read different cases about murder, sex
> crimes, just all different kinds of cases that come from common law,
> from England and stuff. It's like you go to a movie every time you go to
> class because he talks about the cases and how they operate and stuff. So
> that's interesting—I think law is the most interesting.

Part of Adam's excitement stemmed from the course being about the law, but
more came from Adam's sense that the course was "not just theory"; learning
the content had real implications for how he viewed society.

During this first two years, Adam's decision to major in political science—
made before he came to college and perhaps even before he knew what political science was—seemed to be playing out well. If not engaged by all of

his courses, at least Adam found particular aspects of some of his courses interesting. But by his junior year, when asked about his major, Adam was not enthused. He said he felt duped into thinking that he needed to major in political science if he wanted to go to law school and suggested that he wished he could restart college with a new major: "What they don't tell you is that your undergraduate degree, the concentration, really has no merit whatsoever. It doesn't matter. Most medical school students are English majors. It doesn't matter. I probably would have majored in something like sociology or theater had I known."

While it is not true that "most medical students are English majors," it is true that the link between post-college plans and majors is not as strong as many students assume. Because Adam came to college with a fixed idea of what he had to major in, and did little to question the assumptions on which that decision was based, he felt stuck in a discipline about which he was no longer excited. The course he liked best in his junior year was an introductory course in sociology. When asked why, he responded:

> Just in terms of structure, attention to detail, thoughtfulness that goes behind selecting the readings for the class, the diversity, and just the appeal, the intriguing nature that it brings to me when I try to understand what's going on, the concepts. Soc, although it's a lot about American things, there tends to be a lot of international issues also.

Adam started an honors project in his major his senior year but dropped it after the first semester because he lost interest and wasn't getting as much work done as his advisor expected. He found the political science class he took in his last semester mediocre. When asked what his favorite classes were over four years, he replied:

> Sociology. I love things that involve sociology and bringing it to biology. I like the meshing of the two. I enjoy that a lot. I took [an introductory sociology class] that was interesting. We ended up talking about Hurricane Katrina and the interracial and cultural divides that took place during that time. I mean those kind of things are just fascinating. And I took [a course] a couple of years ago in biology that was about viruses and the human body and so forth. I love stuff like that.

Adam's academic experience in college was guided by a decision he made prior to attending college—that if he wanted to go to law school he had little choice but to major in political science. Adam found some political science courses engaging—often those that had to do with "real-life" issues or helped him think about how societies are governed—but several were not. He even lost interest in his honors project. He was engaged by some sociology courses he took and, as a senior, said that he might have benefited from majoring in that discipline. But when asked why, Adam gave an instrumental reason: "Because [sociology courses] are not as stressful. I don't want to say they're not as rigorous, because I don't think that's true. I just think they're less stressful and yield higher GPA [grade point average] results. So to be strategic, I would go about it differently that way."

Adam's academic engagement was episodic at best, peppered with moments of engagement but not sustained through several courses within his major field of study, several courses with a particular professor, or similar pedagogical experiences across more than one discipline. In some semesters one or more of his courses captured his interest, but at other times, when asked about his best class, he mentioned the course in which he was getting the best grade—more a signifier of academic achievement than engagement.

A student like Adam might have given many different answers to NSSE-like questions about his level of engagement across the four years of college because it was so variable. Although he sampled courses in college looking for something that would interest him, his course choices were not primarily driven by reflection about the academic experiences he found engaging. They were guided by his concern for an acceptable GPA or by his belief that he had little choice over a major given that he wanted to attend law school. As a consequence, Adam's engagement was momentary and sporadic—a petunia in an onion patch.

Michael: Sustained and Cumulative Engagement within a Discipline

Unlike Adam, Michael came to college interested in science and math but with no clear road map as to the courses he wanted or needed to take. He was excited that at college, unlike high school, he could choose his own curriculum: "I'm having a good time learning the material because I get to choose what I learn. I think that's the best part of going to college." His favorite class in his first year was organic chemistry, because "it was a lot of fun being able to learn something completely new just over the course of the semester." But his favorite course in the fall of his sophomore year was history, because he liked the professor and was "learning a lot of new things." By spring, he was most excited about, and challenged by, a theoretical physics course: "It's kind of interesting to see all the methods of solving problems that we're learning." Michael saw each of the courses he could select in college as an opportunity to learn something new. This purposeful orientation toward making decisions about which courses to take resulted in Michael's sustained engagement throughout college.

Michael began to dig deeply into physics and chemistry in his sophomore year, and did research with a professor in the summer that followed, but he continued to explore courses in other disciplines which he also found engaging. In the fall of his junior year, Michael took quantum mechanics, inorganic chemistry, classical political theory, and a studio art course. He described this semester as his best one in college:

> I've been able to take, pretty much, any course that I've wanted to do. [Taking a variety of courses] maybe put me on a track that I was a little unsure about, but then I got to go into it and really enjoyed the courses. Or, I learned that I didn't like them so much, but I still enjoyed the process of learning about something that I always wanted to learn about, even if it didn't end up being something I want to continue with. It's been really great to experience chunks of different subjects, and go a little deeper than a *Wikipedia* article. You can always learn about stuff on the surface. But to submerge yourself for a semester, write something about it, put some of your own self into it, and then have someone review what you think, isn't always an opportunity you get. That's been great.

The summer before his senior year, Michael had a research internship in Austria that helped clarify his interests in an honors project. He very much liked "doing laboratory research as opposed to writing a research paper" and enjoyed the open-ended nature of his research: "[My summer experience] definitely makes me want to make my honors project something that I'm interested in. So that might mean changing the scope of the project a little so that it's something that I feel passionate about, as opposed to doing just something that's assigned." Michael said that his honors project was the best academic experience he had at college, because it gave him the opportunity to do "the whole process of research, not just an experiment but plan the experiment and do it and . . . get it published—seeing what it takes to do all of that."

Adam and Michael entered college with very different ideas as to how they could shape their academic programs. From the start, Adam felt constrained to major in a particular discipline and then constrained by his need to take courses that he found less rigorous so that he could maintain a good GPA. Although he got excited about political science and sociology courses that helped him think about "real-world" issues, when deciding on courses, his understanding of his own interests never trumped his beliefs that he had to major in political science and should take courses that he found relatively easy.

By contrast, Michael came to college excited about the newfound control he was given in shaping his academic experience. The decisions he could make about which courses to take—something he couldn't really do in high school—allowed him to pursue his strong interests in science and math, but also allowed him to explore new subjects and learn new things. He sampled courses in lots of areas—studio art, political theory, English, environmental studies—and although his engagement in science courses was constant and deepened over time, his engagement with non-science courses was also constant. For instance, somewhat on a whim, Michael took an environmental policy class because he heard the professor was great. He found it very challenging and didn't do particularly well grade-wise in it, but he said it was his favorite course that semester because he had never learned about policy actions before. His decisions about courses were grounded in expectations that he would be learning something new and valuable from faculty who were experts in their fields. Michael's engagement was sustained, happening every semester in a variety of different courses. In physics, his engagement was also cumulative in that the more he learned the more engaged he became.

Dan: Sustained and Cumulative Engagement across Disciplines

Dan was similar to Michael in that his engagement was sustained throughout college, but the cumulative nature of their engagement differed. Whereas Michael's engagement in physics deepened each year, culminating in collaborative research and a senior honors project, Dan's engagement grew because he selected courses across fields that strengthened his ability to pose questions, read critically, and debate positions. Because Dan's curricular decisions were driven by selecting courses, professors, and pedagogies that honed these skills which he valued, his academic experience was characterized by frequent opportunities for engagement.

Although most of his high school friends chose to attend a large, prestigious public university in the Midwestern state where he grew up, Dan wanted to go to a place where students "took college seriously." In high school he often debated big ideas with his friends, so when he chose classes in his first semester, he was attracted to a philosophy of religion course:

> "Does God exist?" "Can you define the nature of God?" "Can you ultimately decide whether or not God exists?" I really like dissecting those questions and tried multiple times to start the argument with friends. And so being in a class with readings and a professor—it definitely piqued my interest and really engaged me in something that I've been looking forward to taking for a long time.

Dan was so excited about this course that, when he decided to drop his calculus class in the second week of the semester, he enrolled in another philosophy course on logic taught by the same professor. He also really liked his first-year seminar, which was an English class focused on modernity: "I like this class because we read a lot of classic authors like Locke and Rousseau. Just a lot of things that you've heard of but you've never sat down and read because they are kind of dense. So I really like the fact that I have a good reason to read them."

In his second semester, Dan declared a major in philosophy, taking his third course in the department, but he decided at the last moment to take a history course, even though he hated history in high school. He loved the course and the professor: "I think maybe because I didn't expect to enjoy it so much and because I am enjoying it so much, the difference makes it more exciting than my other classes." His course selection followed a similar pattern throughout his first three years. Most of his courses were in the humanities—English, religion, history, and philosophy. Some choices were quite deliberate; he knew he was interested in the topics or thought learning about the subject matter would be helpful to him in the future. Others were more serendipitous because they fit his schedule or because nothing else looked interesting and the subject matter caught his attention. Dan was equally excited about courses that he chose deliberately and thought he'd like and ones he took more on a whim or to fulfill a general education requirement. He was intrigued by a research paper he wrote for bioethics even though the class was something of a disappointment. He liked a gender studies course he took, as well as one on Japanese culture. Although questioning the value of some philosophy courses he had taken, Dan saw the value in taking many courses in one subject area over time:

> I probably feel more inspired just because I'm becoming better, and I sort of have a better understanding of what a good philosophy paper is. So it makes me try and think about a certain problem in a way that I wouldn't have in the past. Just remembering writing my first philosophy paper and then thinking about how I'd go about it now. I'm probably a lot more inspired because I feel more competent than I have in the past.

Dan described himself as growing intellectually at his college: "It's made me like school a lot, in a way that I didn't in high school."

In his junior year, Dan spent the first semester trying to fulfill the requirements for a second major in history, because he was planning to study abroad the second semester and wasn't sure how many credits would transfer. He was not particularly excited about any of these courses and this realization culminated in a curricular restart in which he downgraded his history major to a minor. He enjoyed his study abroad semester because he liked the students in the program and because he had more time to read outside of class and explore a new part of the world, but he found his courses frustrating: "I miss the academic atmosphere at [my college] and the way people interact and ask questions."

In the summer before his senior year, Dan had an internship back home in a state legislator's office and found the work fascinating. When asked the following fall if his summer experiences changed his academic plans, Dan replied:

> Yes, because I know I'm interested in public policy and that is the career path I could see myself in. I have definitely started to take some classes this semester that reflect that. Like right now I'm in an education

and law course and next semester I'm going to take something in U.S. foreign policy and American political thought—all to give myself some more vocabulary to deal with these ideas. If I had found out that I really didn't like working in the legislator's office, I might not be pursuing those classes.

What might seem like an abrupt restart—the shift from humanities courses, mainly philosophy and history, to political science courses—didn't seem like one to Dan. He thought his courses in philosophy helped him learn how to think, and that, he believed, lay at the heart of his engagement (or lack thereof) in the other courses he took: "I don't really care about topics that philosophy actually covers. What I care more about is reading an argument and dissecting the argument and objecting to the argument, or proving it, or thinking of a new argument or coming up with an analogy."

His political science classes gave him a "new vocabulary," but he saw himself using the intellectual skills he'd developed elsewhere—"how to reconcile competing ideas, how to be tolerant and sensitive to different opinions, and how to ask important questions when problems arise." Dan decided not to do an honors project in philosophy, because "I just wasn't passionate enough about a philosophy topic," and instead chose to take more courses focused on public policy.

Like Michael, Dan chose his academic path by reflecting on what interested him. Originally, he gravitated toward philosophy because those courses allowed him to discuss big ideas and moral questions until he realized that what really engaged him were critical analysis and argumentation, which could be found in courses across the curriculum. Dan was engaged most every semester with certain kinds of assignments and ways of thinking in courses but not with a consistent subject or set of topics. When he found himself taking courses that did not help him grow intellectually (like while studying away), his engagement diminished. He described himself one year as being "broadly intellectually stimulated" and another year as being "deeply intellectually stimulated" and wasn't sure "that one is necessarily better than the other."

Dan created a series of courses and experiences across philosophy, history, and political science that allowed him to develop a way of posing questions, critically reading texts, understanding arguments, and debating ideas. He articulated this intellectual growth in the second semester of his senior year when responding to a question about his best academic experience. Dan took a philosophy class in his last semester of college from the same professor he had his first semester. He cited the research paper he did for the class he took as a senior as his best academic experience in college:

> It was the best experience, not because the class itself was so much better than any other class, but because I could feel myself being a better student. I knew where I had come from and what I'd learned about reading and writing. I remember writing a paper for the course I took my first semester. I remember reading the question back then and being like, "Oh, okay I know exactly how to answer this question." And I go back now and I read it and I don't think what's been happening in my head has changed that much. I think I had a pretty good answer back then. But what I put down on the page and how well I explained myself and how articulately and how much I responded to objections and delved deeply into the problem have just changed so much. The fact that I could write a good paper now was probably the best moment.

ᖗ Both Dan and Michael did purposeful academic work every semester and were, to varying degrees, excited about that work. It is likely that, were they to be surveyed regularly while in college, they would have appeared as highly engaged students in the ways that NSSE and other survey-based studies measure this concept. Although Dan and Michael were not unique in our study, the majority of students, like Adam, would probably have had more variable answers over time. Adam's engagement was episodic, prominent in some courses in some semesters, but not sustained over time. Depending on when you caught up with him, you might have formed quite different opinions about his enthusiasm for his courses. Yet despite the "hit or miss" quality of Adam's engagement, he nonetheless was highly motivated and interested in some classes and by some assignments.[17]

What about students who exhibited virtually no moments of engagement throughout their four years of college? Contrary to some recent critiques that portray college students as highly unmotivated and uninterested, we found only a few who fit that description.[18] These students were often spending so much time struggling to adjust to college—managing time, seeking balance, developing effective study habits, not feeling "at home"—that they saw their courses as obstacles to their intellectual growth, rather than opportunities. The inability to manage their lives kept these students from seeing, acting, or reflecting on academic experiences that had the potential to engage them.[19] Others found themselves sitting in classes in which they had little investment but which were required of their course of study. Students who had spent years telling themselves and others that they were going to be physicians sometimes had this experience in their premed science courses. Yet others saw college as a way station on their journey to a lucrative career. If they could have bypassed college, they would have.

We may have found few students who expressed little or no engagement for a number of reasons (e.g., the types of students whom we admit or the prominent role teaching plays in our colleges), but we may have found *more* engagement because we looked for it in a different way. Students described with great frequency particular elements of courses or particular professors they found engaging. Like Adam, these students were episodically engaged, neither "engaged" or "unengaged" college students, but college students who were engaged from time to time. Colleges would, of course, like engagement to be a more common and routine experience for students. What have they done to achieve that goal?

Creating Opportunities for Engagement

Admissions officers work hard to recruit students like Dan who can't wait to get to college to debate big questions and ideas—and then actually go on to do so with great frequency after they arrive. But admissions officers—and faculty—know that not every admitted student is going to be a Dan. What, then, have colleges done to promote engagement among all students? And what can they do to enlist students as active partners in creating opportunities for engagement?

Institutional efforts to promote engagement have been a principal concern of those working on large-scale assessment projects, such as the NSSE. As the subtitle of George Kuh and his colleagues' book suggests—*Student Success in College: Creating Conditions that Matter*—colleges have instituted a wide variety of innovative programs that have been shown to enhance student engagement.[20] These range from curricular programs that frame a college education (e.g., first-year seminars and capstone experiences such as senior theses or independent research projects) to residential programs that seek to increase the frequency of student-faculty interaction. None of these is a "silver bullet"; differences in cultures, student populations, and specific areas of need vary from campus to campus. In short, interventions aimed at increasing engagement will always be *institutionally particularistic.*

But setting aside special programs that are designed with engagement in mind, of what bearing do the more *universalistic* elements that structure the academic experience of students at most colleges have on engagement: requiring students to complete a *major* (by taking many courses in a particular field), requiring students to satisfy *general education requirements* (by taking courses in many fields), and using *grades* as signifiers of achievement and success in college? To what extent do these practices act as opportunities for—or obstacles to—engagement?

The ubiquity of the major as a graduation requirement implies that it is the default structural mechanism for sustained—and hopefully, cumulative— engagement. Majors require that students dig deeply into a single discipline or focused area of study with the expectation that, as they acquire greater knowledge and practice in a field, their "passion" for, and identification with, it will intensify. General education requirements, however, are intended to encourage exploration of the curriculum so as to increase the likelihood that students will find new faculty, subjects, and experiences that engage them. Between requiring a major that forces students to dig deep and requiring general education courses that force them to explore broadly, colleges hope to engage most students. Overlaying these college requirements is the use of grades to mark how much and how well students have learned the material in their courses. Assuming that grades matter to students (which they do) and that hard work leads to better grades (which it sometimes does), grades can be seen as a driver for (and sometimes a measure of) engagement.

The Major

Most discussions of student engagement have little to say about the major field of study, apart from a consideration of the value of good advising or capstone experiences. Given that virtually every college or university in the country requires students to declare a major, we find this omission striking.

The major seems to be an unqualified good—or at least a taken-for-granted element—of a college education, something that would have struck leaders of early American higher education as quite odd. The debates over fixed versus elective curriculums that pitted Yale against Harvard are long gone, but the triumph of course choice represented in Harvard's elective system set the stage for the emergence of major and minor fields of concentration organized around disciplinary departments. Course choice would make students more active participants in their education, more passionate, and more prepared to enter a variety of occupations following graduation. Allowing students to select their own courses would give them "abundant practice in making wise free choices of the kind that any man would have to go on making during the remainder of his days on earth."[21]

The requirement that students major in a field (or closely related fields) grew out of the elective system and was, to some extent, a response to concerns about the fragmentation of higher education that course choice enabled. Majors would provide students with a core focus, repeated practice at using a disciplinary lens to understand the world, and a sense of mastery acquired through increasing familiarity with the central texts, methods, and perspectives of a field of study. In short, engagement would be fostered by digging deeply, by anchoring a college education vertically through disciplinary exploration and discovery.

But as we've seen, students are variously engaged by the courses, topics, and methodologies in their major field of study. Michael was increasingly engaged by courses he took in physical chemistry, and his thesis research was the most exciting learning experience he had in college. Dan valued the skills he acquired as a philosophy major but didn't like discussing the ideas advanced by great philosophers. And Adam chose a major that he believed would advance his professional aspirations to be a lawyer but one in which he exhibited little interest.

Students view declaring their major as the most important decision they will make in college. For many, this college-defining moment was stressful because much appeared to ride on it: their sense of what they were good at, their identity while at college, and their career aspirations following college. Although some students did indeed express a strong interest in the major they elected (to the point that they referred to it as their "passion"), for many, declaring a major was more a matter of finding the "best fit" from among the available options.[22] In large part, the investment that students have in the process of choosing a major has more to do with the messages (often subtle and unspoken) that colleges send students than with the students themselves. *Majors are important to students, in large measure, because we tell them they are.*

But can requiring students to declare a major sometimes act as an obstacle to engagement? Someone like Dan who was engaged in lots of subjects may have actually taken more courses that would have engaged him if he hadn't had to fulfill the requirements for his philosophy major. Adam might have benefited from taking more sociology courses instead of finishing up his major in political science. The assumption that digging deep will push students toward sustained and cumulative engagement may well be flawed and is likely connected to how faculty experience their engagement with the subjects that fascinate them. But promoting this path to engagement above others—by loading so much on to the declaration of a major—doesn't work for many students.

General Education Requirements

In contrast to the major, general education requirements—sometimes referred to as distribution requirements—are intended to broaden students' education by ensuring that they take courses across the range of the liberal arts or to strengthen their foundational skills, such as writing, quantitative reasoning, or understanding of diverse cultures. General education requirements provide students with a chance to try out new subjects, take risks and "take a break" from the courses or type of work they are doing to complete their majors. Students who viewed their general education courses in these ways usually saw them in a positive light, as opportunities. Consider Brad's comment on a theater course he took to fulfill a general education requirement:

> This is the first time where I really see how these requirements can actually benefit your education. Because I would never think that I would be that interested in theater. I always thought it was cool, but it's just so much fun. It's a different kind of class. It makes you think about things differently. It makes you think about theater in a completely new way.

And, for the first time, I can see that trying something new and having that benefit your educational experience, and it's been really great.

Indeed, such students often commented on how the ability to take courses in many fields was a primary reason they chose to attend a liberal arts college.

The decision to attend a liberal arts college was particularly likely to invoke questions among international students who grew up in different educational systems. Nicholas recalled that, in his first year of college, he:

asked many people how their liberal arts education applied to the real world [but] nobody told me a specific answer . . . I think few people know exactly what they want to do after graduation, so that's part of it . . . There are lots of people who only study for their classes, and they don't do anything else. And when you do that, you're restricting yourself. I'm starting to read all kinds of newspapers and publications just to see the real world behind the theory that we are studying in class. And that's one thing I'd like to do this semester, just to get acquainted with real-life applications, whether it be economics or math or German.

In his sophomore year, when Nicholas was thinking about potential majors, he said, "It's pretty easy to major in more than one field here . . . It's liberal arts education, so it's not vocational, like engineering, where you have to take 15 engineering courses, or accounting. That's the whole idea, to get a breadth of education. That's why I think I will double major." (He graduated with a double major in mathematics and economics.) Nicholas went on to elaborate:

Well, that's the whole liberal arts argument, whether it's better to focus on one thing or focus on many things. I think that personally you should focus on many things because you don't know. You have to explore these careers. Education [is] for you to explore stuff. So that's the pros. I explore. I know whether I'm better at math or econ or whatever. And I also get to see the connections between the fields, like the application of math and econ. I may go to Germany next year, so I applied to take the German economy course, and I want to live in Germany after maybe five or six years.

When it came to completing his general education requirements, Nicholas was an "explorer"; he developed deliberate strategies for trying out new fields with the goal of becoming broadly educated. By contrast, other students approached the task of fulfilling these requirements more as "samplers," adopting a more menu-oriented approach to selecting courses (e.g., one literature, one science, one history).[23] Some samplers were like Tyler, whom we met at the start of this chapter. He entered college viewing these requirements as something to "get out of the way." As a consequence, Tyler found his first semester courses less engaging than he had expected. By the second semester, however, he had adopted a different strategy for putting together his course schedule: "Enough with just getting the gen eds out of the way; I want to do classes that I like."

Sometimes it took students several semesters (or even years) to see general education requirements as opportunities, rather than obstacles, to engagement. It was not uncommon to find seniors, whose time in college was quickly coming to a close, wishing that they'd come across a particular discipline or professor earlier. For example, one student who was taking her first philosophy class in her last semester of college said, "I feel like that's something I might have liked to have done—take more philosophy classes. I liked the way that classes like that work, where you have to decipher these readings and sort of come up with really solid arguments. I just really enjoy that way of thinking." Another student majoring in biological chemistry expressed similar regrets about not exploring the curriculum more broadly:

> I hear of all these great professors in all these different disciplines. And I'm like "I've never heard of that person" because I don't hang out in [the humanities building]. I don't hang out in [the social sciences building]. I really hang out in [the sciences building], and that's it. You know? And there are so many great faculty members that I wish I could have taken a class with. Like a couple of the econ professors that I wish I could have taken a class with. Women's studies classes. I never got to do that.

Grades

The particularistic and frequently episodic nature of engagement contrasts sharply with the more general and consistent preoccupation students have with grades. Similar to the combination of internal and external forces that lead students to view time in college as short and compressed, students see grades as a measure of success in college because grades play such a prominent role in their high school and college experiences. Good grades in high school can translate into a place on the honor roll or admission to a selective college. Colleges mimic these high school practices by posting dean's lists, awarding prizes, and allowing students to participate in honors projects if they have high enough grades. Graduate and professional schools—especially medical and law schools—will want to see the grades students achieved when they are applying for admission, and increasingly employers—especially prestigious accounting and consulting firms—are limiting their recruitment practices to colleges where a sufficient number of interested students meet or exceed their lofty GPA benchmarks. It is no wonder, then, that many students believe their college GPA will follow them the rest of their lives.

At the beginning of each year, we asked students: "Thinking ahead to the end of the year, what would make this a successful year for you?" Each year, over half mentioned something about grades in their answers to this question: "good grades in all of my courses," "a higher GPA in my science classes," "two B+'s and two A–'s," "a 4.0," and so forth. Getting good grades was the drumbeat in students' definitions of success, the most consistently and frequently mentioned theme.[24] Given the emphasis that colleges and students place on grades, this perspective on college success makes a lot of sense.

But what are the consequences of defining success in college in terms of grades? Does the emphasis on grades in college thwart curricular risk-taking and exploration? Are students more interested in getting good grades than in learning new things and new ways of thinking? Does the pursuit of academic achievement—as measured by a high GPA—crowd out opportunities for academic engagement? Our longitudinal analysis of students' definitions of a successful year revealed that the mention of grade themes and engagement themes was negatively correlated. Students who expressed an interest in getting good or better grades each year were less likely to mention engagement themes (e.g., desire to learn or take interesting classes, get to know faculty, explore new subjects, do independent research) in their definitions of a successful year.[25]

The relationship between the *actual* grades students earn and their engagement with their courses is more variable and complex, and one that we have been puzzled by throughout this study. Scholars who have examined this relationship using survey data from the NSSE have found that aggregate measures of academic performance (semester, year, or final college GPAs) are only modestly correlated with engagement.[26] Because we were able to link students' descriptions of their experiences in *individual courses* to the grades they received in them, we can offer some insight into why the relationship between engagement and GPA is not more robust.

At times, grades and engagement track together: a student who is highly engaged by a course ends up with a higher grade in it, and a student who is not engaged by a course ends up with a lower grade in it. At other times, engagement and grades appear to have little connection to one another: a student may be highly engaged by a course in which she is not earning a high grade, or she may receive a high grade in a course in which her engagement is minimal.

The various ways that grades can relate to engagement are illustrated in Jim's college experience. Jim was someone who was engaged by courses that made explicit connections to the world around him, a perspective he exhibited early on in college. Jim found his first-year seminar in sociology exciting because the course material on social inequality "applies to college" and the course generated "a really interesting conversation. It's really an interesting topic and, like, we could talk about it for hours." Being able to apply what he was learning in his classes became a resonant theme of Jim's engagement in college. His rhetoric classes in his first year taught him how to form arguments, skills that he "can actually apply when I leave school." Throughout his first year, Jim was ambivalent about defining success solely in terms of earning good grades: "For me, my success isn't based on the grade. It's just knowing that I've learned the material, I'm comprehending what's going on, and that if I don't enjoy a class . . . I mean I've actually liked not liking a class because I know I can just cancel that out [as a potential major]."

By the end of his first year, however, Jim said, "academically my expectations were not met" simply because he did not perform well, ending the year with a relatively low GPA: "I haven't done as well in school here as I hoped I would. So that was kind of like disappointing for me as well. But again, like I've learned a lot about my study habits and like how to write good papers . . . that's been real beneficial."

In his sophomore year, Jim raved about a seminar on globalization in which students debated current events and cultural conflicts. Despite receiving a low grade in a course required for the major, Jim declared a major in sociology: "[The grade] really didn't help determine if I wanted to be a major or not. I think I just really like the subject matter. I'm interested in it." Sociology was a "good fit for him" because he "could just apply everything I learned to the real world and that's what I did, and it will definitely help me in the future."

In the fall of his junior year, Jim took four sociology courses "to get rid of, finish my [major] requirements." His course on social inequality was his favorite "because it [is] all about privilege, power, and equality in today's society and how it's . . . prevalent at [my] college and around the world." Jim described this course and a second sociology class as his best this term, because he has "the best grades in those classes." When asked if he would still find this course interesting if he did not receive a good grade, Jim replied, "I was pretty excited about it before the semester even started, but I would definitely like it more if I was getting a good grade." On the other hand, Jim described an art history class, which he was taking to satisfy a general education requirement, as "pretty boring," a course in which he would receive a very high final grade.

When asked if he wanted to do anything differently in his senior year, Jim replied: "Just trying to get my GPA up and just work as hard as I can in my classes. Like getting a good grip on my GPA is something I'd like to resolve." To help him meet this goal, Jim chose two history classes because they required "minimal work. I'm getting A's in them right now." He's not engaged by these classes because his professors "just kind of talk. I get bored when it's not like an interactive class." Compared to previous years, Jim found his senior year courses

> less interesting because, like your first couple of years, you might not have a major yet, so I think you're really searching to find your major, so you're trying to immerse yourself in classes that might pique your interest for a major. But now, I'm taking classes that are going to help me with my GPA and for my major, so I think like they're not as interesting.

In his first two years of college Jim had a number of engaging experiences in his courses (particularly those in sociology) despite receiving low grades in them. He claimed not to measure success in terms of grades, something he said he had done throughout high school. But in his last two years of college—and particularly in his senior year—Jim found little in his courses that engaged him, and he deliberately sought out courses in which he did not expect to be engaged but in which he expected to achieve high grades. This is a good example of how restarts in college—making deliberate choices to change based on reflection about past decision-making—can diminish, rather than enhance, the quality of a student's education. As a senior, having sacrificed opportunities for engagement in order to obtain a higher GPA, Jim bore little resemblance to his first-year self.

Jim's experience should lend a note of caution to thinking of grades as a shorthand measure of success in college. Grades certainly convey some information to students, employers, graduate school admissions committees, and others—whether or not students have met, exceeded, or failed to meet the expectations set by their instructors, for example—but they remain a partial and imperfect indicator of what students have learned or how their habits of mind have been shaped. Just as we claim that students are not either engaged or unengaged in college—they are both and in various ways—we would argue that global grade measures (such as cumulative GPA) fall far short of defining success in college.

The primary structures that shape the college experience—majors, general education requirements, and grades—are perceived and acted upon differently by students. Some see one or more of these as pathways to engagement, while others see them as obstacles. In the concluding chapter of this book, we will offer some suggestions for how colleges might create alternative structures to increase the likelihood that students will find additional experiences that engage them throughout college.

Yet colleges—and the faculty who teach at them—can only do so much to engage students. As the student narratives in this chapter suggest, sustained and cumulative engagement requires that students purposively recognize, reflect on, and respond to the many restarts that colleges offer them. Students don't always realize that part of taking responsibility for their education involves learning as much as they can from every assignment, lecture, or class discussion, especially in those courses in which they are less engaged. But some do. Sonya eloquently made this point in her response to the question about what advice she would give to students new to college:

I think, in the grand scheme of things, it doesn't matter how many awards that you win or what place you get in your classes. As soon as you have a feeling that you're learning, it's important. Don't be desperate if you get a C on a paper. Be desperate if you get an A on a paper and realize that you didn't learn anything.

Brad, in his senior year, voiced similar regrets about not having made the decision to learn as much as he could from every course he had taken:

You have to understand that not everybody has the same style that you might enjoy, and there are times when I've been frustrated, and that has been my fault. Not being willing to accept a different style or different method of teaching and take that for what it's worth. Just being sort of resentful instead of just accepting and saying, "Okay, this isn't exactly what I want, but I'm just going to milk it for all it's worth."

Colleges can help dissuade students of the expectation that all of their academic experiences will engage them equally. At the same time, colleges can help students better understand their role in making less engaging experiences more engaging.

SEVEN

❧ Practice for Life

What was the most important thing you learned about yourself in college?

CINDY, ALUMNA: I'm not quite sure what I did learn about myself in college. I guess I learned how to make decisions for myself. I think that's a very general and basic thing people learn while they're at college. These decisions that may have seemed for me at one point very out of the blue and very random, such as joining this club or choosing to focus on art history as opposed to history, were huge decisions for me and altered the course of how my life played out during college and post-college. So learning how to weigh options and make decisions was probably a pretty significant thing to learn and practice.

WE BEGAN THIS BOOK with the simple observation that college doesn't just start one day during orientation week and then end ceremonially some years later. College is a liminal space and place in which students make lots of decisions that serve as practice for the many more they will make as older adults. This is true of all colleges but especially true of residential colleges, where students live, learn, work, and play in close proximity to one another. College campuses are landscapes on which students are invited to create homes, find advisors and mentors, seek balance, make close friends, and become academically engaged. Like Cindy, however, most students don't realize until after they graduate that they are getting practice at making decisions every day when they are in college.

By asserting that college is practice for life, we don't mean to imply that college is not "real life." The many decisions, both large and small, that students make have tangible consequences for how they experience college. Colleges are both "real life" and practice for the adult life that comes after college. For many students, college marks the transition between living with family as adolescents and living on their own as adults. Although it is tempting to focus on residential colleges as safe places in which to practice adult decision-making—they are often described as "bubbles," after all—it is of greater importance that they are *places densely populated with decisions about who one is becoming and who one aspires to become.* In the lives of college students, these decisions implicate the personal as well as the social, the academic as well as the extracurricular. As fertile ground for a broad range of decisions, colleges are places where students can try on different selves, discarding some, retaining others—perhaps even returning to some they had previously tossed aside.

Many of the benefits of college as practice for life depend on how students view and respond to the decisions they confront. Students see some of the decisions they make in college as opportunities for reflection, learning, and change, but view others as obstacles or inconveniences, decisions they wish they didn't have to make or ones that they hope to make as quickly as possible and not have to justify to anyone, including themselves. When students approach decisions as opportunities rather than obstacles, they can use them to make adjustments to—and sometimes restart—their path through college. As demonstrated by the narratives in this book, students who are seeking greater balance, deeper learning, and more meaningful friendships (or a host of other things) can choose to try out new practices, take intellectual or personal risks, or create priorities among the many relationships and activities vying for their time. In doing so, they are building foundational skills, habits, and values associated with liberal education.

Insights about Becoming Liberally Educated

How students respond to the many decisions they must make in college is essential to understanding the process of becoming liberally educated. Five areas of decision-making in college offer practice at becoming liberally educated. These key decisions involve:

- Finding balance and focusing on the present
- Making and keeping friends
- Creating home and a sense of belonging
- Asking for and receiving advice
- Learning how to approach new ways of thinking and doing

Colleges are complex places animated by the many narratives of their students, and we have used several of these narratives to demonstrate how the decisions students make shape their paths through college. We chose this approach, in part, to emphasize that there is no "one size fits all" method to acquiring a strong, liberal education, no list of behaviors or "right" or "wrong" decisions guaranteeing success in college. As a consequence, we have shied away from offering prescriptive advice to students, parents, faculty, and college administrators, although we believe that our analysis provides each of these groups with novel insights into the lives of college students. We call attention to some of those insights here as we summarize the major findings from our research.

Time

Although many students arrive at college worried about how they'll adjust to an environment much less structured and scheduled than their high schools, few anticipate how difficult it will be to manage time or balance multiple commitments in their first year. The experiences of Jessica and Stephanie remind us that managing time and multiple commitments is difficult and requires much practice. Both spent considerable effort and time trying to find the right balance between their academic work and social activities. From them, we learned that doing this successfully requires much self-reflection and a holistic focus on creating balance rather than attempting to adopt a more generic, rigid, and fragmented focus on managing one's time.

Equally consequential but perhaps seldom anticipated by students is how quickly they will come to experience time in college as compressed and future-oriented. After being told that college is about exploring new interests and finding their "passions," the barrage of decisions they are asked to make—declaring a major, deciding whether to study abroad, securing summer internships or volunteering, taking graduate school examinations, among others—can make it difficult for even the most reflective and deliberative of students, such as Jason, to be focused on the present. If students appear to be opportunistic in their responses to these decisions by choosing courses, majors, or internships they believe will enhance their career opportunities after graduation, colleges can take much of the blame for their doing so. If students spend much of their time in college planning for being out of college, they can't fully appreciate the opportunities for engagement that a college education affords.

Connection

Compared to the significant difficulties that new college students have managing time, making friends happens relatively easily. Shared living spaces and a mutual desire for connection greatly facilitate early friendships among first-year students. If students do encounter social difficulties, they more likely involve making meaningful friendships rather than making any friends at all. Some came to realize that friendships formed in the first weeks and months of college had very little going for them. Not all students thought this was a bad thing; some wanted nothing more than friends to have fun with. Others simply lacked the motivation to make new friends, even when their current friendships were not particularly satisfying. Not surprisingly, students who reported having fulfilling friendships—and they were in the majority—often approached them with the same thoughtful consideration and purposeful action that Amy demonstrated. Amy felt trapped inside the social cocoon of her soccer team. Lacking a strong connection to any of her teammates, she made the difficult decision to distance herself from the team. Amy's risky action paid off: within a short period of time, she met two students who became her best friends for the duration of college.

Remaining physically and psychologically available for new social interactions, especially those involving students of different races, is another significant challenge confronting college students. Many students shared Sonya's genuine interest in meeting new people and exploring new friendship possibilities long after the first-year friendship market ended. Yet an even greater number became part of exclusive friendship networks that monopolized their time and attention. Many factors contribute to this social closure that became more apparent by the sophomore year. A major one is college's waning influence on students' social lives. College is simply not "getting in the way"[1] of students as much as it did in the first year when it assigned roommates and residences. Furthermore, many students, such as Dan, found a stable group of friends more preferable to the potential embarrassment and wasted effort that students like Sonya risked when trying to make new friends. But an aversion to social risk-taking means that students can miss out on the many opportunities provided by college restarts to broaden social perspectives, deepen cultural awareness, and develop practical social skills.

Home

Almost all students created a sense of home at their colleges. Not all of their narratives about creating their new homes, though, fit with the hyperbolic rhetoric our colleges often use—"these are the best four years of your life" or "your college friends will be the ones you'll keep forever." Students are given many opportunities to find different ways in which to develop a sense of belonging. In residential colleges, they move between their family homes and college homes frequently, measuring in each their changing sense of where they fit best. Furthermore, they move every year in college, choosing new roommates, new residences, and, in some cases, new countries in which to temporarily study.

Some students see each of these moves as an opportunity to reflect on what a sense of belonging means to them. Oma spent most of the first two years of college feeling "in-between," not at home in college but also no longer at home in her family home. After much hesitation, she created a home in college through strengthening her passion and connection to her academic program. After four years, she was reluctant to leave college and start home-making all over again in graduate school, but she also was reflective about how she would do things differently in her next move. Oma contrasts greatly with Adam who felt at home the minute he arrived. While recognizing differences between his cultural upbringing and the predominantly white middle-class culture prevailing on campus, he plunged in and made connections through his campus job, the organizations in which he chose to participate, and his social life. Unlike Oma, he felt an eagerness to leave college and create home again in a new place.

Oma and Adam both created a home at college but did so through very different paths, something of critical importance for students and college administrators to understand. It would be easy to see Adam as the more successful of the two because he felt as though he belonged quite early on in college and through the more typical path of social connections. But success at finding a home at college shouldn't be defined by how quickly it happens but by the degree to which students begin to understand what is important to them in making college home.

Advice

Most students enter college with limited experience seeking advice from anyone other than a parent or friend, especially those from under-resourced high schools who often did not experience close advising relationships with a guidance counselor. So it was somewhat surprising, given all the reports about helicopter parents, that so many students were no longer depending on their parents for academic advice by the end of their first year. Instead, they were consulting faculty advisors and developing meaningful, if sometimes limited, connections to them. The types of advice-seeking practiced in the first year mostly concerned academic issues, but some students went beyond this, establishing deeper relationships that allowed for reflective conversations with their advisors. Even the more limited relationships, though, required time, effort, initiative, and a clear commitment from both students and faculty. Given the relatively ambiguous roles of advisor and advisee, compared to those of teacher and student, students and faculty need to negotiate a mutually agreed upon relationship. Students may need to take the initiative, not relying so heavily on faculty to take the lead. Faculty also may need to recognize that students need encouragement and a clear indication that their advisors are interested in them. Students often want a "comfortable" relationship that steps outside the typical student and professor roles but don't know what atypical roles might entail.

Students who failed to establish a connection with their advisor did so for many reasons, but for quite a few the lack of a shared academic interest served as an impediment. Brad, for example, only developed a beneficial advising relationship once he declared a major but regretted not making more of an effort to find a way to connect with all his professors. And although Nileen's story was not typical in that she quickly established close mentoring relationships that lasted throughout her four years, most students, like Brad, were strongly connected to their major advisor and reaped the benefits of personalized advice as they prepared to leave college.

However, a sizeable minority of students, like Sam, navigated college on their own. These students were much less likely to meet with faculty outside of class and readily admitted that they hadn't taken advantage of opportunities to get to know their professors. Not only does the lack of practice they received at obtaining advice leave them at a disadvantage in their future endeavors, but we also suspect that they may have had a better college experience if they had gotten to know their professors (especially advisors). The many missed opportunities for seeking advice, or any kind of feedback, in college leaves these students less prepared to find a supportive advisor, or even a mentor, after college.

Engagement

Colleges pay a lot of attention to engagement because it's positively correlated to a number of valuable outcomes—persistence, personal development, learning, and satisfaction. To measure engagement, they often use large-scale surveys which ask students a series of questions about their academic behaviors in broad terms devoid of context and curriculum. Depending on how students answer these questions, they are labeled as "engaged" or "unengaged" as if it's a state of being rather than a condition that is contingent on particular courses, pedagogies, assignments, or professors. Adam was highly engaged in a political science course that focused on legal case studies, but unengaged in his political theory course. His engagement with academics was episodic, only happening in one or more courses and typically for limited periods of time during the semester. Michael's academic engagement was much easier to chart in some ways. He came to college interested in science and math and sustained those interests throughout his four years, digging deeply into his physics and chemistry classes. That said, even Michael's engagement story is more nuanced. He also was passionate about courses in history, classical political theory, and studio arts. And although engaged in science courses, he found some aspects *more* engaging than others—he liked to do lab research and run experiments more than writing up his research. Unlike Adam, Michael's engagement was sustained in multiple courses throughout every semester and cumulative in that he became more engaged with physics as he took more courses and did more work in the field.

College offers students practice in recognizing opportunities for engagement. Engagement happens not just when students find an intriguing discipline in which to major or a research experience that could lead to an honors project—the "big" decisions—but also when they find a fascinating reading or enlivening assignment—the "small" decisions. All faculty would love students like Michael who become passionate about our fields and work, and many curricular practices are built for them—requiring a major or capstone research project. But many students like Adam, and those even less engaged than Adam, are sparked by particular courses, assignments, or professors from time to time rather than being engaged in a sustained or cumulative fashion. These students aren't "engaged" or "unengaged." Instead they move between these two states throughout their college years.

Insights for Higher Education

The above discussion of what our analysis offers to parents, students, and faculty ignores, for the most part, the role played by colleges. If, as we claim, students become liberally educated through a messy process of figuring out how to use large and small decisions as opportunities to learn about themselves, others, and the world, what role do institutional structures play in framing these decisions? Colleges make extensive efforts to shape the environment in which first-year students develop social networks. They also construct advising systems, general education requirements, grading policies, and many other structures and practices that make up the college environment. Yet as much as colleges want to scaffold "good" decision-making among their students, they also want students to assume responsibility for making their own decisions, experience successes and failures, accept the consequences of their decisions, and reflect on what they've learned from the choices they have made. If college is practice for later-life decision-making, then both support and responsibility are necessary. Colleges confront the challenge of managing the tension between college structure and student choice so that they can create supportive environments that cushion student decision-making but don't excessively constrain it.

College administrators and faculty think about how best to manage this tension, and their often conflicting resolutions to it are the stuff of which contentious debate, disappointment, and dissatisfaction are made. The seemingly never-ending recalibrations of practices and policies that colleges undertake are evidence of this. Will changes in how advisors are assigned and trained foster better student decisions about what courses to take and how to approach learning in them? Will first-year seminar programs and a required senior thesis increase the number of students who engage with big ideas? Will redesigned orientation programs and different training for residential hall advisors help more students feel at home earlier in college?

The self-reflective exercises undertaken by colleges demonstrate the seriousness with which they approach their mission to provide excellent educational experiences for their students. Regularly asking questions about whether programs or policies are achieving their desired goals models for students the importance and value of critical thinking. Our research into the everyday lives of students, however, makes us wonder if many of the questions colleges are asking of themselves—although well-intentioned and helpful—are ones that tinker more with the edges of the college experience rather than with its core. What questions aren't colleges asking themselves, and why aren't they asking them?

There are many practices, policies, and structures whose assumptions are seldom questioned: why we expect students to start college immediately after high school, why a traditional college education takes four years to complete, why course grades are the predominant measure of success in college, to name but a few. To be sure, some colleges and universities have begun to question these practices, but most have not. Are some college practices so inviolate that they don't merit scrutiny, or are they so deeply embedded in the culture that few are willing to take them on?

We conclude by examining two such rarely-questioned practices. The first is requiring students to declare a major. There is widespread agreement and very little debate over requiring students to complete a major in order to graduate, but often a fair amount of disagreement and much debate about what constitutes a major (e.g., the nature and number of required courses) and the decision-making process of declaring one (e.g., the year in which a major is declared, whether or not multiple or self-designed majors are allowed). This is true for virtually all colleges.

The second, which lies at the heart of residential colleges, is limiting efforts to shape students' social lives primarily to the first year of college. Few students, faculty, or administrators would question the practice of assigning roommates and residence halls to first-year students. Although college administrators may frequently debate how best to make roommate assignments for first-year students and whether first-year students should be housed in their own dorms or in multi-class ones, few would suggest extending the practice of assigning roommates and mandating other social experiences beyond the first year.

Both of these practices are seen as fundamental because of their presumed benefits to the academic or social experiences of college students, but they represent quite different orientations toward balancing traditional college practices and student choice. Colleges offer students a vast array of courses from which to choose and they encourage curricular exploration, but they don't give students total discretion over the number of courses or credit hours they need in order to graduate. Instead, colleges require students to declare majors because it is assumed that digging deeply into a discipline or subject will promote certain habits of mind—what we have referred to as sustained and cumulative engagement—that won't necessarily follow from students' individual course preferences. Requiring students to declare a major is an example of college practice trumping student choice.

By contrast, college practices intended to shape students' social and residential lives run in the opposite direction. New students experience the strong force of college the minute they set foot on campus. They are expected to attend orientation events they had no hand in creating. They are told where they will live and are assigned strangers with whom they will share a room for the year. For the most part, new students welcome the involvement of their colleges. After all, who else would make these decisions? They also understand that colleges adopt these practices to build broad social networks connecting individuals who are different from one another in many ways. But after getting things moving in the first year, colleges back off, and often opportunities for making new friends or learning from others with different backgrounds—the things colleges worked so hard to encourage among new students—recede. Allowing upperclass students to fully manage their own social lives is an example of student choice trumping college practice. Why do colleges rely so heavily on individual students to sustain and hopefully deepen their experiences with difference?

In what follows, we extend our critique of the assumptions that extensive study within a discipline necessarily leads to greater academic engagement and that the broad social networks created in the first year will persist in subsequent years without college interference. We also offer some suggestions for how colleges might facilitate more opportunities for students to experience greater engagement and more meaningful encounters with difference. Put differently, what can colleges do to give students more experience in making decisions that can serve as practice for life?

How Can Colleges Promote Greater Academic Engagement?

Virtually every college and university in the United States requires that students choose at least one major field of study. Specialization—acquiring the epistemological, theoretical, and methodological tools of a discipline's trade—is seen as essential to fostering academic engagement and developing critical thinking skills among college students. This makes sense, given that faculty and college administrators are typically people for whom delving deeply into a field of study resulted in more rigorous inquiry and was a successful path to engagement. But is this true of most college students today? Is so much emphasis on the choice of a major deserved and, of greater importance, are the assumptions that undergird this perspective justified?

As we've noted at various times, students viewed the declaration of their major as the most important decision they would make in college. This perspective on the purpose of college had significant consequences for them well before they started. Many chose their major while in high school and used this decision to limit their college search, only exploring schools reported to have strong programs in their intended major field. It was not unusual for high school students to be asked by family and friends about their intended major and, for that matter, even how that major would figure into their career plans following graduation from college. Once they arrived on campus, many were disappointed if their assigned faculty advisor was in a different field than the one in which they planned to major. How could that person possibly offer them useful advice about their first year of college? Students, like Adam, declared majors in subjects in which they had little interest because they thought those subjects were required for their intended careers. Some students got so locked into a major that it was hard for them to imagine any other, no matter how miserable they were. Others, like Dan, had less room in their course schedules to broadly explore the curriculum as they tried to complete the sometimes extensive requirements for their major.

For those who entered college less committed to a particular field of study, choosing a major triggered a good deal of anxiety. Students viewed courses that didn't help them refine their search for a major as costly—at best, identifying which disciplines students didn't want to major in, at worst, a "waste of time." Having been told that they would have lots of time to make this decision when they first arrived on campus, students nearing the major declaration deadline felt as though they had been misled. The focus on declaring a major and considering which majors best prepare them for their lives after college also perpetuated students' future orientation at the cost of being able to live more fully in the present.

Regardless of their path to a major, most students viewed declaring one as a pivotal point in their college experience. Our research, however, demonstrates that students' experiences with their majors can be quite mixed. Although digging deeply fostered engagement for many students, for others it did not. For Oma, Brad, Nileen, and Michael, completing the required courses for a major led to deeper and sustained academic engagement. Oma's history major (and her interest in African history, in particular) was the vehicle that initiated and fueled her academic engagement, but it was also essential to the (albeit limited) sense of home she was able to develop in college. By contrast, students like Dan and Adam were hamstrung by major requirements in their junior and senior years and, in Adam's case, his academic engagement suffered.

For students whose academic interests are *vertically-aligned,* taking more courses in their major creates a powerful path to engagement. They can't wait to take their next chemistry or English or economics course because of their broad and hierarchical interest in the subject matter, and the analytic methods of these disciplines fascinate them. Traditional college structures in which curriculum and departments are organized around disciplines serve these students well. Our research suggests, however, that many fewer students exhibit patterns of sustained or cumulative engagement within their major field of study; most are episodically engaged with courses both within and outside of their majors. If requiring students to declare a major is not a primary vehicle for engagement for many students, what might colleges do to create more opportunities for engagement?

We believe that promising answers to this question will follow from *identifying more horizontal linkages* among subjects, courses, and pedagogies in the curriculum and making these explicit to students. Engagement is linked to either curriculum—the subjects that are taught—or pedagogy—how these subjects are taught. Often it is a product of both. Students who make connections between courses across fields largely do so on their own, with little help from their colleges.[2] To the extent that colleges provide interdisciplinary curricular road maps to students, they tend to focus on topics that are addressed in multiple departments (e.g., courses that deal with international development or climate change). Students interested in American studies, for example, might find a long list of courses across departments that focus on the history, literature, politics, and economics of the Americas, but if their interests were in public writing or, like Dan, in argumentation and moral questions, would they know which courses to take?

Similarly, students who become engaged through particular kinds of pedagogy—group work, simulations, and community fieldwork—have a difficult time making those linkages. Jim, for example, was not engaged with most of his courses with the exception of one that focused on a semester-long project that asked him to study a topic from multiple perspectives. How could Jim find other courses like this one? What about students like Michael, who particularly liked science courses that allowed him to manipulate instruments? Would he be able to deduce which ones those were from the college catalog? No doubt simple changes, like providing more (or different) information about individual courses or providing user-friendly ways to sort through this information, would help more students negotiate curricular and pedagogical pathways that prompt greater engagement. This will only work if students—perhaps with the encouragement of advisors and mentors—take on the work that Dan did: reflecting on what he found engaging in his philosophy courses and using that reflection as an opportunity to restart college with a different perspective on his major.

Neither colleges nor students should assume that pursuing a major will lead to sustained and cumulative engagement because, as our research suggests, this structure only works for some students. Others must craft for themselves alternative paths through the curriculum that then need to be grafted onto existing major requirements. Yet others remain, at best, episodically engaged as they move through the requirements for their majors. By learning more about how and when students become engaged, colleges can create multiple paths to "going deep" and, in doing so, increase the likelihood that students will find more of their curricular experiences engaging.

How Can Colleges Promote Sustained Interaction with Difference?

When residential colleges use their discretionary authority to choose roommates and residences for first-year students, they are quite successful in creating social environments that bring diverse students together. First-year students talked enthusiastically about the variety of perspectives and experiences they were exposed to through their roommates, others who lived on their dorm floors, and peers they met on orientation trips or at first-year events. A common sight at all of our colleges is large groups of first-year students moving like schools of fish from dorms to dining halls. And even though individuals within these groups may not really know or like each other in the future, because they have been placed together, they interact. Recall the student who talked about how making friends with her floormates meant that she "socialized with different people that had different priorities and different social preferences," something she strongly valued about her first-year experience.

The current modus operandi at most colleges—one endorsed by both students and institutions—is to assign roommates and orchestrate, sometimes quite heavy-handedly, peer interactions through things like orientation trips, dorm events, or mixers for first-year students only. After the first year, students are pretty much left alone. They choose their own roommates, whether to live off campus or alone in a single room, whether to spend their time on teams or clubs or participate in activities with those who share their interests—playing music, hiking, or writing for the student newspaper. Making these decisions has great value. It gives students important practice in deciding what is important to them in their living environments, how they might want to construct homes as adults after college, and how and with whom they want to spend time. This valuable practice in decision-making, however, often comes at the price of narrowing students' social networks.

When colleges turn over housing decisions to students and scale back on other forms of "required" social interactions like orientation trips or dorm events, diversity is sacrificed and social closure becomes the norm. As we've seen, Abby described how, even on her diverse college campus, students ended up "unconsciously a lot of the time . . . gravitating towards a group of people with whom you feel comfortable. So they're more similar." Although we aren't suggesting that only interactions with diverse peers are of value or that there aren't exceptions to social closure, we do see great value in learning that takes place when students interact with others who have different perspectives and life experiences—when students find themselves, at least occasionally, out of their comfort zones. The hallmarks of liberal education include such things as "openness to new friendships" and "an appreciation of 'difference,'"[3] and our colleges have done much over the last two decades to increase the racial and social class diversity in their student populations. How can we find some middle ground between the relative lack of institutional engineering for diversity after the first year and the institutional practice of assigning roommates every year or mandating social events? Are there places other than where students live that colleges could use to counteract narrowing social interactions and to encourage the diversity experiences that students, educators, and administrators desire?

We believe that many opportunities for increasing students' interactions with difference in the academic sphere have yet to be fully exploited. Upperclass students often said that the classroom was the primary place in which they encountered diversity. This was true not just for courses for which diversity was the subject matter, but across the curriculum. One Latino student observed that the different perspectives and teaching styles among the faculty broadened his own outlook on the world, and "then also, there are the students who will participate in class and bring their own opinions in class for everyone to hear." He called classrooms "the main melting pot" for diversity on campus.

Students commented about engaging with difference in many more classes than just ethnic studies courses or ones in which race, class, and sexuality were the subject. Essential to these classroom interactions was the creation of "safe environments" which promoted trust and openness among students and faculty. These interactions could be classroom discussions of ideas within a subject area, or one-on-one conversations with peers or faculty—times and places that allow students to listen and respond to ideas and perspectives different from their own.

This is not to say that students always responded positively to these interactions. A few students, almost all students of color, recounted some very negative academic encounters with diversity. They talked about insensitive discussions where faculty and peers made negative comments about people different from themselves or resorted to racial, social class, or gender stereotypes. But even many of these students suggested that courses and classrooms are, after the first year, the primary places in which they interacted over an extended period of time with faculty and peers who thought differently from them. As one African American student said, "It's got to be academics because socially, there's always going to be that tension around diversity."

Because almost all students eventually find their way into cohesive and supportive social groups, institutions hesitate to disrupt that comfort. Often colleges attempt to facilitate interactions among diverse groups of students through nonacademic venues, such as programs on how to have constructive dialogues on controversial issues, campus dinners with "strangers" where you eat a meal with people you don't know, or community service projects that combine different student groups working together on the same project. These efforts are significant, but they may not be maximizing the impact that colleges hope to make of student diversity. If students are looking to their coursework and faculty to provide opportunities to expand their social awareness and cultural understanding, can colleges do more in the academic arena to make this happen?

A good first step would be to acknowledge the key role that faculty can and should play in encouraging students to engage with perspectives and individuals who differ from them in meaningful ways. Faculty teaching courses where issues of power, difference, and marginalization are recurrent themes are probably most aware of this. Yet almost all academic disciplines "offer opportunities for the reflection on issues of current political or social importance . . . At some point in their lives, all professors have to explain to the uninitiated why the work they do matters to the world."[4] Faculty-led discussions of these kinds would do much to continue students' interactions with diversity that were so much a part of their first year of college.

We acknowledge that encouraging faculty to incorporate into their courses an appreciation of multiple perspectives and an openness to diversity, similar to how we promote writing and quantitative reasoning across the curriculum, could seem burdensome. Just as they are reluctant to view themselves as expert teachers of writing or quantitative reasoning, faculty might claim that they don't know how to lead productive discussions about difference in their courses, even discussions about different perspectives on issues in their own disciplines. These reservations, however, should not discourage either faculty or college administrators from recognizing that the responsibility of building diverse and inclusive college communities is shared by everyone who contributes to learning in those communities.

Reflections, Regrets, and Imagined Restarts

Institutional changes to the major and the curriculum can help students make choices and act in ways that we believe will deepen academic engagement and promote diverse social interactions. There are limits, however, to what colleges can do to accomplish these outcomes. Ultimately, students must choose for themselves their academic and social priorities. For many, those priorities now tilt in the direction of choosing options that appear safe—choosing majors based on their job prospects—and comfortable—choosing to socialize with one close group of (similar-to-me) friends. Why? We believe the primary answer rests in the fact that the loftier goals of liberal education receive equivocal support, at best, from other influential forces—parents, prospective employers, and the mass media.[5] Moreover, faculty and administrators do not always persuasively and consistently present these goals to students as things worth striving for. It is not surprising then that many students adopt the limited definition of college success—good grades and good friends—that is validated by the wider cultural context and the colleges in which their education takes place.

If this is the bad news, then the good news is that students who choose to enroll in college tend to be receptive to both academic engagement and social diversity. We know this from interviews with students who spoke enthusiastically and passionately about a course, a professor, or an assignment. We know this from the many students who found first-year and study abroad interactions with those different from themselves to be exhilarating and enlightening. Clearly, academic engagement and social diversity are not the educational equivalent of cod liver oil: good for your health but not pleasant to drink. If students get a taste of engagement and diversity, they tend to like it.

They also wish they had had more of it. The regrets and imagined restarts voiced by students reflect the desire for deeper academic engagement and broader social connections, including more opportunities for diversity experiences. Very few students wished that they had taken easier classes so they could have graduated with a higher GPA. Although many students consistently mentioned achievement goals every semester, when looking back, they wish they had been more aggressive about finding their passions and being engaged with courses. They also desired greater social connection and wished they had done more—joined more clubs, played more sports, made more friends, gotten to know more professors—and spent more time interacting with those who were different from them. At the same time, they wished they had slowed down, found more balance, and resisted the future-oriented nature of time in college.

Contradictions like these are not unique to college students. We all want more, including more time and balance, but they point to an acknowledgment from students that college is full of opportunities. There is both regret that they didn't explore more and an understanding that exploring more would have had its downsides as well. In reflecting back on their four years of college, they came to the realization that they had more opportunities to create and shape their college experience—to restart college—than they had ever imagined or exercised.

APPENDIX

NOTES

ACKNOWLEDGMENTS

INDEX

Appendix

In this section, we describe in more detail the methodology that underlies our project.

Background of Our Study

Our project began in 2005 when academic administrators, institutional research staff, faculty, and students began meeting to discuss the possibility of designing and implementing a novel approach to student assessment using a variety of research methods. At the center of these various methodologies would be one-on-one interviews with students in each year of college. From those initial planning meetings, the broad outlines of the project began to take shape:

- Longitudinally track students from the time they entered college to the time they graduated (and possibly after graduation as well).
- Oversample Asian American, African American, Latino/a, and international students to permit group comparisons.
- Focus on residential liberal arts colleges in New England and include multiple sites.
- Involve senior administrators, institutional research staff, faculty, and students at each step of the research project.

The New England Consortium on Assessment and Student Learning (NECASL) emerged from those initial meetings. In May of 2005, the Teagle Foundation provided the first of two three-year grants to fund the project—with the second awarded in May 2008. Each college in the study provided substantial internal funding for the project. The Spencer Foundation and the Andrew W. Mellon Foundation provided additional external funding in the project's third year (2008–2009). NECASL began with six member colleges (Bates, Bowdoin, Colby, Smith, Trinity, and Wellesley) and grew to seven colleges in 2007 with the addition of Middlebury. Wellesley and Smith Colleges are the only two single-sex colleges (both are female) in the study. Our regional accreditation agency, the New England Association of Schools and Colleges (NEASC) also participated in NECASL since the beginning.

Project Goals and Strengths

From its inception, NECASL sought to expand the discussion of student assess-ment by digging more deeply into the experiences of college students as they were occurring. NECASL's goals have been to: (1) better understand student transitions from high school to college, (2) study how students make academic and social deci-sions in relation to institutional policies and practices, (3) involve multiple voices and viewpoints in student assessment, and (4) share institutional research among ourselves and others.

NECASL's strengths are derived from its collaborative nature both at the in-ter- and intra-institutional level, its multiple methodologies, and its longitudinal design. Our inter-institutional collaboration allowed us to compare our colleges to identify "best," or at least better, practices and policies and suggest reforms. Undertaking a seven-college collaboration has also provided a larger and more di-verse sample of students than would have been possible with a single-site study. At an intra-institutional level, NECASL has brought together senior administrators, institutional research staff, faculty, and students from each of our campuses. The direct involvement of faculty, and especially students, in all aspects of the project has been invaluable.

We chose personal interviewing with broad, open-ended questions as the center of our methodological approach because interviewing is ideally suited to exploring how students make decisions affecting their college experiences as well as how those decisions are affected by institutional policies and practices.[1] Much of what we found led us to conclude that more conventional ways of assessing college student achievement, particularly close-ended survey questions with preconceived ideas about what is important to measure, are incomplete and inadequate. We would not have been able to write this book had we based our study entirely on survey data.

In addition to personal interviewing, we administered annual cohort surveys to all members of the Class of 2010 including the panel participants. These cohort surveys allowed us to verify the representativeness of our panel participants when compared to their entire class. We also collected institutional data on the panel participants including, but not limited to, admissions applications and grade tran-scripts. Institutional data made it possible to assess the validity of students' subjec-tive reports of their progress and experience. It also avoided the need to ask about sensitive topics, like grades, that might have affected interviewer-interviewee rap-port. Panel participants were also asked to submit at least one writing sample at the end of their first, sophomore, and junior years.

With multiple institutions and many individuals involved in the study, research-ers paid close attention to insuring the confidentiality of all student data. Each school obtained IRB approval for the project, and all of those who worked on the project signed a data-confidentiality and nondisclosure agreement. All panel par-ticipants signed consent forms that allowed NECASL to access their student records.

Panel Selection, Composition, and Retention

For the longitudinal interview portion of our study, we selected a panel of students from the Class of 2010 who entered college in the fall of 2006. We used a random sampling methodology that was stratified by race (at all colleges) and gender (at the coeducational colleges); this resulted in a sample that intentionally over-represented students of color and international students to help us examine how these less-frequently studied groups of students experienced college. Our target was to recruit 252 students, with thirty-six students on each of our seven campuses such that six were Asian American, six were African American, six were Latino/a, six were international, and twelve were domestic white students. At the coeducational colleges, we selected equal numbers of male and female students within each group (e.g., three Asian American men and three Asian American women). In addition, one college included a small sample of Native American students. At each school, we largely met our target; thirty-five to thirty-nine students agreed to participate.

Six colleges began conducting interviews in the fall of 2006 with incoming first-year students; one college joined the project in its second year and began conducting interviews in the fall of 2007 with sophomores. Most students were invited to join the panel in the summer before they arrived on campus. In the fall of 2006, 201 first-year students joined the panel, with another fifteen first-year students added in the early spring of 2006. In the fall of 2007, thirty-nine additional sophomores from the seventh college were added to the panel. Thus, the "initial" sample included the 216 first-year students from the original six colleges, and the thirty-nine sophomores whose college joined in the second year.

Initial Coeducational Sample: Gender and Race/Ethnicity

- Gender: ninety-four females and eighty-seven males
- Race/Ethnicity: thirty Asian American, twenty-three African American, twenty-five Latino/a, three Native American, twenty-five international, and seventy-five domestic white students
- Gender by Race/Ethnicity: fifteen Asian American females and fifteen Asian American males, twelve African American females and eleven African American males, fourteen Latina females and eleven Latino males, three Native American females, twelve international females and thirteen international males, and thirty-eight domestic white females and thirty-seven domestic white males

Initial Single Sex Sample: Gender and Race/Ethnicity

- Gender: seventy-four females
- Race/Ethnicity: twelve Asian American, thirteen African American, eleven Latina, thirteen international, and twenty-five domestic white females

Initial Full Sample: Gender, Race/Ethnicity, and Additional Characteristics

- Gender: 168 females and 87 males
- Race/Ethnicity: forty-two Asian American, thirty-six African American, thirty-six Latino/a, three Native American, thirty-eight international, and one hundred domestic white students
- Gender by Race/Ethnicity: twenty-seven Asian American females and fifteen Asian American males, twenty-five African American females and eleven African American males, twenty-five Latina females and eleven Latino males, three Native American females, twenty-five international females and thirteen international males, and sixty-three domestic white females and thirty-seven domestic white males

Additional Characteristics[2]

- 60.5% received financial aid
- 33.7% were first generation[3]
- 59.5% attended a public high school, 7% attended a parochial high school, and 33.3% attended a private high school
- 54% were from the Northeast, 22% from the South, 7% from the Midwest, and 17% from the West
- 18% played on a varsity athletic team
- 49.8% studied abroad for one or two semesters during their junior year

For the colleges that began the project in 2006 with first-year students, we attempted to replace panelists who left the project in the first year.[4] During the first year, we lost thirty-six students (an attrition rate of 17%). Of those who left, twenty-four were female and twelve were male; eight were Asian American, six were African American, seven were Latino/a, six were international, and nine were domestic white students. The dropout rates were equivalent for females and males (16%), and roughly equivalent for the five main groups based on race/ethnicity (rates ranged from 17% to 21%). To replace these students, we added thirteen panelists to the sample: twelve were female and one was male, two were Asian American, two were African American, three were Latino, three were international, and three were domestic white students. For the college that joined the project in the sophomore year, only one student dropped out that year.

We interviewed 216 students in the fall of their first year and 199 in the spring. We interviewed between 182 and 192 students in each of the following semesters, and between 205 and 212 students at least once each year. By the senior year, we had collected 1,728 interviews. We assessed retention in a number of ways. First, we considered the extent to which students participated in each year the study was conducted at their college: 167 students (65% of the initial sample) were interviewed each year. Second, we considered the number of students who were with us in their first year and in their senior year: 196 (77%) were interviewed in the first year and again in the senior year. Looking at retention in two additional ways, we found that 135 (53%) students participated in all, or all but one, interview and 83 (33%) participated in all interviews. Thus, our retention rate, defined in a number of ways, was quite high for a study of this nature.

We also conducted interviews with 137 panelists (54% of the initial sample) one year after graduation.

Interviewing Process

We attempted to interview each panelist up to eleven times: three times in the first year (once in mid-fall, once in early spring, and once in late spring), two in each of sophomore, junior, and senior years (once in fall and once in spring), and once one year after graduation.

The majority of interviewers were upperclass students, typically majoring in the social sciences.[5] Prior to the first round of interviewing, all interviewers attended a two-day training workshop in August of 2006.[6] This workshop included sessions on good interviewing techniques with particular attention to active listening and the use of follow-up probes to elicit detailed responses. The workshop also provided training with digital voice recorders, videotaped mock interviews (students interviewing students), and discussion of research ethics and how to handle sensitive or urgent information. New interviewers who joined the project were trained at their home institution by their faculty supervisors and current student interviewers.

We used a semi-structured interview format in which the interviewer initiated questions and probed for detailed answers. Interviewers followed an organized list of questions but had the flexibility to reorder questions or adjust the language of the questions as the conversation unfolded. They were allowed to answer questions posed by the panelists and to clarify questions as needed. Interviewers did their best to maintain a natural conversational manner; they were allowed to let the panelists steer the interview in any direction they wished (which often led to some of our most interesting findings) but were trained to return to the interview schedule to ensure that all questions were asked and thoroughly answered.

Prior to each round of interviewing, interviewers met with their faculty supervisors to review the interview schedules and best interview practices. Our student interviewers reported that they found participation in the project to be academically rewarding—being able to participate in research that was important to college students and consequential social science research—and personally enriching—inspiring them to be more self-reflective about their college experiences. A number of these student interviewers have pursued careers in higher education or the social sciences. The student interviewers were paid to conduct the interviews.

Before each interview, the interviewers contacted the panelists and arranged a convenient time and location for the interview. Each semester there were target timeframes within which we tried to conduct the interviews in order to capture students' narratives at the time they were making key decisions. The majority of the interviews were conducted face-to-face in a quiet space on campus, one that would allow the panelists to feel comfortable talking about confidential aspects of their lives. When panelists were off-campus (either due to a leave of absence or participation in study abroad), interviews were conducted via telephone or Skype. Each interview lasted from 45 to 120 minutes, with an average of about 60 minutes.

At the first interview, the interviewer obtained written informed consent from each panelist granting access to their college records and letting them know that interview information would be published without revealing their identity. At each interview, we also obtained consent to digitally record the interview. Each panelist received an identification code for record keeping and a pseudonym for publication purposes.

Each college in the consortium developed its own practice and policies for panelist compensation but most provided them with some monetary compensation (typically gift cards). Panelists were also made to feel part of an important project; they were given multiple opportunities to express their opinions, ask questions, and share experiences in lengthy interviews. In the late spring of their senior year, some of the colleges invited panelists to a reception to thank them for their support of the project. Panelists were reminded that by attending this event their participation would be revealed to other panelists and to the college staff who attended the reception. Some colleges also provided panelists with a bound copy of their interviews.

Interview Schedules

Faculty, students, academic administrators, and institutional research staff collaborated on designing the interview schedules. For the first two years of the project, questions were pilot tested using focus groups from the Class of 2009. As we constructed the interview schedules, we carefully worded the questions to be nondirective and open-ended. For example, instead of asking panelists if they were getting along well with their roommates, advisors, or professors, we asked them to describe their interactions with those individuals; instead of asking them if they were worried about declaring their major in their sophomore year, we asked them what was most on their mind? We believe this was one of the greatest strengths of our study, as it allowed students to describe their experiences to us without exposing them to our biases or expectations.

Each interview schedule was designed to capture not only broad aspects of the student experience, but also particular aspects that varied by semester. Every semester students were asked questions about their academic experiences (the classes they were taking and how they decided what to take, their experiences/perceptions of their classes, their interactions with advisors and other faculty, and their study habits), their social experiences (interactions with family and friends, experiences with roommates and floormates, and participation in clubs, organizations, or athletic teams), and their personal experiences (ability to manage life and time, balancing competing demands from their academic and social lives, whom they consulted for advice). Some questions were asked every year (definitions of success, whether college felt like home, what's on your mind as you start the year, advice to other students, self-assessment of learning). And other questions asked about important events as they occurred (thoughts about transferring, declaring a major, study abroad, finding summer internships, senior theses and honors projects, life after graduation). Finally, a few questions concerned particular areas of interest to our institutions (e.g., definitions of diversity and experiences with diversity, perception of the typical student at their college, views on participating in upcoming elections).

Transcription and Analysis

Most interviews were fully recorded but some were incomplete due to technical issues with the recorder, loud ambient noise from the surroundings, a poor telephone/Skype connection, or difficulty understanding what the panelist was saying. Following each interview, all digital recordings were loaded to secure sites at each school. Interviewers took minimal notes during interviews but submitted post-interview reports at the end of each interview.

Recorded interviews were professionally transcribed. Student research assistants were trained to edit the transcribed interviews to remove all identifying information. NVivo, a qualitative data analysis software package, was used to code and analyze the interviews.

Our analysis of the interviews involved a variety of strategies. We read all responses to particular questions, semester by semester as well as year by year. We read entire interviews for students in particular semesters. We read all of the interviews for numerous panelists and developed case studies on various aspects of the student's college experience. This case study approach helped us see college as a series of decisions that provided opportunities for restarts.

Survey Instruments

Although this book focuses on the panel interviews, our findings were informed by the results of cohort surveys. The consortium colleges surveyed the entire Class of 2010 in the sophomore, junior, and senior years. We created the sophomore and junior surveys but, for the senior survey, we started with the Consortium on Financing Higher Education (COFHE)[7] senior survey to which we added our own items. We are indebted to our institutional research staff for helping us to develop these surveys, maintain the extensive longitudinal database, and analyze the survey responses.

The sophomore survey was administered in 2008 to the entire Class of 2010 at all seven colleges. About two-thirds of the Class responded to the survey (2,641 students). The response rates varied across the colleges from a low of 48% to a high of 78%, with a median response rate of 68%. The survey covered (among other topics) academic advising and support, choice of major, engagement in courses, course selection, coursework, various aspects of social and residential life, personal well-being, and extracurricular activities. Several schools continue to administer this survey to subsequent cohorts of sophomores in an effort to establish longitudinal databases for assessment purposes.

In the spring of 2009, we administered three junior class surveys: one for juniors who remained on campus, another for those who studied abroad, and a third for juniors who had returned from studying abroad in the fall of 2008. In this book, we only report results from the on-campus survey. About 37% of the entire Class took the on-campus survey (1,475 students). The percent of students who took the survey varied across the colleges from a low of 25% to high of 61%, with a median of 30%. The percentages of students who took this survey are lower, in part, because it was not administered to students who were studying abroad. These surveys focused on students' experiences in their chosen major field of study and in their study abroad program (for those who opted to study abroad), and how the two interacted.

The senior survey, administered in the spring of 2010 to the entire Class of 2010 at all seven colleges, was based on the COFHE senior survey. About 60% of the Class responded to the survey (2,304 students). The response rates varied across the colleges from a low of 32% to a high of 90%, with a median response rate of 57%. Five of the seven consortium colleges were members of COFHE in 2010. The survey covered the following topics: student satisfaction with various aspects of their academic experience and their major field of study; participation in off-campus academic experiences (e.g., internships, study abroad); quality of campus services, facilities, and campus/residential life; self-reported change in abilities; interactions with students of different backgrounds; participation in extracurricular activities or working for pay; and post-graduate plans.

Finally, we administered a one-year-out survey to those students in the Class of 2010 who had graduated. It asked alumni/ae what they have been doing since graduation, how well they believed their college prepared them for their current activities, the extent of contact they had with friends from college, and how much they valued a variety of behaviors or goals.

Notes

1. Restarting College

1. Plato, *Cratylus* 402a.

2. For expense critiques see, for example, William J. Bennett and David Wilezol, *Is College Worth It? A Former United States Secretary of Education and a Liberal Arts Graduate Expose the Broken Promise of Higher Education* (Nashville, TN: Thomas Nelson, 2013); Andrew Hacker and Claudia Dreifus, *Higher Education? How Colleges Are Wasting Our Money and Failing Our Kids and What We Can Do about It* (New York, NY: St. Martin's Press, 2011); and Richard Vedder, *Going Broke by Degree: Why College Costs Too Much* (Washington, DC: AIE Press, 2004). For structure critiques see, for example, Randy Bass, "Disrupting Ourselves: The Problem of Learning in Higher Education," *EDUCAUSE Review* 47, no. 2 (March/April 2012), http://www.educause.edu/ero/article/disrupting-ourselves-problem-learning-higher-education; Clayton M. Christensen, *The Innovative University: Changing the DNA of Higher Education from the Inside Out* (San Francisco, CA: Jossey-Bass, 2011); Louis Menand, *The Marketplace of Ideas: Reform and Resistance in the American University* (New York, NY: W. W. Norton, 2010); and Mark C. Taylor, "End the University as We Know It," *New York Times*, April 27, 2009, A23. For outcome critiques see, for example, Kevin Carey, "Americans Think We Have the World's Best Colleges. We Don't," *New York Times*, June 28, 2014, http://www.nytimes.com/2014/06/29/upshot/americans-think-we-have-the-worlds-best-colleges-we-dont.html?_r&_r=0&abt=0002&abg=1.

3. Richard Arum and Josipa Roksa, *Academically Adrift: Limited Learning on College Campuses* (Chicago, IL: Chicago University Press, 2011); Richard Arum and Josipa Roksa, *Aspiring Adults Adrift: Tentative Transitions of College Graduates* (Chicago, IL: Chicago University Press, 2014).

4. Arum and Roksa, *Academically Adrift*; Arum and Roksa, *Aspiring Adults Adrift*.

5. For a review of these issues see, for example, Andrew Delbanco, "MOOCs of Harvard: Will Online Education Dampen the College Experience? Yes. Will It Be Worth It? Well . . . ," *New Republic*, March 31, 2013, http://www.newrepublic.com/article/112731/moocs-will-online-education-ruin-university-experience. Or Geoffrey A. Fowler, "An Early Report Card on Massive Open Online Courses: MOOCs

Promise to Change the Face of Higher Education, One Giant Classroom at a Time. Here's What They're Doing Well—And How They Can Do Better," *Wall Street Journal*, October 8, 2013, http://online.wsj.com/news/articles/SB100014240527023037 59604579093400834738972. Or Michael Horn and Clayton Christensen, "Beyond the Buzz, Where Are MOOCS Really Going?" *Wired*, February 20, 2013, http://www.wired.com/2013/02/beyond-the-mooc-buzz-where-are-they-going-really/.

6. See, for example, "Performance-Based Funding for Higher Education," National Conference of State Legislatures (July 31, 2015), http://www.ncsl.org/research/education/performance-funding.aspx. And "Massachusetts' Big Bet on Performance-Based College Funding," *Governing: The States and Localities* (November 2013), http://www.governing.com/topics/education/gov-massachusetts-bet-on-performance-college-funding.html.

7. For example, see Andrew Delbanco, *College: What It Was, Is, and Should Be* (Princeton, NJ: Princeton University Press, 2012); Martha C. Nussbaum, *Not for Profit: Why Democracy Needs the Humanities* (Princeton, NJ: Princeton University Press, 2010); Mark William Roche, *Why Choose the Liberal Arts?* (Notre Dame, IN: University of Notre Dame Press, 2010); Michael S. Roth, *Beyond the University: Why Liberal Education Matters* (New Haven, CT: Yale University Press, 2014); and Carol G. Schneider, "Liberal Education: Slip-Sliding Away?" in *Declining by Degrees: Higher Education at Risk*, ed. Richard H. Hersh and John Morrow (New York, NY: Palgrave Macmillan, 2005), 61–76.

8. Pierre Bourdieu examines individual decision-making within social settings that impose constraints and limitations on those decisions. He refers to social settings as "fields," similar to competitive games like soccer or chess. Individuals enter a field with different levels of "capital" (e.g., skills, money, social ties, knowledge) and "habitus" (i.e., different childhood experiences and family upbringing). Habitus is central to Bourdieu's understanding of how and whether individuals perceive opportunities within a given field, and how they deploy capital. In entering into a field, participants have agreed that the game is worth playing, but due to differences in capital and habitus, they do not pursue the objective of the game—to acquire more capital—with equal passion, commitment, and skill. Furthermore, they do not necessarily agree on what kind of capital is worth striving for. Bourdieu's conception of actors drawing on different past experiences and different levels of capital when making decisions informs our understanding of how colleges work. Colleges create social spaces that bring together diverse groups of students for the purpose of educating them. College compels them to make a series of decisions about what they want their own education to look like, and offers suggestions and guidance for an expansive and enriching education. But, that vision is not always in agreement with students' initial college aspirations. So the college experience becomes a process of trial and error, one of starts and restarts, as students discover for themselves the value of a liberal education. Our colleges very much set the agenda and the rules of the game; students are allowed to make their own choices, but they choose from the options that colleges put

before them. For an excellent summary of Bourdieu's contributions to social theory, see Pierre Bourdieu and Loic J. D. Wacquant, *An Invitation to Reflexive Sociology* (Chicago, IL: The University of Chicago Press, 1992).

9. William G. Bowen, *Lessons Learned: Reflections of a University President* (Princeton, NJ: Princeton University Press, 2010), 144; Derek Bok, *Our Underachieving Colleges: A Candid Look at How Much Students Learn and Why They Should Be Learning More* (Princeton, NJ: Princeton University Press, 2006), 66–76; and William Cronon, "'Only Connect . . .': The Goals of a Liberal Education," *American Scholar* 67 (1998): 73–80.

10. We had originally thought that experiences with difference and diversity would be a sixth area of decision-making on which we would focus. Although unequal access to higher education institutions continues, the students, faculty, and staff at most colleges and universities have become increasingly diverse. For many students, coming to college brings them into the most diverse communities they have ever experienced, so we were greatly interested in how students embrace or shy away from those with different perspectives or lived experiences. But the extent to which the students in our study talked about issues of racial, ethnic, gender, sexuality, or class differences depended on whether we explicitly asked about these issues. When asked directly, students sometimes had very poignant comments about how their "differentness" created difficulties for them. Many of these comments concerned their interactions with peers, so we discuss them in the Connection and Home chapters. However, when we asked students to talk in a more general way—to reflect on their efforts to manage time and develop helpful study stills, their learning experiences, and the advice they sought from others—they seldom brought up issues related to their race, ethnicity, gender, or other forms of difference.

11. Ernest T. Pascarella and Patrick T. Terenzini, *How College Affects Students*, vol. 2, *A Third Decade of Research* (San Francisco, CA: Jossey-Bass, 2005).

12. Richard Light reported, "Students point out repeatedly that getting constructive, somewhat personalized advice may be the single most underestimated experience of a great college experience." Richard J. Light, *Making the Most of College: Students Speak Their Minds* (Cambridge, MA: Harvard University Press, 2001), 4.

13. Among these we would include such iconic works as Alexander W. Astin, *What Matters in College? Four Critical Years Revisited* (San Francisco, CA: Jossey-Bass, 1993); William G. Bowen and Derek Bok, *The Shape of the River: Long-Term Consequences of Considering Race in College and University Admission* (Princeton, NJ: Princeton University Press, 1998); William G. Bowen, Matthew M. Chingos, and Michael S. McPherson, *Crossing the Finish Line: Completing College at America's Public Universities* (Princeton, NJ: Princeton University Press, 2009); Camille Z. Charles, Mary J. Fischer, Margarita A. Mooney, and Douglas S. Massey, *Taming the River: Negotiating the Academic, Financial, and Social Currents in Selective Colleges and Universities* (Princeton, NJ: Princeton University Press, 2009); Thomas J. Espenshade and Alexandria Walton Radford, *No Longer Separate, Not Yet Equal*

(Princeton, NJ: Princeton University Press, 2009); George D. Kuh, Jillian Kinzie, John H. Schuh, Elizabeth J. Whitt, and Associates, *Student Success in College: Creating Conditions That Matter* (San Francisco, CA: Jossey-Bass, 2005); Douglas S. Massey, Camille Z. Charles, Garvey F. Lundy, and Mary J. Fischer, *The Source of the River: The Social Origins of Freshmen at America's Selective Colleges and Universities* (Princeton, NJ: Princeton University Press, 2003); James L. Shulman and William G. Bowen, *The Game of Life: College Sports and Educational Values* (Princeton, NJ: Princeton University Press, 2001); Vincent Tinto, *Leaving College: Rethinking the Causes and Cures of Student Attrition*, 2nd ed. (Chicago, IL: The University of Chicago Press, 1993); and Vincent Tinto, *Completing College: Rethinking Institutional Action* (Chicago, IL: The University of Chicago Press, 2012). Others are mentioned later in this chapter.

14. Catharine Hoffman Beyer, Gerald M. Gillmore, and Andrew T. Fisher, *Inside the Undergraduate Experience: The University of Washington's Study of Undergraduate Learning* (Bolton, MA: Anker Publishing Company, 2007); Daniel F. Chambliss and Christopher G. Takacs, *How College Works* (Cambridge, MA: Harvard University Press, 2014). Other books have focused on how students' perspectives on particular issues change between the first and fourth years of college, such as Elizabeth Aries and Richard Berman, *Speaking of Race and Class: The Student Experience at an Elite College* (Philadelphia, PA: Temple University Press, 2013).

15. Light, *Making the Most of College*; Ken Bain, *What the Best College Students Do* (Cambridge, MA: The Belknap Press of Harvard University Press, 2012).

16. Tim Clydesdale, *The First Year Out: Understanding American Teens after High School* (Chicago, IL: University of Chicago Press, 2007); Mary Grigsby, *College Life through the Eyes of Students* (Albany, NY: State University of New York Press, 2009); and Rebekah Nathan, *My Freshman Year: What a Professor Learned by Becoming a Student* (Ithaca, NY: Cornell University Press, 2005).

17. Elizabeth A. Armstrong and Laura T. Hamilton, *Paying for the Party: How College Maintains Inequality* (Cambridge, MA: Harvard University Press, 2013); Derek Bok, *Our Underachieving Colleges*; Clydesdale, *The First Year Out*; and William Deresiewicz, *Excellent Sheep: The Miseducation of the American Elite and the Way to a Meaningful Life* (New York, NY: Free Press, 2014).

18. Arum and Roksa, *Aspiring Adults Adrift*, 40–46.

19. Arum and Roksa, *Academically Adrift*, 59–89.

20. William Damon, *The Path to Purpose: How Young People Find Their Calling in Life* (New York, NY: Free Press, 2008).

21. Delbanco, *College: What It Was, Is, and Should Be*; Roche, *Why Choose the Liberal Arts?* and Roth, *Beyond the University*.

22. Victor E. Ferrall, *Liberal Arts at the Brink* (Cambridge, MA: Harvard University Press, 2011).

23. Bennett and Wilezol, *Is College Worth It?*

24. These rates only approximate the true percentages of students of color since the percentages of students for whom race was unknown varied from school to school and from year to year with a median of 6% unknown.

25. The regional accreditation agency (the New England Association of Schools and Colleges or NEASC) was also a member of NECASL.

26. Our presentation at the Mixed-Method Assessment Meeting for Wabash National Study institutions held at the Center of Inquiry at Wabash College (Crawfordsville, IN) is an example of this: Cristin Bates, Claire Droste, Lee Cuba, and Joe Swingle, "Qualitative Assessment and Student Faculty Collaborations" (March 2008), http://www.liberalarts.wabash.edu/storage/Assessment_Notes_One_on_One_Interviews_07.28.09.pdf. Our materials on training student interviewers have also been used by other collaborative assessment projects funded by the Teagle Foundation (e.g., Moravian College, Drew University, Muhlenberg College, Roanoke College, and Susquehanna University, "Value Added Programs of Intense Student-Faculty Interaction.")

27. Because we asked students to talk about each of their courses in every semester, we also acquired grade transcripts for each of them. The relationship between grades and engagement is explored in Chapter 6.

28. See Delroy L. Paulhus, "Socially Desirable Responding: The Evolution of a Construct," in *The Role of Constructs in Psychological and Educational Measurement*, ed. Henry I. Braun, Douglas N. Jackson, and David E. Wiley (Mahwah, NJ: Lawrence Erlbaum Associates, Inc., 2002).

29. For books that address issues of drug use, partying, and sexual relationships, see Chambliss and Takacs, *How College Works*; Armstrong and Hamilton, *Paying for the Party*; Arthur Levine and Diane R. Dean, *Generation on a Tightrope: A Portrait of Today's College Student*, 3rd ed. (San Francisco, CA: Jossey-Bass, 2012).

2. Time

1. For a critique of the way in which "corporate time" has superseded the "public time" of universities, see Henry A. Giroux and Susan Searls Giroux, *Take Back Higher Education: Race, Youth, and the Crisis of Democracy in the Post-Civil Rights Era* (New York, NY: Palgrave Macmillan, 2004).

2. For an examination of how high school students manage time, see Tim Clydesdale, *The First Year Out: Understanding American Teens after High School* (Chicago, IL: Chicago University Press, 2007).

3. How students allocate their time and how time allocation affects student outcomes is addressed by Richard Arum and Josipa Roksa, *Academically Adrift: Limited Learning on College Campuses* (Chicago, IL: University of Chicago Press, 2011) and *Aspiring Adults Adrift: Tentative Transitions of College Graduates* (Chicago, IL: Chicago University Press, 2014); Alexander W. Astin, *What Matters in College? Four Critical Years Revisited* (San Francisco, CA: Jossey-Bass, 1993); and Camille Z.

Charles, Mary J. Fischer, Margarita A. Mooney, and Douglas S. Massey, *Taming the River: Negotiating the Academic, Financial, and Social Currents in Selective Colleges and Universities* (Princeton, NJ: Princeton University Press, 2009).

4. Others have used the concept of "compressed time" to describe the experience of college students who are facing specific deadlines associated with particular course assignments or examinations. In these moments students' subjective sense of time is shorter than "physical time." See Tim F. Liao, Joshua Beckman, Emily Marzolph, Caitlin Riederer, Jeffrey Sayler, and Leah Schmelkin, "The Social Definition of Time for University Students," *Time and Society* 22 (2013): 119–151.

5. Our discussion of the college search process might read as an exclusively middle-class portrait of this experience, one in which families can afford vacations (during which they visit colleges) or one where parents can offer guidance based on their own college experiences. Although some students in our study were solidly middle-class by many metrics, others were not, and their comments animate this discussion as well. First-generation students, international students, and students of color often described their college search process in ways similar to those who had white, middle-class backgrounds, although the pathways to college for these non-majority groups may have been less heavily influenced by parents, and as we discuss in the Advice chapter, guidance counselors can play important roles in the college search for some of these students. Regardless of their class, race, or ethnicity, virtually all of the students in this study were not engaged in a college search to decide whether or not to attend college; they were engaged in this search to determine which "good" college they were going to attend.

6. For more on the role of parents in the college search, see Thomas J. Espenshade and Alexandria Walton Radford, *No Longer Separate, Not Yet Equal* (Princeton, NJ: Princeton University Press, 2009). Also, for more on the role of the college visit in the admission process, see Mitchell L. Stevens, *Creating a Class: College Admissions and the Education of Elites* (Cambridge, MA: Harvard University Press, 2009).

7. International Baccalaureate is an international foundation that offers educational programs, some of which help students obtain advanced placement into college courses or receive college credit.

8. These factors shaping the college search process of high school students are, of course, situated in the larger cultural context and media attention devoted to the importance and time-consuming nature of applying to college—college guidebooks and rankings, SAT/ACT preparation and test-taking, special "education" sections of newspapers that appear each fall and spring, and the admissions outreach of colleges themselves.

9. For more on the importance to students of achieving such balance, see Arum and Roksa, *Aspiring Adults Adrift*.

10. See Rebekah Nathan, *My Freshman Year: What a Professor Learned by Becoming a Student* (Ithaca, NY: Cornell University Press, 2005) for a discussion of the

"harried" student life and time management strategies that work and do not work, as well as Clydesdale, *The First Year Out.*

11. Some researchers have found that students who perceive that they have less control over time experience greater stress and more psychological and physiological health problems. See Sarath A. Nonis, Cail I. Hudson, Laddie B. Logan, and Charles W. Ford, "Influence of Perceived Control over Time on College Students' Stress and Stress-Related Outcomes," *Research in Higher Education* 39 (1998): 587–605.

12. It is reasonable to wonder if the differences between Jessica and Stephanie were attributable to differences in academic achievement in their first year. In other words, did Jessica experience a greater feeling of control because she got better grades than Stephanie in her classes? This does not seem to have been the case. Jessica's grades were lower than Stephanie's in the first semester, but Jessica's grades went up in the second semester while Stephanie's went down. Some research suggests that effective time management is associated with a higher college GPA. See Bruce K. Britton and Abraham Tesser, "Effects of Time-Management Practices on College Grades," *Journal of Educational Psychology* 83 (1991): 405–410.

13. Nathan found that "many of the academically most successful juniors and seniors . . . believed that they did, indeed, need to control their time to create a balanced life. . . . The key to managing time was not, as college officials suggested, avoiding wasted minutes by turning yourself into an agent of your day planner. Neither was it severely curtailing your leisure or quitting your paying job. Rather it was controlling college by shaping schedules, taming professors, and limiting workload" (*My Freshman Year*, 112–113).

14. The sophomore-year survey asked students about the extent to which they had managed time successfully, successfully balanced academics and extracurricular activities, been able to get adequate sleep, kept on top of their commitments without compromising their health, and successfully managed stress. Almost four-fifths agreed or strongly agreed that they had managed time successfully and a similar number reported that they had successfully balanced academics and extracurricular activities. By contrast, only about half agreed or strongly agreed that they had been able to get adequate sleep, and only two-thirds agreed that they had kept on top of their commitments without compromising their health or had successfully managed stress. Thus, there is somewhat of a disconnect between students' claims about time management and balance and their ability to manage their health and stress.

15. The GRE is a standardized test required for admission to many graduate and professional schools. The LSAT is the Law School Admissions Test.

16. A majority of first-semester sophomores were indeed thinking ahead. Of those responding to the sophomore-year survey, 68% planned to study abroad, 75% planned to do an internship, and 65% planned to go to graduate school of

some kind. Thirty-nine percent of sophomores reported two of these goals, and another 36% responded "yes" to all three.

17. Our analysis of how students experience time in the sophomore, junior, and senior years is based largely on responses to this open-ended question asked at the beginning of each of these years. As our discussion suggests, many of the answers to this question focused on decisions students will make or experiences they hope to have in years beyond the one in which the question was asked.

18. Some first-year students voiced skepticism about having lots of time to make decisions in college. Reflecting on the messages her college had offered up at orientation, one first-semester, first-year student said:

> I actually get a little scared when they tell me I have a lot of time. Because I feel like, if I listen to them, it might be beneficial. But, at the same time, I feel like I might get into this mindset that, "Oh, I have time. I'll worry about my major later." And that once I finally decide, that the four years will be almost gone, and I don't have a set of classes for a major. [During orientation] we had a lecture by this professor who was talking about [students] who planned out their whole college careers, and she's really talking about me here. Because I did plan it out. It's not going how I wanted it, because I didn't get the bio classes and stuff. But I don't know. I think there's space for changes and improvements.

19. The students in our study were sophomores and juniors during the U.S. financial crisis of 2007–2008. This severe economic downturn heightened their concerns about finding a job following graduation, concerns that were validated by the experiences of students who were seniors at their colleges at the time.

20. Our survey data confirm that almost all seniors expressed high levels of satisfaction with their undergraduate experience. The senior-year survey asked students how satisfied they had been with their undergraduate education. About 92% responded that they were "generally" or "very satisfied." Less than 1% were "very dissatisfied," about 2% were "generally dissatisfied," and about 6% were "ambivalent." Students were also asked if they would encourage a high school senior who resembled them when they were a high school senior to attend their college. About 80% reported that they "probably" or "definitely would," about 12% responded "maybe," and about 10% responded that they "probably" or "definitely would not." Finally, we asked seniors if they would still attend their college if they could start over again. About 84% said that they probably or definitely would, and only about 1% said they definitely would not.

21. Declaring a major with confidence appears to be common among students as they begin their sophomore year. Almost three-quarters of first-semester sophomores responding to our sophomore-year survey reported having already decided on a major. When asked how certain they were in their choice of major, 89% of those who had already decided on a major were either very certain (59%) or somewhat certain (30%) about their decision.

22. Jason's declaration that he was only learning about the value and meaning of time as he was leaving college speaks to the larger issue of how students sometimes create narratives about the past that don't accurately represent prior experiences. This underscores the importance of interviewing students multiple times while they are in college, rather than after they graduate.

3. Connection

1. Students who fail to find a social niche are at risk of dropping out or transferring to another college. See Vincent Tinto, *Leaving College: Rethinking the Causes and Cures of Student Attrition*, 2nd ed. (Chicago, IL: University of Chicago Press, 1993).

2. For a fascinating study of college student drinking, see Thomas Vander Ven, *Getting Wasted: Why College Students Drink Too Much and Party So Hard* (New York, NY: New York University Press, 2011). Also see Elizabeth A. Armstrong and Laura T. Hamilton, *Paying for the Party: How College Maintains Inequality* (Cambridge, MA: Harvard University Press, 2013).

3. Many have recognized that a student's social life is an integral part of his or her college experience. For example, Alexander Astin writes, "Viewed as a whole, the many empirical findings from this study seem to warrant the following general conclusion: the student's peer group is the single most potent source of influence on growth and development during the undergraduate years." See Alexander W. Astin, *What Matters in College? Four Critical Years Revisited* (San Francisco, CA: Jossey-Bass Publishers, 1993), 398. Also see Richard Arum and Josipa Roksa, *Aspiring Adults Adrift: Tentative Transitions of College Graduates* (Chicago, IL: Chicago University Press, 2014); Daniel F. Chambliss and Christopher G. Takacs, *How College Works* (Cambridge, MA: Harvard University Press, 2014); Mary Grigsby, *College Life through the Eyes of Students* (Albany: State University of New York Press, 2009); Rebekah Nathan, *My Freshman Year: What a Professor Learned by Becoming a Student* (Ithaca, NY: Cornell University Press, 2005); and Ernest T. Pascarella and Patrick T. Terenzini, *How College Affects Students*, vol. 2, *A Third Decade of Research* (San Francisco, CA: Jossey-Bass, 2005).

4. Students report "making friends" as a goal more often in the first year than in subsequent years. They continued, however, to mention good grades as a measure of success in every year. Catharine Hoffman Beyer, Gerald M. Gillmore, and Andrew T. Fisher, *Inside the Undergraduate Experience: The University of Washington's Study of Undergraduate Learning* (Bolton, MA: Anker Publishing Company, 2007) similarly asked first-year students to describe what they most wanted to learn and develop. Making new friends was among their top goals.

5. In the sophomore survey administered at the start of the second year, 92% of responding sophomores agreed or strongly agreed that they had developed close friendships with other students. In addition, when asked if they had found people

with whom they could discuss intellectual issues, personal issues, or hang out and have a good time, less than 10% said rarely or never. The modal response for each question was "usually" (71% for intellectual issues, 65% for personal issues, and 82% for hanging out).

6. See also Chambliss and Takacs, *How College Works* and Mitchell Stevens, *Creating a Class* (Cambridge, MA: Harvard University Press, 2007).

7. See Menachem Wecker, "Outdoor Orientations Can Help Students Acclimate to College," *U.S. News & World Report*, November 28, 2011, http://www.usnews.com/education/best-colleges/articles/2011/11/28/outdoor-orientations-can-help-students-acclimate-to-college. For a contrasting result, see Chambliss and Takacs, *How College Works*, who found that "orientation 'friendships' often prove fleeting" (24).

8. For more on the importance of dormitories and residential houses for the formation of first-year friendships (and increased social competence) see Arum and Roksa, *Aspiring Adults Adrift*; Chambliss and Takacs, *How College Works*; Grigsby, *College Life*; and Nathan, *My Freshman Year*.

9. On the sophomore survey, we asked students to rate the extent to which they got along with their assigned first-year roommate. Of the responding sophomores who had a first-year roommate, 51% said they got along very well with their roommate and 32% said they got along well enough. Only 16% claimed that they did not get along at all with their first-year roommate.

10. After the first semester, students increasingly cited extracurricular activities as places where they made new friends. Chambliss and Takacs (*How College Works*) observed that "extracurriculars exist primarily to foster relationships among friends and acquaintances, mainly through the sheer number of contact hours between people." They also found that those extracurricular activities that have "a semi-'mandatory' feel to them, have an interdependent division of labor, and often entail some public performance" are particularly helpful in creating strong relationships among students (30–31).

11. Often called first-year seminars, these courses introduce first-year students to the skills (reading, writing, oral, and thinking) needed for success in college. A substantial amount of empirical research documents their academic merit. For a review see Pascarella and Terenzini, *How College Affects Students*, vol 2.

12. Nathan, *My Freshman Year*, finds that students met fewer than 25% of their friends through their courses or major. See also Grigsby, *College Life* and Chambliss and Takacs, *How College Works*. Pascarella and Terenzini argue that first-year seminars may enhance "social integration," but it's unclear if this is due to increased acquaintance networks as opposed to the development of friendships (403). Stearns, Buchmann, and Bonneau found that classrooms were not an important site of cross-racial friendship formation among first-year college students. The authors suggested that large enrollments, competition for grades, and the relatively short amount of time spent in a particular college classroom may explain this finding.

Note that these three limitations cited by the authors would seem to impede friendships of any kind forming in a classroom, not just cross-race friendships. See Elizabeth Stearns, Claudia Buchmann, and Kara Bonneau, "Interracial Friendships in the Transition to College: Do Birds of a Feather Flock Together Once They Leave the Nest?" *Sociology of Education* 82 (2009): 173–195.

13. Chambliss and Takacs (*How College Works*) also found athletic teams to be an avenue for making friends. For more on the role of athletics on college campuses, see James L. Shulman and William G. Bowen, *The Game of Life: College Sports and Educational Values* (Princeton, NJ: Princeton University Press, 2002); and William G. Bowen and Sarah A. Levin, *Reclaiming the Game: College Sports and Educational Values* (Princeton, NJ: Princeton University Press, 2005).

14. The apt term "routinized proximity" is from Chambliss and Takacs, *How College Works*, 32.

15. See Beverly Tatum, *Assimilation Blues: Black Families in a White Community* (New York, NY: Greenwood Press, 1987); and Stearns, Buchmann, and Bonneau, "Interracial Friendships in the Transition to College."

16. Massey and his colleagues observed that most white students attending selective colleges or universities "come to college with little or no direct experience interacting with minorities." The typical white first-year student in their study came from a neighborhood that was 85% white. For Asian, Latino/a, and black students, the comparable percentages were 67% white, 63% white, and 43% white. See Douglas S. Massey, Camille Z. Charles, Garvey F. Lundy, and Mary J. Fischer, *The Source of the River: The Social Origins of Freshmen at America's Selective Colleges and Universities* (Princeton, NJ: Princeton University Press, 2003), 75.

17. Richard J. Light, in *Making the Most of College: Students Speak Their Minds* (Cambridge, MA: Harvard University Press, 2001), 39, described the carefully planned first-year residential living arrangements at Harvard to be especially important in providing students with opportunities to learn about diversity. In addition, Bowen and Bok (*The Shape of the River*) and Espenshade and Radford (*No Longer Separate, Not Yet Equal*) found that students who had first-year roommates or dormmates from another racial or ethnic group had more cross-race interactions. Espenshade and Radford also found that students who interacted socially with students from another racial group were "most likely to feel they have learned a lot from diversity" (337).

18. At a large university, Grigsby (*College Life*) found that while some students actively pursued diversity in their friendship networks, it was more common for students to make friends within their racial or ethnic group. Nathan (*My Freshman Year*) also found that students' close friends were students who were members of their own racial or ethnic group, especially for white students. Finally, Elizabeth Aries described that the black and white students in her study had at least a couple of close friends from the other racial group. While most students felt they "better understood and appreciated those whose life experiences had been unlike their own,"

these personal experiences did not always result in "feelings that *learning* about race had taken place." Elizabeth Aries, *Speaking of Race and Class: The Student Experience at an Elite College* (Philadelphia, PA: Temple University Press, 2013), 117.

19. Grigsby also found that residence halls were where students "encounter the most diversity and learn how to get along with other people" (*College Life*, 84). In addition, at one highly selective research university, Stearns, Buchmann, and Bonneau ("Interracial Friendships in the Transition to College") show that inter-racial contact in residence halls was one of the strongest determinants of interra-cial friendships among first-year college students. Other factors correlated with a higher proportion of interracial friendships were (i) having interracial friendships prior to college, (ii) a different-race college roommate, (iii) not joining a racially homogeneous cultural/ethnic club if one were a student of color, and (iv) not join-ing a Greek organization if one were a white student.

20. Recently, Pleskac and his colleagues reported that roommate conflicts were one of six critical factors that led students to decide to withdraw from college. See Timothy J. Pleskac, Jessica Keeney, Stephanie M. Merritt, Neal Schmitt, and Freder-ick L. Oswald, "A Detection Model of College Withdrawal," *Organizational Behavior and Human Decision Processes* 115 (2011): 85–98. For other research on the impact of roommate conflicts, see Chambliss and Takacs, *How College Works*.

21. Victor Turner, *The Forest of Symbols* (Ithaca, NY: Cornell University Press, 1967), 105. Nathan, in *My Freshman Year*, also uses the idea of liminality to describe the powerful emotions surrounding first-year friendships. For an extended discus-sion of adult transition, see Jeffrey J. Arnett, *Emerging Adulthood: The Winding Road from the Late Teens through the Twenties* (New York, NY: Oxford University Press, 2014).

22. Chambliss and Takacs note that "the initially open doors of freshmen year tend to swing shut rather quickly" (*How College Works*, 36). Nathan concurred, ob-serving that "Once networks were formed, usually by the end of the freshmen year, students tended to stay with their groups, maintaining intense and frequent inter-actions with their network and more superficial and sparse contact with others" (*My Freshman Year*, 58). Grigsby also found that a student's core group of friends were formed by the end of the first year.

23. In addition to race, nationality and socioeconomic status are major social di-visions on American college campuses. Even so, when discussing changes in friend-ship and interactional diversity, students talked far more about race than national-ity or social class. Many nationality-segregated friendship networks surfaced in the first year and so any increase in such networks may not have been especially pro-nounced. We don't know if social class-segregated friendship networks increased after the first year because students generally did not talk about social class. More-over, social class is generally less visible to an onlooker than race, so an increase in social class segregation may have been less noticed. Whether students failed to see the role of social class or simply thought it was not relevant is not clear to us. For a

provocative and extended discussion about the role of social class in student friendships, see Elizabeth Aries, *Race and Class Matters at an Elite College* (Philadelphia, PA: Temple University Press, 2008).

24. Thomas J. Espenshade and Alexandria W. Radford, *No Longer Separate, Not Yet Equal* (Princeton, NJ: Princeton University Press, 2009). Others have also found that although students value and seek out diversity in their social relationships early on, they increasingly associate with those who are similar to them rather than different. See Beyer, Gillmore, and Fisher, *Inside the Undergraduate Experience*; and Grigsby, *College Life*. Students of color are also more likely to develop same-race social connections away from campus. See Chambliss and Takacs, *How College Works*; and Camille Z. Charles, Mary J. Fischer, Margarita A. Mooney, and Douglas S. Massey, *Taming the River: Negotiating the Academic, Financial, and Social Currents in Selective Colleges and Universities* (Princeton, NJ: Princeton University Press, 2009). In interpreting the results of their empirical study of first-year interracial friendships at one highly selective research university, Stearns, Buchmann, and Bonneau ("Interracial Friendships in the Transition to College") concluded that, "When participation is voluntary and determined by choice, many students tend to choose homophilous contexts and friendships; when organizational policies are in place to ensure that students have interracial contact in at least one major facet of the college experience, such as residence halls, their friendship networks contain a higher proportion of interracial friendships" (2009, 189). The authors fell short of recommending complete institutional control over roommate and residence hall assignments since hampering same-race ties may have deleterious social and academic consequences for students of color.

25. Espenshade and Radford also found that "minority students who belong to an ethnic organization are more likely to interact with classmates from their own race-ethnic group" (*No Longer Separate, Not Yet Equal*, 218.)

26. Many factors in addition to race—e.g., social class, gender, nationality, etc.—potentially influence the friendship choices of college students. Even so, racial differences may be the most significant barrier to friendship formation, at least for some groups. Quillian and Campbell concluded that, among seventh to twelfth grade students nationwide, "A 20-year difference in mother's education is not as great a barrier to friendship as race between black and white students." See Lincoln Quillian and Mary E. Campbell, "Beyond Black and White: The Present and Future of Multiracial Friendship Segregation," *American Sociological Review* 68 (2003), 550.

27. The helpful terms "contexts of placement" and "contexts of choice" come from Stearns et al.

28. Transitivity appeals to individuals because it reduces the likelihood of conflicts among one's friends: "enmity among one's friends leads to strain and is avoided." See James Moody, "Race, School Integration, and Friendship Segregation in America," *American Journal of Sociology* 107 (2001), 684.

29. In addition to transitivity, reciprocity is another important determinant of friendships. Reciprocity is the tendency to return or reciprocate offers of friendship. Recent research at one large university has shown that transitivity and reciprocity "are of overwhelming importance for the formation of students' friendships and that they are two of the largest contributors to racial homogeneity in the aggregate by amplifying the effects of racial homophily [same-race preference]." See Andreas Wimmer and Kevin Lewis, "Beyond and Below Racial Homophily: ERG Models of a Friendship Network Documented on Facebook," *American Journal of Sociology* 116, no. 2 (2010): 583–642.

30. Important research conducted by Sidanius and his colleagues also lends support to those who argue for the elimination of white-dominated fraternities and sororities. Like ethnic and cultural organizations, Greek organizations tend to "increase perceptions of group victimization, intergroup bias, and perceived zero-sum conflict between groups." See Jim Sidanius, Collete Van Laar, Shana Levin, and Stacey Sinclair, "Ethnic Enclaves and the Dynamics of Social Identity on the College Campus: The Good, the Bad, and the Ugly," *Journal of Personality and Social Psychology* 87 (2004): 96–110.

31. Perhaps there were more negative feelings about racial divisions on campus than interviewees were willing to share with student interviewers, particularly when interviewees and interviewers were not of the same race. That is certainly a possibility but it does not seem likely. We had hoped to demographically match interviewees and interviewers—white American female interviewees matched with white American female interviewers, international male interviewees matched with international male interviewers, etc. While there may have been some benefits to this research strategy in terms of collecting better and more truthful (i.e., valid) answers, we realized at the study design phase that identifying, successfully recruiting, and training the requisite number of student interviewers would be a challenge. Furthermore, had we enlisted the help of more student interviewers, each interviewer would have performed fewer interviews and would have had less of an opportunity to improve as an interviewer.

32. See Appendix.

33. "Open Doors 2013 Fast Facts," Institute of International Education, 2013, http://www.iie.org/Research-and-Publications/Open-Doors/Data/Fast-Facts. As an example of making study abroad more affordable, Wellesley College increases the financial aid grant for a student whose study abroad budget exceeds her budget were she to stay on campus. The SAFE (Study Abroad is For Everyone) program at Bates College actively encourages students, particularly students of color and first-generation students, to apply for study abroad programs, helps them locate Federal and program grants, and offers additional financial support to qualified students interested in a study abroad program.

34. Wellesley College, Office of International Study, n.d., http://www.wellesley.edu/ois.

35. Giddens referred to this sense of order and continuity as ontological security. See Anthony Giddens, *Modernity and Self-Identity: Self and Society in the Late Modern Age* (Stanford, CA: Stanford University Press, 1991).

36. See Ross Gittell and Avis Vidal, *Community Organizing: Building Social Capital as a Development Strategy* (Thousand Oaks, CA: Sage, 1998) and Robert D. Putnam, *Bowling Alone: The Collapse and Revival of American Community* (New York, NY: Simon & Schuster Paperbacks, 2000). These two approaches mirror Putnam's discussion of bonding social capital ("going deep") and bridging social capital ("going broad"). Putnam pointed out that "bridging social capital can generate broader identities and reciprocity, whereas bonding social capital bolsters narrower selves" (23). This echoes concerns that some express over the social closure that occurs in the social networks of many college students after the first year.

37. Mitchell Chang, Alexander W. Astin, and Dongbin Kim, "Cross-Racial Interaction among Undergraduates: Some Consequences, Causes, and Patterns," *Research in Higher Education* 45 (2004): 529–553. Also see Bowen and Bok (*The Shape of the River*).

4. Home

1. A. Bartlett Giamatti, "The Green Fields of the Mind," in *A Great and Glorious Game: Baseball Writings of A. Bartlett Giamatti*, ed. Kenneth Robson (Chapel Hill, NC: Algonquin Books, 1998).

2. See Elvira Cicognani, Isabel Menezes, and Gil Nata, "University Students' Sense Of Belonging to the Home Town: The Role of Residential Mobility," *Social Indicators Research* 104 (2011): 33–45; Kenny Chow and Mick Healey, "Attachment and Place Identity: First-Year Undergraduates Making the Transition From Home to University," *Journal of Environmental Psychology* 28 (2008): 362–372; Lee Cuba and David M. Hummon, "Constructing a Sense of Home: Place Affiliation and Migration Across the Life Cycle," *Sociological Forum* 8 (1993): 547–572; and Lee Cuba and David M. Hummon, "A Place to Call Home: Identification with Dwelling, Community, or Region," *Sociological Quarterly* 34 (1993): 111–131.

3. Researchers who write about college students' sense of belonging define "belonging" in many different ways. For instance, in *How College Works* (Cambridge, MA: Harvard University Press, 2014), Dan F. Chambliss and Christopher G. Takacs defined belonging as "real things that happen in daily life create the feeling—the reality—of belonging to groups and to the community they make up" (79). "Home" and "belonging" in our student interviews certainly draw from this literature, but we use the terms to mean more establishing a physical and emotional space of comfort rather than a connection to a group. So, it is more a sense of being at home *in* a place than belonging *to* a place.

4. Jeffrey J. Arnett, *Emerging Adulthood: The Winding Road from the Late Teens through the Twenties*, 2nd ed. (Oxford, UK: Oxford University Press, 2015).

5. Marieke Meeuwisse and her colleagues showed positive relationships between learning environments, peer and teacher interactions, and a sense of belonging. This was true for all students, but for minority students, formal teacher and peer interactions seemed to have the greatest benefit to their academic program. Marieke Meeuwisse, Sabine E. Severiens, and Marise P. Born, "Learning Environments, Interaction, Sense of Belonging and Study Success in Ethnically Diverse Student Groups," *Research in Higher Education* 51 (2010): 528–545.

6. Many researchers write about the difficulties students of color have transitioning to colleges that are predominantly white, and about the effects these difficulties have on retention, academic achievement, and social integration. See for example: Walter R. Allen, "The Color of Success: African-American College Student Outcomes at Predominantly White and Historically Black Colleges and Universities," *Harvard Educational Review* 62 (1992): 26–44; Mardy T. Eimers and Gary R. Pike, "Minority and Nonminority Adjustment to College: Differences and Similarities," *Research in Higher Education* 38 (1997): 77–97; Mary J. Fischer, "Settling into Campus Life: Differences by Race/Ethnicity in College Involvement and Outcomes," *The Journal of Higher Education* 78 (2007): 125–161; Shaun R. Harper and Sylvia Hurtado, "Nine Themes in Campus Racial Climates and Implications for Institutional Transformation," *New Directions for Student Services* 120 (2007): 7–24; and Richard M. Lee and Claytie Davis III, "Cultural Orientation, Past Multicultural Experience, and a Sense of Belonging on Campus for Asian-American College Students," *Journal of College Student Development* 41 (2000): 110–114.

7. For a discussion on Latino/a students' feelings about home and school cultures, see John C. Hernandez, "A Qualitative Exploration of the First-Year Experience of Latino College Students," *Journal of Student Affairs Research and Practice* 40, no. 1 (2002): 69–84, doi:10.2202/1949-6605.1189. For African-American students see, for example, Sharon Fries-Britt and Kimberly Griffin, "The Black Box: How High-Achieving Blacks Resist Stereotypes about Black Americans," *Journal of College Student Development* 48 (2007): 509–525; and Rachelle Winkler-Wagner, "The Perpetual Homelessness of College Experiences: Tensions Between Home and Campus for African-American Women," *Review of Higher Education* 33 (2009): 1–36. For all students of color, see Patrick T. Terenzini et al., "The Transition to College: Diverse Students, Diverse Stories," *Research in Higher Education* 35 (1994): 57–73.

8. See also Arnett, *Emerging Adulthood.*

9. For a discussion on the issue of family ties to students' transition to college see Alberto F. Cabrera, Amaury Nora, Patrick T. Terenzini, Ernest Pascarella, and Linda Serra Hagedorn, "Campus Racial Climate and the Adjustment of Students to College: A Comparison Between White Students and African-American Students," *Journal of Higher Education* 70 (1999): 134–160; Eimers and Pike, "Minority and Nonminority Adjustment to College"; and Sylvia Hurtado and Deborah Faye Carter, "Effects of College Transition and Perceptions of the Campus Racial

Climate on Latino College Students' Sense of Belonging," *Sociology of Education* 70 (1997): 324–345.

10. Arnett, *Emerging Adulthood.*

5. Advice

1. George Kuh and his colleagues have argued that two "tried and true" principles of student success are (1) providing support services for students, including faculty advisors and deans, and (2) figuring out ways to "induce large numbers of students to use them." Advising will not be effective if students do not "take full advantage" of this opportunity (266–269). But another critical factor concerns faculty's ability to "forge authentic relationships with students" by "revealing their inner selves"—it is through "meaningful human connections" that faculty will be "able to connect with students at deeper levels and challenge them to previously unrealized levels of achievement and personal performance" (281). George D. Kuh, Jillian Kinzie, John H. Schuh, Elizabeth J. Whitt, and Associates, *Student Success in College: Creating Conditions That Matter* (San Francisco, CA: Jossey-Bass, 2010). In addition, Alexander Astin reported: "faculty who show a strong interest in students' academic and personal problems and who are available to interact with them can impact positively on students' academic self-concept or Intellectual Self-Esteem." Alexander W. Astin, *What Matters in College? Four Critical Years Revisited* (San Francisco, CA: Jossey-Bass, 1993), 113.

2. Much research has demonstrated that faculty-student and staff-student interactions are key factors for student learning, persistence, retention, and success in college: Astin, *What Matters in College*; Catharine Hoffman Beyer, Gerald M. Gillmore, and Andrew T. Fisher, *Inside the Undergraduate Experience: The University of Washington's Study of Undergraduate Learning* (Bolton, MA: Anker Publishing Company, 2007); Daniel F. Chambliss and Christopher G. Takacs, *How College Works* (Cambridge, MA: Harvard University Press, 2014); Arthur W. Chickering and Zelda F. Gamson, "Seven Principles for Good Practice in Undergraduate Education," *AAHE Bulletin* 39 (1987): 3–7; Felly Chiteng Kot, "The Impact of Centralized Advising on First-Year Academic Performance and Second-Year Enrollment Behavior," *Research in Higher Education* 55 (2014): 527–563; Kuh et al., *Student Success in College*; George D. Kuh and Shouping Hu, "The Effects of Student-Faculty Interaction in the 1990s," *The Review of Higher Education* 24 (2001): 309–332; Ernest T. Pascarella and Patrick T. Terenzini, *How College Affects Students*, vol. 2, *A Third Decade of Research* (San Francisco, CA: Jossey-Bass, 2005); Tricia A. Seifert, Kathleen Goodman, Patricia M. King, and Marcia B. Baxter Magolda, "Using Mixed Methods to Study First-Year College Impact on Liberal Arts Learning Outcomes," *Journal of Mixed Methods Research* 4 (2010): 248–267; Vincent Tinto, *Leaving College: Rethinking the Causes and Cures of Student Attrition*, 2nd ed. (Chicago, IL: The

University of Chicago Press, 1993); and Vincent Tinto, *Completing College: Rethinking Institutional Action* (Chicago, IL: The University of Chicago Press, 2012).

3. Cotton and Wilson also found that students who were unsure as to whether their professors were truly interested in interacting with them were discouraged from interacting with faculty outside of class. They noted, "faculty must demonstrate an active interest in contact and repeatedly encourage students to approach them" (508). Sheila R. Cotton and Bonnie Wilson, "Student-Faculty Interactions: Dynamics and Determinants," *Higher Education* 51 (2006): 487–519.

4. Recent research shows that parent-child conversations about attending college increase the likelihood of college attendance. See Laura W. Perna and Marvin A. Titus, "The Relationship between Parental Involvement as Social Capital and College Enrollment: An Examination of Racial/Ethnic Group Differences," *The Journal of Higher Education* 76 (2005): 485–518; and Gary D. Sandefur, Ann M. Meier, and Mary E. Campbell, "Family Resources, Social Capital, and College Attendance," *Social Science Research* 25 (2006): 525–553. For recent research on variables that predict the likelihood of parent-child conversations about college, see Scott M. Myers and Carrie B. Myers, "Are Discussions about College between Parents and Their High School Children a College-Planning Activity? Making the Case and Testing the Predictors," *American Journal of Education* 118 (2012): 281–308; and Heather T. Rowan-Kenyon, Angela D. Bell, and Laura W. Perna, "Contextual Influences on Parental Involvement in College Going: Variations by Socioeconomic Class," *The Journal of Higher Education* 79 (2008): 564–586.

5. For more on the strategies employed by parents to increase their children's success in the college search and application process, see Thomas J. Espenshade and Alexandria Walton Radford, *No Longer Separate, Not Yet Equal* (Princeton, NJ: Princeton University Press, 2009).

6. We defined first-generation students as students with neither parent having a college degree.

7. Ingrid A. Nelson, "Rural Students' Social Capital in the College Search and Application Process," *Rural Sociology* (2016): doi:10.1111/ruso.12095

8. For recent research on the role of school guidance resources versus parents, see Mark E. Engberg and Gregory C. Wolniak, "Examining the Effects of High School Contexts on Postsecondary Enrollments," *Research in Higher Education* 51 (2010): 132–153; and Stephen B. Plank and Will T. Jordan, "Effects of Information, Guidance, and Actions on Postsecondary Destinations: A Study of Talent Loss," *American Educational Research Journal* 38 (2001): 947–979. For recent research on variables that predict the likelihood of consulting with a guidance counselor, see Julia Bryan, Cheryl Holcomb-McCoy, Cheryl Moore-Thomas, and Norma L. Day-Vines, "Who Sees the School Counselor for College Information? A National Study," *Professional School Counseling* 12 (2009): 280–291.

9. Mitchell L. Stevens, *Creating a Class: College Admissions and the Education of Elites* (Cambridge, MA: Harvard University Press, 2009) also found that guidance

counselors at well-resourced high schools were more likely to have caseloads that allowed them to get to know their students.

10. The faculty advisor is either assigned (usually by an administrator) or is the instructor of the student's first-year fall seminar.

11. Our colleges have relatively elaborate advising structures. Celeste Pardee describes three basic organizational structures for academic advising: centralized, decentralized, and shared. Our colleges best fit the shared category, in that all students have both a faculty advisor and an advisor from the Dean of Students' office. Celeste F. Pardee, "Organizational Structures for Advising," *NACADA Clearing house of Academic Advising Resources*, 2004, http://www.nacada.ksu.edu/Resources/Clearinghouse/View-Articles/Organizational-Models-for-Advising.aspx. Students are typically assigned to a particular dean who serves as a general advisor for academic and nonacademic issues. At all but two of our colleges, there is a Dean of First-Year Students; after the first year, students either transition to a new dean who stays with them until they graduate or receive a new dean each year (a Class Dean model). At the two other colleges, the deans share advising responsibilities for all students. Deans can provide students with help navigating the variety of resources our colleges offer around particular topics—premed, pre-health, prelaw, pre-education, career planning services, off-campus study, residential life, student activities, counseling services, community service, and academic skill tutors in writing, quantitative reasoning, and languages.

12. Some students further broaden their advising networks to include on-campus friends and older students. Although students talked to friends during course registration and later, when deciding upon a major, we found that students were more likely to share their thoughts with them as they were all trying to make these decisions rather than seeking personalized advice about these decisions.

13. In the sophomore survey, which was administered in spring 2008 to the entire sophomore Class of 2010 at all seven colleges (for more details about this survey and its response rate please see the Appendix), we asked sophomores how often they met with their first-year advisors (never, once, twice, three to five times, or six or more times). The modal response was three to five times, which was selected by 51% of the responding sophomores. About 11% met with their advisors six or more times and 29% met with them twice. Less than 10% met with them only once or never. This is consistent with the interviews, which also found that most students sought advice from their advisors.

14. The topics expressed in the interviews included figuring out a good schedule, adding/dropping courses, and identifying courses that were appropriate for their abilities and interests. In the sophomore survey, we also asked sophomores whether they asked their first-year advisor academic, personal, or career-related questions, and to rate the helpfulness of their advisor on a three-point Likert scale—not helpful, somewhat helpful, very helpful—in each of these areas. Over 95% of responding sophomores asked their advisors academic questions, but only about 60% asked

them personal or career-related questions. This finding is consistent with the interview results—students consulted with their advisors mostly about course-related issues. Of those who asked their advisor academic questions, 42% rated them very helpful and 45% rated them somewhat helpful; results were again consistent with the interview results (advisors are helpful with academic issues). Sophomores also reported that their first-year academic advisors were somewhat less helpful answering their personal and career-related questions. For personal questions, only 35% found their first-year advisor very helpful and 38% found them somewhat helpful. For career-related questions, only 27% found their first-year advisor very helpful and 38% found them somewhat helpful. This reduced helpfulness may explain, to some extent, why students are less likely to seek out advisors for help with nonacademic issues.

The range of course-related topics for which students sought advice appears broader than found by Chambliss and Takacs (*How College Works*), who reported that at their college advisors played a minor role in course registration; only those advisors who met with students early in the registration process or had achieved the role of mentor had a substantial impact on students' course choices. Although we found a range of interactions between advisors and students, students for whom the advisor was characterized as "not helpful" were in the minority; it may be the case that our students were likely to label an advisor as helpful even if they only helped them select a fourth course.

15. For similar findings that students may be seeking "validation" rather than critical feedback when interacting with faculty, see Cotton and Wilson, "Student-Faculty Interactions"; Patricia M. King and Marcia B. Baxter Magolda, "A Developmental Perspective on Learning," *Journal of College Student Development* 37 (1996): 163–173; and Kuh and Hu, "The Effects of Student-Faculty Interactions."

16. In the sophomore survey, we asked sophomores whether they had a particular career field in mind before they had come to college (this question was asked in the context of declaring a major). About 59% of responding sophomores said they did. Of those with a career in mind at the start of college, about 77% were still considering that field in the fall of their sophomore year. And in the junior survey, which was administered in the spring of 2009 to those juniors in the Class of 2010 who remained on campus (rather than study abroad) at all seven colleges (for more details about this survey and its response rate please see the Appendix), 70% of responding juniors stated that a long-term interest in the field was quite or very important to their decision to declare a major in that field. Thus, more than half of our students entered college with a career (and major) in mind and most seemed to stay committed to that early decision. It is perhaps not surprising then that this early commitment to a major (something that one might expect would be less common at a liberal arts college) leads some students to question the usefulness of a first-year academic advisor from outside their intended major.

17. For a discussion of the benefits of forming "weak ties" that facilitate building "crucial bridges," see Mark Granovetter, "The Strength of Weak Ties: A Network Theory Revisited," *Sociological Theory* 1 (1983): 201–233.

18. Marcia B. Baxter Magolda, "Three Elements of Self-Authorship," *Journal of College Student Development* 49 (2008): 269–284. See also Marcia B. Baxter Magolda and Patricia M. King, "Toward Reflective Conversations: An Advising Approach that Promotes Self-Authorship," *Peer Review* 10 (2008), http://www.aacu.org/publications-research/periodicals/toward-reflective-conversations-advising-approach-promotes-self.

19. At some colleges, the first-year seminar instructor is a student's first-year advisor, but even in these situations, it would not be valid to claim that these students choose their advisor. Students choose classes, in part, based on the reputation of the instructor, but that is only one of many factors. Additionally, the courses in which students end up are not always their first-choice courses nor the ones they really wanted.

20. The sophomore survey data revealed that first-year students who met with their advisor less often were significantly less likely to rate him or her as being helpful, Spearman $r = .405$, $N = 2256$, $p = .001$. Advisees were more likely to seek out attentive, accessible, helpful advisors. It is also likely that students who meet often more often with their advisor will get to know them better, feel more comfortable working with them, and thus, perhaps develop deeper, more meaningful relationships.

21. Cotton and Wilson in "Student-Faculty Interactions" found that as students matured and came to see the value in interacting with faculty, they were more willing to find time to meet with them.

22. Cotton and Wilson in "Student-Faculty Interactions" also reported that negative experiences with faculty discouraged future interactions.

23. Although we did not find this, Elizabeth Aries and Richard Berman found that lower income, first-generation college students were unable to obtain advice from their parents about navigating the college culture. Elizabeth Aries and Richard Berman, *Speaking of Race and Class: The Student Experience at an Elite College* (Philadelphia, PA: Temple University Press, 2013). In addition, for a recent review and examination of how white, first-generation students adjust or fail adjust to college, including the role of family, see Jenny Marie Stuber, "Integrated, Marginal, and Resilient: Race, Class, and the Diverse Experiences of White, First-Generation College Students," *International Journal of Qualitative Studies in Education* 24 (2011): 117–136, doi:10.1080/09518391003641916. Finally, for a fuller discussion of the various roles that parents play in the lives of college students (and college-aged students), see Jeffrey J. Arnett, *Emerging Adulthood: The Winding Road from the Late Teens through the Twenties*, 2nd ed. (Oxford, UK: Oxford University Press, 2014) and Mary Grigsby, *College Life through the Eyes of Students* (Albany, NY: SUNY Press, 2009).

24. According to Levine and Dean: "They are called *helicopter* and *chinook* and *blackhawk* parents because they hover over their children. They are called *lawn-mower* and *snowplow* parents because they roll over everything in the paths to 'defend' their cubs. They are called *stealth* parents because they swoop in to 'protect' their offspring. They are called *umbrella* and *nest* parents because they shielded their progeny." Arthur Levine and Diane R. Dean, *Generation on a Tightrope: A Portrait of Today's College Student*, 3rd ed. (San Francisco, CA: Jossey-Bass, 2012), 79. Arnett, in *Emerging Adulthood*, agreed with Levine and Dean that parents today are more involved in the lives of their children, but argued that "research strongly supports the conclusion that parental involvement . . . has mostly beneficial effects" (66). Arnett cited data from a Clark University poll as well as NSSE results to argue that only a third of college parents were perhaps "over-involved" in their lives of their children.

25. Grigsby, in *College Life through the Eyes of Students*, also found that students turned to their parents more for emotional support than for academic advice. Only a minority of first-year students exclusively relied on parents rather than their faculty advisor for academic advice. This was also reported in Chambliss and Takacs, *How College Works*.

26. At some of our colleges students cannot declare their major until the spring of their sophomore year, but at others students can declare it during their first year. About a third of the students had declared a major and transitioned to a new advisor at the start of the sophomore year.

27. Richard J. Light also found that establishing meaningful relationships, ones in which both parties knew each other "reasonably well," was critical to obtaining good advice. Richard J. Light, *Making the Most of College: Students Speak Their Minds* (Cambridge, MA: Harvard University Press, 2001), 86.

28. Chambliss and Takacs, *How College Works*, reported spending time with faculty was key to developing mentorship relationships.

29. One important decision, the major declaration, will be made by the spring of sophomore year. In the sophomore survey, we asked sophomores whom they consulted in thinking about their major or future careers: 51% of responding sophomores reported that they consulted their first-year advisor and 43% consulted with other faculty. Only 36% failed to consult with any faculty about their major. Of those who consulted with their advisor, 61% found him or her to be helpful, and of those who consulted with other faculty, 86% found them to be helpful. Students also reported that they consulted with other students (59%), and to a slightly lesser extent, family members (49%). Of those who consulted with other students or family members, 78% found them helpful.

30. The senior survey, which was administered in spring 2010 to the entire senior Class of 2010 at all seven colleges (for more details about this survey and its response rate please see the Appendix), asked seniors to reflect back upon their premajor advising experiences and to rate their level of satisfaction with premajor

advising on a four-point Likert scale, with 1 being very dissatisfied, 2 being generally dissatisfied, 3 being generally satisfied, and 4 being very satisfied. About two-thirds of responding seniors were generally or very satisfied, but one-third were generally or very dissatisfied. This finding is consistent with how students talked about advising when they were sophomores. It may be that seniors who were dissatisfied with premajor advising were those students who as sophomores failed to reconnect with their premajor advisor at the start of the sophomore year.

31. The fact that about a third of students claimed to make decisions on their own is consistent with the sophomore survey finding that about a third of sophomores failed to consult with faculty about their choice of a major. Although making independent decisions is a key criterion of achieving adulthood for emerging adults (Arnett, *Emerging Adulthood*), it should not be equated with refraining from asking for advice.

32. Although our colleges often provide students in these situations with information about how to acquire a new advisor, we find that they often stumble here. We suspect that these students either don't give this task much priority in their busy schedule or they are reluctant to approach faculty on their own. One sophomore described how awkward it was to approach a professor to ask her to be her advisor: "It was kind of an awkward conversation. I just stopped by her office because I saw she was in there. I was like, 'will you be my advisor?' and she was like, 'all right, I suppose.' I was just really desperate at that point. But she was the first person I asked. And I don't know, it's kind of like a weird commitment thing, like I can't even describe it, it's like proposing to somebody."

33. This misperception occurred more often when those first faculty advisors received the label "first-year" advisors rather than "premajor" advisors; the latter label more clearly implies to students that this person would be their advisor until they declared a major.

34. In the sophomore survey, we asked sophomores how often they met with faculty outside of class—never, occasionally, often, very often—and how well they had come to know individual faculty members since entering college—not at all, somewhat, quite well, very well. Only about 5% of responding sophomores reported that they "never" met with faculty outside of class. The modal response was "occasionally" with 52% selecting that response, and 44% said "often" or "very often." Similarly, only 6% said they had "not at all" gotten to know individual faculty. The modal response was "somewhat" with 54% selecting that response, and 40% said "quite well" or "very well." In fact, the responses to these two questions were significantly positively correlated, Spearman $r = .455$, $N = 2158$, $p < .001$. In some ways, it's probably not surprising that students who met more often with faculty outside of class got to know them better or that students who value getting to know faculty will make an effort to meet with them. But it reiterates the finding from the interviews that meeting more often with faculty leads to stronger relationships. In addition, the sophomore survey also revealed that sophomores who met more often

with their first-year advisors were significantly more likely to report that they met with faculty outside of class, Spearman $r = .210$, $N = 2326$, $p < .001$, and had come to know individual faculty, Spearman $r = .160$, $N = 2146$, $p < .001$. This is directly consistent with the interview result that students who valued close relationships with faculty were more likely to develop close relationships with their first-year academic advisor.

35. At a large university, Rebekah Nathan found that students were often encouraged by other students to "get to know your professors," but this was not for the sake of increased "learning or discovery." Instead, it was for the "instrumental value" of how that relationship might affect class performance. Nathan's students remarked that they would more be likely receive help from professors they knew well, but also believed they would be more likely to receive exceptions and favors, and even hints for exams and homework. Nathan described the "professor-student relations as a rough facsimile of the boss-worker relationship." This description does not seem to fit what we found. Rebekah Nathan, *My Freshman Year: What a Professor Learned by Becoming a Student* (Ithaca, NY: Cornell University Press, 2005), 116–117.

36. The senior survey asked seniors to rate their level of satisfaction with advising within the major using a four-point Likert scale, with 1 being very dissatisfied, 2 being generally dissatisfied, 3 being generally satisfied, and 4 being very satisfied. We found high levels of satisfaction. In fact, 84% of responding seniors were generally or very satisfied and only 15% were generally or very dissatisfied. This finding of satisfaction with advising in the major generally mirrors the results from the interviews.

We also compared students' satisfaction with advising longitudinally and found that while students generally show an increasing satisfaction from sophomores to senior year, those who were less satisfied as sophomores were likely to be less satisfied as seniors. Of those students who were generally or very dissatisfied with premajor advising, about 30% continued to be generally or very dissatisfied with advising in the major compared to only 10% of those students who were generally or very satisfied with premajor advising. We wonder whether establishing a satisfying advising relationship in the first two years of college significantly improves a student's likelihood of doing so in their last two years.

Finally, the senior survey data also revealed a significant positive relationship between how well seniors got to know their faculty and satisfaction with advising in the major, $\chi^2(N = 1640, df = 6) = 148.10$, $p < .000$. The better students knew faculty the more satisfaction they had with advising in the major.

37. In the senior survey, we asked seniors to rate how well they had come to know individual faculty members since entering college, and only 2% said not at all. Almost two-thirds of the responding seniors said they had come to know individual faculty quite well or very well, and about one-third responded somewhat well. Additionally, when we asked seniors how many faculty they knew well enough to provide a professional recommendation concerning their qualifications for a job or for

advanced degree work, only 3% said none. The modal response was three faculty, with about 75% responding that they knew three or more such faculty. Thus, the broader survey data suggests that most seniors got to know their faculty, which is consistent with the interview data.

38. These results are similar to those reported by Levine and Dean, who found that in a survey of students conducted in 2009, 61% had someone on the faculty "whom they could turn to for advice on personal matters" and 73% had someone on the faculty who took a personal interest in their "academic progress," which was substantially higher than results from surveys conducted for the entering classes of 1976 and 1993 (*Generation on a Tightrope*, 43). See also Bowen and Bok, who similarly reported an increase from the class of 1976 to the class of 1989 in the percentage of students who reported having someone on the faculty they "could turn to for advice or for general support or encouragement"; they also reported that faculty advisors were most common at liberal arts colleges. William G. Bowen and Derek Bok, *The Shape of the River: Long-Term Consequences of Considering Race in College and University Admission* (Princeton, NJ: Princeton University Press, 1998), 203.

39. This finding is consistent with the results from the junior survey, which asked students to rate the quality of their major advisor. Of responding juniors, 73% rated their major advisor as good or very good and only 6% rated them as poor.

40. In Chambliss and Takacs, *How College Works*, students defined the "best teachers" as those who were "1) exciting; 2) skilled and knowledgeable; 3) accessible—easy to find, available, and approachable; and finally 4) engaging" (47). Interestingly, with the exception of "exciting," these were among the characteristics our students reported for the ideal advisor.

41. Chambliss and Takacs, in *How College Works*, also found a mix between students who preferred a purely academic relationship with their professors and those who wanted a more personal relationship, but male students, international students, and students of color preferred a less personal one. Beyer, Gillmore, and Fisher also reported a mix; about 43% defined a "meaningful connection to a faculty member as a 'personal' relationship, in which the faculty member showed an interest in the student's personal life, as well as in her academic life" (*Inside the Undergraduate Experience*, 344).

42. The senior survey asked students from whom they sought information to help them achieve their post-graduation plans and how valuable that information was. As we found in the interviews, seniors had a variety of valuable resources at their disposal. They were able to obtain moderately or very valuable information from parents or family (78% of responding seniors), their college's career services office (46%), their faculty advisor (55%), other faculty (52%), students or friends (75%), and alumni (44%). About two-thirds of responding seniors reported receiving valuable post-graduation information from either their faculty advisor or another professor. In addition, when we tallied the number of different valuable resources used by students, we found that only about 7% did not report obtaining

valuable information from anyone, and only 6% cited one valuable resource. The modal response was four valuable resources—with about half of the responding seniors citing four or more valuable resources and 70% citing three or more. Thus, as we found in the interviews, most students had expansive advising networks, and few relied on one person or were the "go it alone" type.

6. Engagement

1. See, among others, Alexander W. Astin, *What Matters in College? Four Critical Years Revisited* (San Francisco, CA: Jossey-Bass, 1993); Arthur W. Chickering and Zelda F. Gamson, "Seven Principles for Good Practice in Undergraduate Education," *AAHE Bulletin* 39 (1987): 3–7; George D. Kuh, Jillian Kinzie, John H. Schuh, Elizabeth Whitt, and Associates, *Student Success in College: Creating Conditions That Matter* (San Francisco, CA: Jossey-Bass, 2005); and Ernest T. Pascarella and Patrick T. Terenzini, *How College Affects Students*, vol. 2, *A Third Decade of Research* (San Francisco, CA: Jossey-Bass, 2005).

2. NSSE: National Survey of Student Engagement, About NSSE Statement, http://nsse.iub.edu/html/about.cfm.

3. These three questions were drawn from the 2014 NSSE survey, http://nsse.iub.edu/html/survey_instruments.cfm.

4. The sophomore survey asked students to recall their first-year experiences. Only 3% said they never discussed course content outside of class in their first year, with 59% saying that they often or very often did. Only 2% said they did not complete assigned readings before class in their first year with 76% saying they often or very often did. Similar figures were true for sophomore and junior years. Because we found a significant positive correlation for the first year between such things as discussing course content outside of class and excitement in class (Spearman $r = .299$, $N = 2138$, $p < .001$), the high percentage of students who talk to others about their learning suggests a high level of episodic, if not cumulative, engagement among students.

5. Our conceptualization of engagement bears some similarity to Mihaly Csikszentmihalyi's notion of "flow." See his books: *Flow: The Psychology of Optimal Experience* (New York, NY: Harper and Row, 1990) and *Finding Flow: The Psychology of Engagement with Everyday Life* (New York, NY: Basic Books, 1997).

6. These observations from our qualitative analysis are reinforced by surveys we conducted with students who were in the same cohort as the panel study students. When asked how often they "felt excited by a class," 58% of juniors responding to the survey reported "once a week or more." Virtually the same proportion (59%) reported that they "felt bored by a class once a week or more." Although it's not clear whether students associated all of their "exciting" experiences with one or more courses and all of their "boring" experiences with others, the variable nature of students' reports underscores the importance of deriving an understanding of

engagement in the context of specific classes, interactions, assignments, and other academic experiences rather than in more generic learning experiences (e.g., first-year seminars, community-based research courses). Similar results were found in other years.

7. Richard J. Light found that first-year Harvard students who were in academic trouble typically chose courses based on fulfilling requirements rather than on interest. He attributed this to the large enrollments common to these courses, which made getting to know professors difficult. Light also noted that students who select courses based on fulfilling requirements may find that the courses neither "engage" nor "excite them." Richard J. Light, *Making the Most of College: Students Speak Their Minds* (Cambridge, MA: Harvard University Press, 2001), 39.

8. Tim Clydesdale, *The First Year Out* (Chicago, IL: The University of Chicago Press, 2007) found much disengagement for first-year students enrolled in large lecture courses in which they felt anonymous, especially if they were taught by graduate students or adjunct faculty. Kuh et al. (*Student Success in College*) described a number of "engaging pedagogies" that promoted student success, and Light (*Making the Most of College*) also provided examples of how faculty successfully engage students in the classroom, even in large classes. See also Chickering and Gamson, "Seven Principles."

9. Clydesdale, *The First Year Out*, 162, noted that students were often bored in college courses because they found them "irrelevant to 'real life.'"

10. The role of faculty in facilitating engagement has also been noted by others: Catharine Hoffman Beyer, Gerald M. Gillmore, and Andrew T. Fisher, *Inside the Undergraduate Experience: The University of Washington's Study of Undergraduate Learning* (Bolton, MA: Anker Publishing Company, 2007); Daniel F. Chambliss and Christopher G. Takacs, *How College Works* (Cambridge, MA: Harvard University Press, 2014); and Clydesdale, *The First Year Out*. In addition, see Ken Bain, *What the Best College Teachers Do* (Cambridge, MA: Harvard University Press, 2004) for a discussion of the qualities that best exemplify engaging professors.

11. Brad decided to major in English because of the professor he talked about in this quote. Results from our junior-year survey showed that having "a course with a great professor" played a substantial role in students' decision about their major. Seventy-three percent of responding juniors said it was quite or very important to their decision and only 10% said it was not important.

12. Others also reported a connection between engagement and academic challenge (setting high yet achievable standards). See for example Beyer, Gillmore, and Fisher, *Inside the Undergraduate Experience*; Chickering and Gamson, "Seven Principles"; Clydesdale, *The First Year Out*; Kuh et al., *Student Success in College*. The junior-year survey showed about an equal percentage of students excited and bored by their classes on a weekly basis, and also showed a higher percentage—78%—of students who said they encountered challenging material once a week or more. It is unclear whether the excitement, boredom, and challenge pertain to the same

courses or same assignments, but our data suggest that others' findings of a connection between challenge and engagement holds true in our sample as well.

13. See also Clydesdale, *The First Year Out*; Kuh et al., *Student Success in College*.

14. A number of researchers have found that student engagement is facilitated through community-based learning opportunities. For example, see Kuh et al., *Student Success in College*. Researchers have also found that such courses enhance "course learning and dimensions of cognitive development." For a review, see Pascarella and Terenzini, *How College Affects Students*, 611.

15. It's also good news that researchers have found that "academic effort and engagement" is positively related to "knowledge acquisition and intellectual growth . . . to the extent to which students . . . fully exploit these opportunities." See Pascarella and Terenzini, *How College Affects Students*, 613.

16. Our claim that opportunities for engagement are plentiful may seem at odds with the conclusion reached by Chambliss and Takacs that "the best opportunities for engagement are limited" (*How College Works*, 156). This difference stems, in part, from the more expansive set of decisions we argue that students confront each day ("many" opportunities to become engaged rather than "the best" opportunities). We also tend to place greater emphasis on the responsibility students have for making decisions that can create greater engagement.

17. Our discussion raises questions about the extent to which students versus faculty (or colleges, more generally) bear responsibility for engagement. Data from the senior-year survey suggest that students see faculty as generally committed to teaching in ways they hope students will find engaging. When asked to rate the overall quality of instruction while in college, 52% said that they were "very satisfied," 46% were "generally satisfied," and only 2% were "dissatisfied." These findings support the conclusion that, while students and faculty share responsibility for engagement, greater responsibility falls to students.

18. A number of researchers have characterized students as being "unengaged." For example, Clydesdale in *The First Year Out* described college students as being "quite immune to intellectual engagement" (170), that they "quietly endure their liberal arts hazing" (22), and that "only a handful of students on each campus find a liberal arts education to be deeply meaningful and important" (29). More recently, Richard Arum and Josipa Roksa, *Aspiring Adults Adrift: Tentative Transitions of College Graduates* (Chicago, IL: Chicago University Press, 2014) asked students, "How academically engaged would you say you were in college?" Students defined engagement using class attendance, doing homework, being a "good student," studying for tests, and doing the readings for class. Arum and Roksa wrote that this definition, with its "focus on fulfilling little more than minimum requirements," demonstrated a lack of engagement (36). Others, however, present a different characterization of college students. For example, Beyer, Gillmore, and Fisher, *Inside the Undergraduate Experience*, concluded that "students want to be intellectually engaged" (364). See also Kuh et al., *Student Success in College*, for conditions that enhance engagement.

19. We will consider in more depth the relationship between grades and engagement later in this chapter, but it is worth noting here that some degree of grade "success" might be necessary for some students to become engaged in a particular course or subject area. Put differently, students who can enroll in virtually any course expecting to earn what they view as a good grade in it may have the luxury of focusing on what interests them through exploring the curriculum broadly or digging deeply into a particular field.

20. Kuh et al., *Student Success in College.*

21. Lauren R. Veysey, *The Emergence of the American University* (Chicago, IL: University of Chicago Press, 1965). For additional commentary on the shift from fixed to elective curriculums, see John R. Thelin, *A History of American Higher Education* (Baltimore, MD: Johns Hopkins University Press, 2004) and Christopher J. Lucas, *American Higher Education: A History*, 2nd ed. (New York, NY: Palgrave Macmillan, 2006).

22. This finding echoes Chambliss and Takacs's claim that choosing courses and majors is a "satisficing" decision-making process in the sense that Herbert Simon used this concept. See Chambliss and Takacs, *How College Works*, 2014, 65.

23. In an analysis of the experiences of students majoring in science, these issues are addressed in greater detail in Adele Wolfson, Lee Cuba, and Alexandra Day, "The Liberal Education of STEM Majors," *Change* 47 (2015): 44–51.

24. Some students included "getting good grades" in their descriptions of a successful college year for all four years of college. Others have reported similar findings. For example, Camille Z. Charles, Mary J. Fischer, Margarita A. Mooney, and Douglas S. Massey, *Taming the River: Negotiating the Academic, Financial, and Social Currents in Selective Colleges and Universities* (Princeton, NJ: Princeton University Press, 2009, 78) found that more than three-quarters of sophomores rated that getting "good grades" was "very important to their peers." However, Beyer, Gillmore, and Fisher (*Inside the Undergraduate Experience*) found that only first-year students at the University of Washington cited "getting good grades" when asked to define college success. Methodological differences (the use of focus groups at the University of Washington and the use of individual interviews in our research) may, to some extent, account for these incongruent findings.

25. For an extended discussion of the themes students employ to define a successful year in college, see Nancy Jennings, Suzanne Lovett, Lee Cuba, Joseph Swingle, and Heather Lindkvist, "'What Would Make This a Successful Year for You?' How Students Define Success in College," *Liberal Education* 99 (2013): 40–47.

26. See Robert M. Carini, George D. Kuh, and Stephen P. Klein, "Student Engagement and Student Learning: Testing the Linkages," *Research in Higher Education* 47 (2006): 1–32, and George D. Kuh, Ty M. Cruce, Rick Shoup, Jillian Kinzie, and Robert M. Gonyea, "Unmasking the Effects of Student Engagement on First-Year College Grades and Persistence," *The Journal of Higher Education* 79 (2008): 540–563. See also Ken Bain, *What the Best College Students Do* (Cambridge, MA: Belknap Press, 2012).

7. Practice for Life

1. Richard J. Light, *Making the Most of College: Students Speak Their Minds* (Cambridge, MA: Harvard University Press, 2001), 209.

2. For evidence of this claim as it relates to the experience of students majoring in science, see Adele Wolfson, Lee Cuba, and Alexandra Day, "The Liberal Education of STEM Majors," *Change* 47 (2015): 44–51.

3. William G. Bowen, *Lessons Learned: Reflections of a University President* (Princeton, NJ: Princeton University Press, 2010), 144.

4. Ellen Condliffe Lagemann and Harry Lewis, eds., *What Is College For? The Public Purpose of Higher Education* (New York, NY: Teachers College, Columbia University, 2012), 34.

5. A survey of parents of children in the fifth through the twelfth year of school conducted by *Inside Higher Education* and Gallup found that 38% said that getting a good job is the main reason their child would obtain more education beyond high school. Over 40% of parents strongly agreed that they were confident that a vocational education would lead their child to a good job, compared to 28% who were confident that a liberal arts education would lead to this outcome. See https://www.insidehighered.com/news/survey/jobs-value-and-affirmative-action-survey-parents-about-college.

Appendix

1. For an excellent reference on qualitative methodology, see Bruce L. Berg, *Qualitative Research Methods for the Social Sciences*, 7th ed. (Boston, MA: Pearson, 2008).

2. Based on available information for each student. Financial aid data for one coeducation college was not available. First-generation status for two coeducation colleges was not available. Type of high school data was not available for one single sex and one coeducational college.

3. Defined as neither parent having graduated from college.

4. Students left the project because they were no longer at the school or declined further participation.

5. One college had faculty conduct the interviews.

6. For training student interviewers, we recommend Kathryn Roulston, Kathleen deMarrais, and Jamie B. Lewis, "Learning to Interview in the Social Sciences," *Qualitative Inquiry* 9 (2003): 643–688 and Robert S. Weiss, *Learning from Strangers: The Art and Method of Qualitative Interview* (New York, NY: Free Press, 1995).

7. COFHE is a consortium of thirty-one selective private colleges and universities dedicated to providing full need-based financial aid to their students. Participating schools voluntarily administer web-based surveys and share survey results to help in this endeavor. More information is available at http://web.mit.edu/cofhe/.

Acknowledgments

This project was born out of a small meeting of liberal arts college deans and provosts convened in 2003 by Bob Froh, associate director of the New England Association of Schools and Colleges (NEASC). As a member of an organization that establishes standards for educational quality and accreditation, Bob asked these college administrators how best to assess student learning at their schools. Their answers were novel at the time: involve faculty and students more directly in assessment, create meaningful and honest collaborations among colleges, and augment standardized surveys with more nuanced and contextualized measures of student learning.

A year later the ideas generated at this meeting were incorporated into a proposal to the Teagle Foundation. With Lee Cuba, Bob Froh, Jill Reich, dean of the faculty at Bates College, as principal investigators, seven colleges agreed to put together teams of administrators, faculty, and students to conduct a longitudinal assessment study: Bates, Bowdoin, Colby, Middlebury, Smith, Trinity, and Wellesley. Together with NEASC, these colleges formed the New England Consortium for Assessment and Student Learning (NECASL). The Teagle Foundation supported NECASL with two large awards, spanning 2005–2011. The Andrew W. Mellon Foundation and the Spencer Foundation, along with our colleges, also provided financial support to augment these external awards. We are grateful for this widespread affirmation of the value of our work.

This multi-disciplinary, multi-college project was not without its challenges. Interview protocols and surveys had to balance issues of concern to individual colleges with the desire to assess general patterns in the academic and social lives of college students. Job changes, sabbaticals, and graduations meant that project teams were often in transition, and the unpredictable rhythms of college campuses meant that there were times when the needs of our colleges took precedence over those of the consortium. None of these challenges, however, undermined our willingness to share our worries and our data. That many different administrators, faculty, and students were able to have honest conversations about their colleges over a ten-year period is testimony to both the people involved in the NECASL project and our institutions, which allowed us this space. Our NECASL colleagues were exceedingly generous with their time and kept the project tethered to their colleges; over the years, this collegiality led to new friendships. This has been one of the richest and most meaningful experiences of our lives, a sentiment we believe many of our NECASL colleagues share.

We gratefully acknowledge and are indebted to the many faculty and staff who are listed here: Margaret Allen, Sally Baker, Larry Baldwin, Kim Besio, Susan Bourque, Alison Byerly, Alec Campbell, Martha Denney, Michael Donihue, Lauren Duncan, Susan Etheredge, Jim Fergerson, Stephanie Foster, Mark Freeman, LeRoy Graham, Paul Greenwood, Judy Head, Adam Howard, James Hughes, Cristle Collins Judd, Jane Kimball, Whitney King, Adela Langrock, Michelle Lepore, Kathryn Graff Low, Maureen Mahoney, Phyllis Mannocchi, Yonna McShane, Thomas Mitzel, Elisa Narin van Court, Ellen Peters, Bill Peterson, Kat Power, David Reuman, Ann Marie Russell, Andrew Shennan, Jim Sloat, Kent Smith, Mark Tappan, Liz Tobin, Bill Wilson, Adele Wolfson, and Ed Yeterian. These colleagues contributed not only to the work of the project but to the ideas that ultimately made their way into this book. Their array of experiences and perspectives pushed us to consider ideas and topics that we would otherwise have overlooked. We particularly want to thank Rachael Barlow, Becky Brodigan, Bob Froh, Heather Lindkvist, Minh Ly, Annick Mansfield, Jill Reich, Cate Rowen, and Kathy Skubikowski for their leadership and sustained involvement over the years. To say that this book would not exist without their work is an understatement.

Many students and alumnae at the NECASL colleges were interviewers or research assistants for this study. Their dedication and skill contributed significantly to the validity of our data and the depth of our analysis: Jasmin Agosto, Amanda Anderson, Ada Avila, Michel Bamani, Sara Brandt-Vorel, Lindsey Bruett, Megan Brunmier, Charlotte Cabot, Paul Carroll, Katherine Case, Flavia Chen, Christine Choi, Miki Cisco, Courteney Coyne, Trevor Dodds, Jesse Drummond, Hal Ebbott, Chanel Geter, Abigail Goodridge, Maggie Gross, Alisa Hamilton, Michael Hannaman, Suzanne Heller, Jessica

Hortskotte, Joan Huang, Bill Jack, Manpreet Kaur, Kiersten Kelley, Jodi Kraushar, Amy Lareau, Elizabeth Leiwant, Georgina Lopez, Sonia Mahabir, Quan Mai, Emily Maistrellis, Adrienne Matunas, Caroline Mayson, Sarah McAra, Caitlin McCarty, Teko Mmolawa, Hillary Morin, Khoa Nguyen, Tela O'Donnell, Eugene Pan, Johanna Peace, Addie Pelletier, Lauren Poinier, Veselina Radeva, Avery Rain, Christina Ramsay, Samuel Read, Danielle Recco, Mary Ridley, Carlos Rios, Charles Schopp, Katherine Schwartz, Cloe Shasha, Eugenia Silva-Beccari, Miki Sisco, Emily Skinner, Ariel Smith, Bobby Joe Smith, Emily Stanislawski, Dudney Sulla, Cailin Sullivan, Julia (Schroeder) Ticona, Marice Uy, Jesse Wanzer, Harrison Watkins, Kate Watson, Jessica Welk, Katherine Woo, and Ivory Wu. For their service in multiple roles or their continued involvement with the project both as students and as alumni, we are particularly indebted to Claire Droste, Devlin Hughes, Amelia Iuvino, Amy Johnson, Sarah Maxner, Emily Pagano, Celene Reynolds, Charlie Rose, Maura Spiegelman, and Marissa Szabo. Finally, no student or alumna contributed more to the consortium than Cristin Bates, who interviewed students for four years and served as a full-time graduate administrator for NECASL the year following her graduation. Heartfelt thanks from all of us.

Our work was enriched by feedback on presentations in a number of venues: annual meetings of the Association of American Colleges and Universities, the American Educational Research Association, and the New England Association of School and Colleges; small group discussions sponsored by the Mellon Assessment Project at Hamilton College; and programs and gatherings at the Center of Inquiry in the Liberal Arts at Wabash College. We also benefited from the opportunity to speak about the methods and findings of our study not only at our own colleges but at several other colleges and universities: Amherst College, Bryn Mawr College, Columbia College, Hobart and William Smith Colleges, North Carolina Agricultural and Technical State University, Quinnipiac University, and Trinity University.

Several friends and colleagues offered substantive advice that helped clarify our arguments and our writing. We are grateful for their intelligence, honesty, and generosity: Charles Blaich, Anne Brubaker, Daniel Chambliss, Craig McEwen, Joanne Murray, Diana Chapman Walsh, Steve Weisler, and three anonymous reviewers for Harvard University Press.

We were fortunate and grateful that Elizabeth Knoll, former executive editor-at-large at Harvard University Press, took an avid interest in our work and convinced her colleagues at the Press that ours was a project worth pursuing. We also wish to express our deep gratitude to Andrew Kinney, who assumed responsibility for our manuscript after Elizabeth's move to the provost's office. Andrew's close reading of our work and his helpful guidance through the production process improved this book in numerous ways.

Finally, we would like to express our deep personal gratitude to those who encouraged, fed, pleasantly distracted, and supported us in countless and immeasurable ways: Aaron, Ben, Dan, Gene, Nick, Nithia, and Patty. Our frequent absences from home and our infrequent ability to separate work from home have intruded into your lives. This book will always be for us a reminder of your patience and love.

Index